My Family
and
Other
Hazards

My Family and Other Hazards

A MEMOIR

JUNE MELBY

HENRY HOLT AND COMPANY
NEW YORK

Henry Holt and Company, LLC
Publishers since 1866
175 Fifth Avenue
New York, NY 10010
www.henryholt.com

Certain names have been changed.

"Take a Break for a Delicious Sno-Cone!" first appeared in *Water~Stone Review*
(Fall 2011); then again with the title "The Ice Machine"
in *Utne Reader* (March/April 2012).

Library of Congress Cataloging-in-Publication Data

Melby, June.
  My family and other hazards : a memoir / June Melby.—First Edition.
    pages cm
  ISBN 978-0-8050-9831-0 (hardback)—ISBN 978-0-8050-9832-7 (electronic copy)
  1. Melby, June.   2. Melby, June—Childhood and youth.   3. Melby, June—
Family.   4. Miniature golf—Wisconsin—Waupaca.   I. Title.
  GV987.M45 2014
  796.352'2—dc23   2013048857

First Edition 2014

Designed by Meryl Sussman Levavi

Printed in the United States of America

1 3 5 7 9 10 8 6 4 2

For my family

A hole-in-one is amazing when you think of the different universes this white mass of molecules has to pass through on its way to the hole.

—Mac O'Grady

Miniature: diminutive, minuscule, small-scale, pony; bantam, baby, baby-sized; toy, compact, dwarf, dwarfish, pygmy, midget, nonoid, elfin, Lilliputian, Tom Thumb.

—*Roget's International Thesaurus*

And in twenty years they all came back,
In twenty years or more,
And every one said, "How tall they've grown!"
For they've been to the Lakes, and the Torrible Zone,
And the hills of the Chankly Bore!

—Edward Lear

CONTENTS / SCORECARD

Rules

1. Ball off carpet, place at point of exit, add one stroke.
2. Ball in water, place on green, add one stroke.
3. Maximum six strokes per hole.
4. Have fun.
5. Be kind to others.
6. Go ahead and pet the dog. He's tame.
7. This is a memoir. Every event is true. Because I don't remember exact words spoken twenty to thirty years ago, I based the early descriptions and dialogue on "most likely" scenarios, for example, what customers probably looked like and what they probably said given the circumstances. I had my family read these portions of the text to make sure they agreed on accuracy. However, and by the way, the dialogue and descriptions of customers from the later chapters are *not* from imagination but in fact completely accurate. These are taken from extensive notes and tape-recorded dialogue, because I'm the kind of person who would hide a tape recorder in the ticket booth just to hear what people sound like when they reminisce about a place like Tom Thumb.

My Family
and
Other
Hazards

THE TICKET BOOTH: PROLOGUE

The state of Wisconsin looks like a hand. Set the book down. Hold up your right palm. Stick out your thumb, and lo, you have Door County, a thumb-shaped peninsula of tourism lapping into Lake Michigan, where summertime visitors can drive on crowded roads and buy cherry pies, cherry liquors, cherry-painted shot glasses, and stay at overpriced cherry-themed motels. At the top of your hand, between your extended fingers, in the north-ernmost part of the state, sprawl lakes and rivers and other water-soaked lands generally too overrun with mosquitoes to be habitable except by extremists. I have heard that religious monks in Italy would slap leather whips across their backs until they bled, believing pure suffering could bring them closer to God. Or they could just spend some time in northern Wisconsin, say, five to seven minutes. The suffering is the same; the insects more deft at drawing your blood.

Across the center of the state, and the palm of your hand, are the fertile plains: fields of corn, alfalfa, and glowing soybeans, and pastures of reddish brown slow-moving cows, separated into farms by dots of broken-down silos, collapsing barns, and graying farmhouses. The winter is long and the climate absurd. No paint sticks to the sides of these buildings. As you drive up Highway 22, you can play the game "Abandoned House/Not

Abandoned House," looking for signs of human life between the abundant fields of abundant grains.

Also abundant fields of geometrically correct pine trees.

When my ancestors and yours came to the United States, there were thousands of acres of trees in Wisconsin to be sawed down and milled into lumber, and so they did. Then all the trees were gone. In the 1930s the U.S. Department of Agriculture looked at the bare sandy ground and paid people to plant more trees. Pine trees, they decided. Perhaps feeling glee at its success in organizing a military for World War I, the government encouraged planting in tidy columns, lining up the trees as if for inspection. Red pine, red pine, red pine. A steady ten feet apart. Row after row after row. Ten, hut! The trees look bushy on the top, rough and scaly on the bark, and completely at attention at the base. The forests of Wisconsin are for people who like their wilderness organized, who admire the beauty of crossword puzzles. While driving down state highways you can stare at the space between the rows and recall early lessons in mathematics, how parallel lines never intercept but only appear to converge near infinity.

Along the roadsides, like wildflowers, are strewn the carcasses of freshly killed deer. They bloom red and white and brown, all year long.

I tell you these things so that you will stay away.

Don't go to Wisconsin. Don't consider buying land in Wisconsin.

Maybe I should have mentioned this earlier, say, ten, fifteen years ago. If I could have stopped people from clamoring for land, real estate prices would have stayed the same. Property values wouldn't have risen. Taxes would not have gone through the roof. My schoolteacher-parents would have money left over at the end of the summer after paying their enormous property tax. Their income from their miniature golf course could be used for other things, like hiring local kids to mow the lawn, or paying a handyman to paint all the hazards, replace the carpets, or rake the leaves. My parents are sixty-seven and seventy-six years old; maybe once in a while they'd like a day off. Maybe they'd enjoy working less than twelve hour days, seven days a week, all summer long, just for the right to live in their house, which just happens to be on a lake, which means their taxes keep rising as people keep bidding up the value of the plots of land that surround them. Maybe—just imagine!—if their taxes were lower, my parents could even make a profit. Maybe they wouldn't have had to sell Tom Thumb. So maybe it's actually my fault for not speaking up earlier, telling everyone how terrible it is. Maybe I could have prevented the whole darn thing from crashing to an end.

The problem with Wisconsin: the lakes. Don't ask me about the lakes. Don't ask me about swimming through the clear water. Don't ask me about floating over the surface in a canoe. I'm not going to tell you how beautiful they are. I'm not going to use words like *sparkling* or *blue*, or you will be clamoring too.

You see, yesterday I found out that the world is coming to an end. But if I told you that, you would probably think I was being overly dramatic. Of course I am. This is miniature golf. *Everything* I say about the topic is going to sound like an exaggeration.

The news arrived in the form of a red blinking light, which meant I had missed a phone call. I was driving up Vine Street at the time, heading home from the YMCA where I swim.

I had just crossed Hollywood Boulevard in my fifteen-year-old Honda. The sidewalks were crowded, as usual, with afternoon sightseers. It looks most days as if every tourist in town has dropped something on the pavement. They walk slowly in clusters, canting together towards the earth, searching for the stars of their favorite entertainers. But they won't find them here. Those of us who live here know that new plaques are found at the *other* end of the boulevard. This is where the has-beens are found, in front of pawn shops and the store selling discount men's suits. As usual, I resisted the temptation to yell out the window, in a somewhat helpful tone, that they might happier if they just gave it up. I flipped down the visor of my car and headed up the hill. There is never any shade from palm trees.

At the corner of the pointy-speared Capital Records building I looked down at my phone. Red. Red. Alert. Alert. *That's it then,* I thought. Don't ask me how I knew before I had even heard the message. *It's my mother. It's over. They've sold Tom Thumb.*

Life is like that. Absurd. There are days you can barely find your car in a parking lot, and other times you know *exactly* what's happening seventeen hundred miles and one half of a lifetime away.

It is July 26, 2003. On the hill above my apartment there is a sign that says HOLLYWOOD, and for the last thirteen years I have lived below it in my one-bedroom, rent-controlled apartment. I am forty years old. I eat a Fudgesicle almost every day. I won't cut my hair. It is blonde and down to my waist. I used to be a comedian. I've done over two thousand performances. I celebrate most birthdays in the mountains at Sequoia National Park, where I go camping alone. For comfort I watch Jane Austen movies. I sip red wine that I buy for cheap.

When I was a teenager, I discovered that I can write backwards as well as forwards, using either my left or my right hand. It's the kind of discovery that should be kept from a child, especially during tender ages when that child could get ideas, start believing that the normal rules do not apply. That she might have magical powers, or at least the power to beat the odds, to rise above the circumstances of her birth, to be more than common, to be loved and admired by strangers; and so she flees to the city, scoffing over her shoulder at her perfectly normal, mundane family.

One other thing: I grew up on a miniature golf course. It's not something I talk about often. I never told jokes about the mini golf course at comedy clubs, even though I did stand-up for twelve years. Even though I spent my childhood summers in a place called Tom Thumb. It never seemed relevant. Or perhaps it seemed so *very* relevant that there was no point in trying to explain.

After college I left the Midwest and then moved to San Francisco to become "a rich and famous musician." I arrived with big hopes, a suitcase in one hand and my grandfather's accordion in the other. Less than a year later, I started doing stand-up comedy—a profession that seemed, after miniature golf, comparatively, realistic and practical. Then I migrated to Los Angeles to audition for acting roles, like the part of the "girl next door" or the "naive girlfriend from the Midwest." I performed at the major clubs, wore short skirts, went to parties, took big risks, and acted in exactly one movie. I lived off the residuals for the next three years. Sometime along the way, comedy stopped being fun. But I didn't know how to quit—the way a drinker doesn't realize the whiskey has stopped working. Several years ago I finally gave it up, and these days write mostly poetry.

All the while, Tom Thumb Miniature Golf has been like a clock ticking in the background, my parents welcoming customers to the ticket booth as always, somewhere in Wisconsin, a reassuring *tck tck, tck*, like the blades of The Windmill at #9 sweeping across the sky, a cyclical, reassuring motion that says all is well, we are open, and all is continuing, continuing—ah, the sweet, sweet sound of continuing. I wonder if it's easier to take risks with your life knowing that no matter how badly you fail, how badly you misjudge your talents, it is there: your old life continues. In a kind of parallel universe. Somewhere far away. *Tck tck tck.* Or in the case of The Windmill, *swoop swoop swoop.* A rotation as predictable as the sun rising in the east, the blades lifting from the left to sweep down to the right, first red, then green, then orange, and then blue.

Only now, it seems, that clock is about to stop.

"Hello, Tom Thumb," my mom answers when I call back. "Oh, June! I have some news. We found a buyer for Tom Thumb."

"Hey, that's great," I say in a happy voice, because I have taken acting classes.

"And they told us specifically that they are planning to run the mini golf course."

"Great," I say again.

"They said they won't change a thing."

"Well, good news then."

"Yes," she says. "We are happy about it." She explains how the offer came from a local realtor and three members of his family. Because the property value had gotten so high, it took four people to come up with the money. "It's the right time, June."

"Great," I say. "Well, hurray, I suppose." I hit the brakes, turn left on Beachwood. "So, do you feel a relief?" I ask.

"Hmm, mm." And she says the new owners will take over sometime after the season ends on Labor Day. Just over four weeks away.

I tell her I am happy for her. But there is a lot I don't tell her. That I knew what the message was before I listened. That I feel sick.

I do not get into a car wreck, but I pull into my parking space and stare blankly ahead as if I had.

I have two sisters. I call the younger one first. Carla lives in Iowa, and she's good in a crisis—for a job she answers phones at a suicide hotline. "I don't know why it's such a big deal!" I say. "It's not like I was ever in love with the place."

"I know. I always felt like the mini golf course was like the sick sibling that got all of the attention I never got."

"Oh, Carla!"

She says that as a child she felt so ignored that she even became jealous of our collie. "Dad would say 'Good dog' or 'Good boy' to him all the time," she says, "but he never said anything like that to me." She tells me she is okay with letting the whole place go.

It has been more than a year since my parents contacted a realtor. I admit to her that I've been dreading this moment. "But don't tell Mom and Dad. I want them to think I'm happy."

"Well, actually, they know. They told me they are surprised that you seem the most sentimental of all of us about losing the mini golf," she adds.

"They know? Oh. Well." I admit to her that I'd always assumed that I'd make a lot of money in Hollywood by this age. "I'd be able to buy it from Mom and Dad," I say, staring off at the gray shades pulled over my windows. They were here when I moved in, left behind by the previous tenant thirteen years ago. The vinyl is torn, and the wooden sticks are held to the lower edge with an archaeology of dried glue and cellophane tape.

"Really? I thought you couldn't wait to get away from Tom Thumb."

"What are you talking about?"

"Do you think that's the reason you're the saddest of us all about the sale? Because you moved so far away? LeAnn and I have been living much closer. Do you think that's the reason?" she asks.

I mumble some of my favorite vowel sounds.

"I thought one of us would buy it too," she says.

"Yourself?"

"I don't know. I just assumed . . . I think we all did."

"Do you think Mom and Dad are mad at us? That we can't buy it from them?" I ask.

"It's too expensive. I don't think they expected that," she

says. "And besides, they're too nice. They'd never admit it if they did."

They are too nice, and now Tom Thumb Miniature Golf—the land and house and business that my parents scrounged to buy for forty-five thousand dollars over thirty years ago on a teacher's salary—just got an offer for half a million dollars. I know I should feel happy for them, but I'm hoping the sale will fall through.

We haven't always had Tom Thumb, of course. Once upon a time we were innocent and churchgoing and living peacefully in a small town in Iowa. Our house was painted white with dark green shutters on the windows. In front were two cedar bushes, on the right and on the left. One was named LeAnn's and one was named Mine; it was the smaller of the two. Carla didn't have a cedar bush because she wasn't around when we claimed them. That's how it is. You're the youngest, you just lose out.

My parents were schoolteachers. The school system was our system. Monday through Friday. Saturdays: pancakes. Sundays: naps. Evening: news. Summer: vacation. Which meant visiting my grandparents in Wisconsin, in our pullout camper trailer.

And then that life was over.

"Well, kids," said my dad. I remember standing together in the moonlight in the piney woods of Wisconsin, my parents, my two sisters, ages thirteen and six, and myself, age ten. It was August, we had spent the day with my grandparents, and we had returned to our campsite. The sky was dark and the woods were dark, and we stood in a circle looking, most likely, like a family-sized football team huddled in the moonlight. "What would you think if our family bought Tom Thumb Mini Golf Course?"

"So, girls, would you like that?" my mother added.

"What?" I said. I did not understand the question, really. Buy the mini golf where we had played that day? What does that mean? Would we be able to play more games tomorrow? It sounded like a full glass of pop, that is, something that my parents never offered. An indulgence.

My uncle Joe, who had a canoe rental business in the area, had visited our campsite an hour before. With a notebook in hand, he spoke to my parents in a low, booming voice that made you forget he was a younger brother. "If you get another mortgage on your house back in Iowa . . ." I didn't pay attention to the rest and was probably running between the pines looking for a good stick.

"So, girls," my mother said again, and then she waited for an answer. It was difficult to judge whether our mother was serious. Here it was, the biggest moment of our lives, and all we had to see by was the light of the moon. It was like the moment in the stage production of *Peter Pan* when he turns to the children in the audience and says, "We need your help to rescue Tinker Bell. Do you believe in fairies? If you do, clap your hands!"

"Yes! Yes!" My sisters and I clapped, and thus our lives were changed. And thus went my childhood. And thus explains the putters you may have seen in the corner of my bedroom, or the golf balls in red, blue, green, and purple that I keep on the bookshelf in a glass mug shaped like a pirate head.

That was the end. Or the beginning. I'm not sure how to look at it. I remember the years *before* we purchased Tom Thumb, but if you ask about my "childhood," I picture myself at age ten, the year Tom Thumb came into our lives. And that is just one more thing I can't explain.

But I am getting ahead of myself. First let me tell you about Us.

Mom was tall and practical. If she were an object, she would be a pencil. Not fancy but handy, and streamlined in design. She could do just about everything.

Dad was thin and agitated. He was like a rabbit, only he had several hundred students instead of that many baby bunnies. He taught high school chemistry and physics. But he was unlike a rabbit because he didn't like vegetables all that much. Didn't frolic, but instead frowned and threw his hands in the air.

My older sister, LeAnn, was like an officer in the army. She was good at giving orders, and she tended to keep herself from us, me and my younger sister, like we were enlisted men. She was also like an American Indian. When she went to college in South Dakota, people asked her if she was. She's not. She's Norwegian like us. But she just happened to be strong and dark. Like Dad.

My younger sister, Carla, was like a teapot. She was pale and pretty and a bit fragile, but really nice to have around, especially on cold days. Because she smiled and laughed at my jokes.

Me? I was in the middle. I never learned how to do a cartwheel. I had a difficult time throwing the ball back when it was tossed to me, but I was good at trying hard, and that's about all there is to it. Medium height, medium-colored, I was like a brown dog, easy to miss. But strangely sarcastic when I got the chance to be heard, like the dog in a movie about a dog who, on occasion, gets the magical ability to speak.

That was it, the five of us. And later came a collie and then later still a cat who wandered in one day with a broken jaw.

There were eighteen holes. Each had an obstacle between the tee-off and green. We learned that the correct term for the obstacle was *hazard* as in "item of danger," as in "risky." For us the risk was that the hazard would fall apart. The Paddle Wheel Boat, at #17, had been turning for fifteen years already and once a month dropped a wet piece of rotted wood on the fairway. Hole #14 was sinking into the lake. The Swinging Pole, on #6, an eight-foot beam nearly the width of a telephone pole, was coming loose from the only bolt that held it aloft, and threatened to clobber one of the tourists who pushed against it each week.

Tom Thumb was built on reclaimed land, a phrase that always made me think of Daniel Boone and Indians, of machetes and determination. There had always been *some* ground along this side of Bass Lake, but when the original owner poured concrete and shaped it into a land of amusement, it was definitely evidence of wishful thinking. After heavy rains the ground began reverting to its former swampy state. Sea monster–shaped bulges rose in the blacktop between holes #1 and #2, and between #17 and #18. The roots of the maple tree pushed up further each year, threatening to upturn half the course. "I suppose we should take care of that in case someone trips and gets injured," my mother said. "But what can we do?" my dad answered, throwing his hands in the air.

All of the fairways leaned. Hole #2 leaned to the left; hole #9 leaned towards the right; hole #17 leaned backwards. If your ball bounced off the paddle wheel, it would begin tilting, picking up speed as it rolled across the carpet, onto the blacktop, past the tee-off pad where you had started, and onwards towards the lake.

Hole #8, The Wishing Well, with the most dramatic lean of all, also had a ridge across the green. Short putts were nearly impossible to sink. "Greg must have made a mistake when he was smoothing that one," we said to each other, shrugging when a tourist's ball rolled across the carpet to stop, miraculously, along the invisible rim. Greg was the guy who built Tom Thumb using his own two hands and woodworking skills. Another misdirected schoolteacher with time on his hands, he squeezed the course into the side of the lot because he was good with tools, and it seemed like a fun idea at the time. Or so he said when he sold the place, handed us the keys, and retired.

The sun rises over the Hollywood Hills, above the flat square roof of the building next to mine, forms a fist, and starts to hit my bedroom window. "Bang bang bang!" In my bank account in Los Angeles there are three mice, two dust bunnies, and one piece of cheese. Which is to say, it is empty. My only asset right now is that I look younger than my age. Which isn't technically even an asset, except in Los Angeles. I am not married; in fact, I'm so *not* married that it's possible I have just been broken up with, but I'm not sure. Maybe he is just taking a break from phoning for eight weeks. He was fourteen years younger than me, only twenty-six. And even though he was the one who started it—he asked *me* out—there is one true and remarkable thing about dating someone fourteen years younger: if he leaves you, the entire population of the world will take no small amount of pleasure in joining up like a choir to say quite loudly, in a song they have been rehearsing lo, these many years, "Well, we knew *that* was going to happen."

After a sleepless night I slump on the couch and reach for the cordless.

"Hello, Tom Thumb. Oh! June?" my mom answers. She always sounds surprised to hear my voice, as if Hollywood is on another continent, as if I am stationed with the raj in India, and I am sweating under a pith helmet, swinging a machete to get to the only phone in the jungle, and have finally gotten through. "Oh." Pause. "June!"

"You're coming back?" she asks.

"Of course," I say. She tells me Carla plans to visit with her family, and LeAnn and her husband and their three boys might come too. "They want to make cotton candy."

Our visits are going to overlap a bit, she warns me. "And some of you might have to sleep in the trailer."

Everyone in my family is eager to work in the ticket booth one last time. Stand at the helm of the golf course, say "Thank you" to the tourists, hand out putters and balls, and remember how it was.

She tells me the "new owners" are walking around the yard this morning, looking at the shoreline and the docks.

"Why are they doing that now, while you're still there?"

She explains that they've agreed on a price, but the sale isn't actually a *done deal*. They will meet again on the "closing date," and that is when it becomes official. They'll sign the paperwork and hand over the keys. But in the meanwhile there are details to be worked out. Inspections of the property. Permits to be applied for. "They could still back out. Or we could."

"You could?"

"We both have a right to back out, before the deal is 'closed,' in mid-September."

"Why are they doing that to you?" I say, alarmed.

"Well, June, that's how it's always done."

"Oh," I say. I know nothing of real estate. But ask me sometime about Ramen noodles.

"But we're pretty convinced it's going to work out. So come if you want. This is probably our last summer."

Our last summer . . . Thirty-six more days until Labor Day Weekend. Thirty-six more mornings to welcome customers to our backyard. And then my parents will lower the ticket booth flaps. And it will be over. The summer. Our last summer. Put a padlock on the door. My parents will be able to retire. For the second time. And I will finally have to let go of my childhood.

Or not.

I stand in the doorway of my gray bungalow apartment and lean against the doorjamb. I gaze out at the courtyard. I've been here thirteen years? Over my car looms a twelve-foot poinsettia tree with stems like thick human fingers, twisting and bending as if accusing you of terrible things. They hold, overall, about five sickly leaves. It was a lovely little Christmas plant that some tenant stuck into the ground many years ago. Now it looks like the kind of tree you might see dying in the corner of a greenhouse on Mars.

CHAPTER 1

THE ROCKET

What we call the beginning is often the end. And to make an end is to make a beginning. The end is where we start from.

—T. S. ELIOT

Most miniature golf courses have a first hole that is designed to be easy. There is a statue of an elf, say, or a lighthouse, and a fairway that's lined up with the hole. Simple. Par 2. Customers sink their balls effortlessly, then move on feeling good about themselves. Confidence equals fun. Because people come to mini golf as they come to life: with expectations. That they will be good at it, for one. That they won't look too foolish, for another. Even if they don't come out a big winner in the end, they have good reason to believe it won't be *entirely* unpleasant. It is a *game*, after all. But the thing about Tom Thumb is that it's never going to be as easy as it looks.

The sign at the first hole says . . .

Our first hole, The Rocket, merely *appears* uncomplicated. You will think all is well as your ball leaves the tee-off pad. You may say, "Looking good," as it toddles down the middle of the fairway. Then four feet away the ball will start to drift. "No!" you may yell, or you may pace tight-lipped, or you may stand stock-still and open-jawed. But in any case your ball will bonk the side of the opening. Then it will rebound to bonk the other side of the opening. It may rebound again and possibly again. But regardless of the number of rebounds, when it finally comes to rest, your ball will be under the hazard and unreachable. Always.

"Now what do I do?" is what you might say if you happen to be like most people.

Your best bet is to realize that you are a mere mortal. Lie down on the fairway. Use the handle like a pool cue, and tap the ball towards the hole. Try not to think about the wetness that will appear on the front of your clothes, your own personal Shroud of Turin, when you finally stand up after your prostration on a wet carpet.

Hole #1, The Rocket, is about Expectations.

My mother says I used to hide before bath time, crawl into the hamper and cover myself with shirts and towels, believing I could never be found. Then when I was found and thrust into the tub, I would splash around for hours, like a sea otter just returned to the ocean, making great waves up the side of the tub to let them fall in warm arcs on my arms and legs. Until the water turned tepid, my skin covered in goose bumps, and my mother dragged me out again.

So too does summer come to Wisconsin. Grudgingly. Reluctantly. Appearing weeks later than anyone would like, after a long span of silent hiding in winter. But once it arrives, it lolls around thrilled, sprawling across the land, reflecting the sun off the newly thawed lakes, crystalline, joyful, as heat shimmers off the fields and blacktopped roads.

It is late May, and it is morning, and the five of us—my father, mother, two sisters, and myself—are gathered, more or less, around the first hole. It does not feel like summer yet; the breeze is damp, the air is cool. Grass blades are still bent towards the ground from the weight of the winter, and specks of dew glint a dull yellow. I jigger the zipper of my sweatshirt up and down. This is our first day as owners of Tom Thumb Mini Golf.

There is no hazard here, but we can tell where one has been: a two-foot square of carpet appears greener and fresher than the carpet around it, protected, as it has been, from rain and years of scuffling feet. This is the target my father aims for as he lowers the front end of the dolly. He nudges the corners of the red hazard off onto the fairway and wiggles the dolly out from underneath.

"Pretty close," he says. My sisters and I flick our fingernails against the metal cylinder of the rocket and listen for what might be inside.

"Stop that, girls," Mom says, wrapping her arms around the rocket. She jiggles it onto the platform. "Is it a missile, George?"

"Well, it could be a missile, but I'm thinking it might be a bomb," Dad says. "A little more to the right."

"A bomb!"

"Isn't a bomb the same thing as a missile?"

"No, a missile is self-propelled, but a bomb needs an outside force to project it through the air," Dad explains.

"Stop flicking it, Carla. It's a bomb."

"No, it's not."

"It might explode!"

"I would guess it came from Fort McCoy. Probably World War II." At this moment the bomb/missile sits at an angle, aiming its payload towards the Upper Peninsula of Michigan. "I think it might need some shims." He parks the dolly in the grass and trots towards the garage.

"I'm gonna go help Dad," LeAnn says, leaping over the two-by-fours to gallop after him.

Mom sighs and pries out a few dandelions from cracks in the concrete. I put my ear on the rocket and tap my knuckles against its side.

Our rocket/bomb is five feet tall and painted red and white, with a bayonet-like point on the top. There are four fins attached at the bottom to help it stay on course as it zooms towards a distant planet—or the target it is about to demolish. Around the midsection are booster jets, or what's meant to resemble booster jets. They could be made from pipes scavenged after a plumber has finished work in your basement, then welded here and painted red. Topping each pipe is a little dome with dimples.

"Mom. Are these golf balls?"

"What?"

"Stuck in here," I say, pointing to the pipes.

"How about that."

"I wanna see," Carla says, pulling herself up by the rocket's fins onto the hazard platform.

"They *are* golf balls," Mom says. "Greg must have put them in there."

"That's weird," I say, yanking on one and then another. Carla clenches one on the opposite side.

"Don't pull them out," Mom says.

"Will that make the bomb explode?"

"No. It's just decorative," she says. "Stop it, girls! Why do you keep doing that?"

"Is that for people to get extra balls?"

"No, they look like they're painted in there. They aren't meant to come out."

I try to twist the one farthest from me. "That's weird."

"Stop, June," Carla says, grabbing my hand. "I don't want the bomb to explode!"

"Look, Carla," I say, cupping the ball like a hand grenade. "We have a bomb in our yard. And the bomb is about to blow!" She screams and runs away.

"No, no, no. It's not a bomb," Mom insists. "Greg called it a rocket, so it's a *rocket*. We are calling it The Rocket."

At the end of every summer since 1959, the man who built Tom Thumb unbolted the hazards from their mountings and carted them one by one into the garage. He wedged The Castle and The Paddle Wheel Boat and The Windmill and The Ferris Wheel and The Loop de Loop and The Rocket along with benches and chairs and garbage buckets and other miscellany into a space designed for one and a half cars. Last year my father helped. He didn't think to bring along a notebook. After they lifted and joggled each wooden hazard apart, my father realized he should have memorized the way the pieces came together. He should have taken notes on which hazards used screws, which motors needed brackets, and which would need shims when they were assembled again. The sun was low by the time Greg and my father got the last of the hazards inside, jigsaw-puzzled together under the garage's single naked lightbulb. "That's it," Greg said, as they squeezed their bodies back outside like spelunkers exiting a tunnel. And then Greg, who had designed and built Tom Thumb, handed over the keys. He may have offered my father a handshake. He may have said, "I wish you well."

All around the Chain O' Lakes, families are stirring inside their cottages. Brothers and sisters punching each other awake. It is Saturday morning, Memorial Day Weekend; you can call it the first day of summer; only sixty-five degrees, but you take what you can get in Central Wisconsin. When the glaciers of North America melted fifteen thousand years ago, they left behind this chain of small deep lakes. The deepest reaches ninety-six feet; the shallowest only splashes your ankle. There are twenty-two in all, linked together and fed by underground springs that keep the water cool and clear. From the 1890s, summer homes were built along these lakes. It was a perfect place to escape the heat of the cities, and in the 1930s and '40s its reputation grew. Cottages were clapped together along the sandy shorelines: one bedroom, three bedrooms, or no bedrooms at all; sometimes there was just one large bunkroom where up to twelve could sleep, a kitchen placed as an afterthought on the side. Grandparents from Milwaukee made duplicates of the keys and handed one to each of their offspring. Plumbers and welders and grocery store owners drove their families out from the city to seek their own ritual for announcing that the summer had begun.

"At least the sun's out," mothers say to their children, who crowd around Formica tabletops and pour extra syrup on their pancakes, waiting to see if they will be scolded. On the first day of summer the usual rules might not apply. Grandparents have already begun pushing coins into their grandchildren's pockets. The lakes are still too cold for swimming, and so the families decide to begin the summer the way they always have: "Let's go play mini golf!" And they pile into the grandparents' car that holds four kids in the back, and they sing loudly at their bully older brother until they are shushed, and the grandfather takes the long way around because it is such a pleasant day—he wants to point out the new cottage on Round Lake.

A blue sports car slides into the parking lot, and a woman with dark hair steps out. She presses a lever, and the drivers' seat springs forward. A boy in a brown-striped shirt scrambles out from the back. "I wanna go first," he calls, his tennis shoes hitting the ground.

The woman walks towards us and asks if we're open.

My parents are both kneeling on the second green, trying to push the bottom half of The Castle into place. "Hi-ee," Mom says.

"Not yet," Dad says. "In about an hour."

"Oh, we were hoping to play," the woman says, frowning.

My mom asks if she can come back later. "We'll open sometime between ten and noon."

The woman rests her hand on the split-rail fence and looks out on the eighteen holes, trying to recognize the course from the summers before. The Snack Shack windows are boarded up. The mini golf hazards are missing. Bare concrete and empty fairways crisscross the lawn. Electric boxes flop out on the ground at #2, #15, and #17, where there were once charming little buildings. It looks as if a forest fire came through and left nothing in its path over one-half foot tall, with the exception of hole #6, The Swinging Pole. The pole hasn't been hung, and the frame looms over the course like two limbless trees, or an eight-foot hangman's scaffold.

The woman opens her door and calls her son to get in.

"Why can't we stay?"

"We'll come back another time, honey," she says, nudging his shoulder. He drags his heels in the gravel to make a pair of divots by the front tire. The sports car slowly reverses and tilts back up the road in the direction it came; we watch until it disappears, like sunset.

Along the shore are cattails and the sound of a fumbled kettle-drum. "Ba dup," says an invisible frog.

Dad makes a clicking sound with his tongue. "You'd think people could tell that we weren't open yet."

"Maybe we should get an OPEN sign so people know," Mom says.

"Do we look open? It should be obvious."

"Maybe Greg opened up before ten on the first day."

"It's possible." Dad steers the cart towards the garage on a zig-zaggy path between the greens. LeAnn follows behind. Carla and I balance on two-by-fours and tightrope-walk around the greens.

* * *

The school year had ended the day before, back in our hometown in Iowa. We had cleaned out our desks, celebrated with cupcakes, and by noon were skipping up the hill towards home. "Hurry up and finish packing!" Mom said as a greeting when we danced through the door. Three whole months, I tried to imagine, jamming another pair of shorts into my flowered suitcase. "Bring your stuff down as soon as you can," Mom yelled through the house. At 5 pm the car was fully loaded, and Mom dashed to the neighbors to hand over the front door key. As we crossed into Minnesota, Mom passed around peanut butter sandwiches, and then, as if waiting our turn, we fell asleep one by one, leaning on our belongings. Four and a half hours later we arrived at the dark cottage. "Where's the mini golf?"

"It's over there."

"Where?"

"It's dark now. You'll see it tomorrow."

There was the sound of someone dying coming from the tops of the trees. "Barred owls. Now girls, carry in and then get to bed. Big day tomorrow."

We drifted off to sleep in unfamiliar saggy beds and were awoken two hours later by headlights and revving engines. *Rrrrrrr. Zrrinnnnngg.* Men swearing obscenities. Loud trucks and spinning tires; gravel flying through the air like birdshot. Drunk men, maybe a motorcycle gang. Carla whimpered in the dark on the bed across from me, and I reached for my flashlight on the floor. "I think it might just be people turning around in the parking lot," Mom yelled up the stairs. "You girls try to sleep."

Now ten o'clock the next morning, Carla and I take turns pointing the toes of our sneakers into the metal cup of #17. The course has become a checkerboard of sun and shade. The wings of a dragonfly as it chases towards the shore look like a pair of blue-green oval mirrors reflecting the sun. "Mom, can we play a game?"

"Mini golf? We've got to get open first." She is holding up the roof of the windmill to keep it from crashing on Dad's head, which is buried somewhere inside. She tells us to find something to do.

"What?"

"Why don't you clean out the water hole. That's a good job for you."

"It's full of icky leaves."

"That's why it needs cleaning out. People can't play it until the pond is clear."

"But it smells gross. Like pee."

Dad looks up from his motor, and we know it is in our best interest to stop complaining.

At the edge of #7, Carla and I pick up sticks from the ground and poke at the pond and the leaves floating in it. They are black and heavy in a syrup of red and yellow water. The smell gets stronger with our splashing, as if we have disturbed the crust of its putrescence. We pinch our noses. We say "Ooouuheee" and "Uuuuaaww," using all the vowel sounds we have gathered in our seven and ten years. Is that smell from urine? No, it can't be urine. Would a person really do that? Would a bunch of teen-age boys? Not possible. But still, it just smells so much like pee. We are ignoring Mom's suggestion to scoop the leaves out with a rake because we plan on doing this job so poorly that she will be forced to do it herself. A sedan comes down the road and stops next to the pool. It is only separated from the road by a flower bed full of weeds. A man with a mustache leans his head out his window.

"Are you open?"

We look at him as if he has walked into our living room during a family argument. "Uh. We're going to open later," I say.

"When?"

I shrug. "Maybe noon."

The car resumes its slow cruise down the road as I flip some wet oak leaves in the air, landing a few on Carla's bare ankle.

"Ick! Stop it."

"Ha," I say. I prod another fist-sized blob of leaves onto the end of my stick and aim for her again, but she moves away, as younger sisters do, and scuttles to the safety of the next green over.

Then she leaps back onto the pavement. "Yuck," she says, holding up the soles of one sock. "The green is wet."

"Why did you take your shoes off?"

"The ground is wet and my shoes were getting muddy."

"But now your socks are getting muddy."

She shrugs and peels off her white ankle socks. She drops them in the thick grass underneath the bench by #6, where they remain for the next three days.

The sun is overhead, our shadows are short and crisp, when a pontoon boat built for twelve chugs to the middle of Bass Lake. Twelve people hang over its sides and ogle us across the cattails. They pass cans of pop to each other while the boat turns a circle so those seated on the other side can get a better view. "Well, hello," I say quietly. Mom marches out of the garage lugging a couple of large plastic buckets and rags. "Don't just stand around, girls. The greens need to be swept off. Go find some brooms."

Carla and I stumble down the path towards the garage groaning, hoping to escape into the cottage. Like most children, we are accustomed to estimating how much work can be expected from us "at our age" before we can complain and disappear without a chase. That limit was passed hours ago. Expecting more from us is unreasonable and unjustified, so at this time we feel that hiding is appropriate and apt. We are nearing the porch steps, nearly home free, when LeAnn pushes open the Dutch door of the ticket booth. "Check this out," she says, waving a broom like a flag overhead. Half the straw seems to be missing, the bristles sheared off at a sharp angle.

"Wow. Where do you buy a broom like that?" I say.

"That one looks like it's almost used up," Mom says.

"Used up?"

"From sweeping, I suppose."

Carla and I stop. We stand perfectly still on the pathway just outside the cottage. We are children and we have not experienced death nor are we aware of dying, but at this moment in our short lives we consider the possibility that a situation could require so much sweeping that the bristles of the broom could be worn down to the wood—decapitated—and we have found ourselves in precisely that situation.

"And this is the best one!" LeAnn proclaims.

As the sun passes its zenith, more and more tourists come by, hoping to buy treats or play a round of golf. But we are not much closer to opening than we were two hours ago. We have hauled out a few hazards, but there are still six hazards in the garage. The greens are coated with a winter's worth of leaves, and the water hole teems with rot. And every twenty minutes we wander over to the ticket booth to answer questions: "Are you open?" "When do you plan to open?" A sea of puffy clouds swim together over the golf course. But when you look up it appears as if the sky is standing still, and instead, the mini golf course is moving—floating away from us.

Mom takes a broom and swoops at the concrete. "I wonder how much business we're losing today."

"I don't want to think about that," Dad yells from the grass near #17.

A Lincoln Continental creeps around the corner; the front

end drips over the lip of the road into the parking lot. The grandfather applies the brakes before he is halfway across the gravel, and the car is still rolling when the back door opens. Syrup-filled kids flow out. One lands on the gravel. "You pushed me!" "I did not." "Kids!" A maroon sedan pulls up next to them, then a third and a fourth car, their windows down, arms and fists banging on the sides. "Beat ya. Beat ya!" "We left a lot later than you!" The cars line up side by side as a fifth car peels in and jolts to a stop by the Snack Shack.

It's like a ceramic piggy bank thrown onto the floor, all these redheads in the parking lot, spilling out like so many pennies. Tall gangly men in t-shirts. Women in their thirties with matching ponytails. Babies in strollers, two teen girls in white culottes, and teenage boys who adjust their crotches inside blue athletic shorts. There are twenty or thirty people in all, swarming and moving, as one, towards the grandfather's sedan. "Me first." "No, I go first!" They decide which kids are old enough to play on their own. They claim the blue ball; they claim the best putter; they joke that the losers should have to walk home. In the center, like a brigadier general accustomed to the wiggliness of his troops before battle, the patriarch stands, unmoving. He has thick silver hair, a plaid shirt, and he looks out on the horizon. He checks for his wallet then strides forth, aiming his battalion towards the ticket booth.

We watch from the course where we kneel on the ground, clad in our most-stained shorts and least-loved shirts. We grip broom handles and wrenches, metal dustpans, and rags. Around us like puddles lie metal rakes, white industrial buckets, shears and wire cutters, garden hoses, a wheelbarrow, hammers and pliers and screwdrivers of varying sizes; and the parts of several hazards strewn all over the greens.

When the grandfather reaches the front counter, he notices the plywood flaps on the windows. He turns towards the course.

"Hmm," he grunts. He clears his throat. There is mumbling from his people as one man mentions that he had seen the FOR SALE sign the year before. The grandfather nods, then breaks away from the mob to stride towards us. He grips the wooden rail of the fence like a podium, about to make an announcement. "Are you closed this whole summer?" he bellows at my father.

We have not yet waited on customers here or anywhere else before, but we know instinctively—the way a baby starts to suckle even before its eyes have opened—we must be nice to these people. They are *customers*. This is their summer vacation, and they have driven here to *play*. They pace and stomp around the parking lot—*our* parking lot—but we are still getting used to the possessive tense, whereas they have felt possessive all along.

Mom waves towards the grandfather. Then she notices the dirt and grease stains on her palm and brushes it across her shorts. In her gentlest voice, she turns to my father. "So, when do you think we'll open?"

"I don't know, Jeannie. Why do you keep asking me?"

"I'm not trying to irritate you, George, but I've got to talk to these people. And I don't know what to tell them."

Instead of words, my father lets out the sound of a small breath, like precious air he has been holding on to all morning, and now is reluctantly letting it go. He pushes himself up from his knees and looks at the screwdriver in his hand. He sets it on the ground, then he picks it up again and sets it on the wrenches in his tool tray. He takes two steps towards the garage and then turns and steps back. In his blinking eyes we see that he wants to go into the house, dig out the keys and padlocks, and lock the whole place up.

At the beginning, they say it was three days before God looked out on the earth and realized, Hey, a bit of land might be a nice thing. And he made the water all clump together on one side of the world like the girls at a junior high dance, and the land cluster on the other side, like the boys who are punching each other in the arms, trying to impress the water. Yes, the water says, your muscles are very strong.

God created the rest of the whole she-bang—the animals and the people and the who-sits and the what-sits and the insects that bite each other's heads off when they're mating—in only the two and a half days that followed. Sounds easy. But then, God was working from scratch. He got a clean slate. In my experience it's much harder to put pieces together when you show up sometime in the middle. If God came right now to start it up again, could he find a good place for Eden? Could he raise the Rocky Mountains without plowing over Wyoming? Get the rivers to flow down hills without washing out the suburbs below?

And so with Tom Thumb. There was only one man on earth who knew how to get The Castle doors to open and The Paddle Wheel Boat to fit together and the location of all the parts of The Ferris Wheel, #15.

"Maybe we should call Greg," Mom says.

"It's too late for that now."

"We should have come up this last weekend."

"Of course we should have come up this last weekend."

"Well, I'd better go say something to them," she says, giving a half wave towards the family. She pulls at the hem of her shirt. As my father kneels at the paddle wheel, she steps past his shoulder, reaching out her fingers, just a breath away from his skin, touching the tender air that hovers between them.

Mom tells the grandfather and his redheaded family that we might be open later, about 3 pm. And with upturned hands, a gesture of humility, she offers an apology to each one who needs it. Then she calls us into the house to eat sandwiches, while the group hovers by their cars in indecision.

"They're closed. I told you."

"All right, beely-bobs, let's get going."

We watch as the five cars eventually drive off—the last one spinning its tires as it flees, leaving a pair of dirt ovals that my father shovels over the next day.

We carry our sandwiches back outside and nibble at the corners as we stand around the castle as if it's a campfire, watching Dad lean inside it with a Phillips screwdriver. "Shoot. It just won't balance. I can get it to close, but then it won't open again."

"Do you want peanut butter?"

"What's that, Jean?"

"Peanut butter or ham."

More cars pull in, a family on a set of bicycles, a couple in a canoe. The men glare and shake their heads in disgust; the women lean towards each other and whisper. We take turns apologizing as best we can, and say we might be open around 5 pm.

Cars come and go. Mowers across the lake choke and stop, then start again. But the birds carry on with their own conversations above us. They live in a stratum of pure joy, hidden from our view by the leaves of the obliging trees. And we wipe the mud off the bottoms of our feet so we won't track it onto the carpet of #3.

The lake is still bright, the surface calm, the water like glass as the evening creeps in. But the mini golf is mostly shaded now, except for a puddle of light on the green of #14. A blue sports car edges along the road and slowly tips into the parking lot. The boy in the striped shirt pops out of the back, and his mother, in khaki shorts, follows. She looks at us out on the course, and then her chest heaves in a tremendous sigh. The boy runs to the ticket booth and plops his hands on the carpeted counter.

"Goodness," Mom says, setting down a trash bucket by the first hole. "Weren't you here this morning?" She looks at the woman. Her shorts are stained, just like my mother's, and her eyes are just as tired, the expression just as desperate. "We really thought we'd be open by now," Mom says. "I'm sorry. I know you were here earlier, but there's so much we have yet to do."

The woman glances up the road as if hoping to see something other than a line of summer cottages: another amusement, a go-cart track, a county fair to appear from nowhere. "Okay. Sure. I understand," the woman says.

"Where are we going?" the boy asks.

"I don't know," she replies. "Back in the car. I'm sorry."

"Shoot." My mom sighs quietly. She looks up at the oversize Pepsi clock on the front of the garage. Both hands are straight down. Six-thirty. "Wait," she says. "Don't go yet. We're really not quite ready to open, but if you don't mind us working around you while you play?"

"Yay," the boy says, leaping onto his toes.

"We're opening," LeAnn yells to us, as she scampers to turn on the power in the garage.

"Are you kidding?" I say, draping wet rags on the fence.

Dad comes running from the back. "Jeannie, you're letting them play? I don't think we're ready!"

Mom guides him to the grass behind the ticket booth and lowers her voice. "She was here once already, George, maybe twice. I just can't send them away again—that little boy—" My father takes a step to the side and frowns at the woman. He had worked all the previous day finishing the school year. As the last students left his classroom, he filled out report cards and turned in his final grades for all five sections of his chemistry and physics classes. Then he packed up the car, drove almost five hours to get here, and after a late night and very little sleep, he had worked today since dawn. He is not in the mood for demands.

He takes a deep breath and walks to the front counter. He brushes a leaf from the felt countertop. He plucks at a twig with his fingertips. "Well, I don't know what to say to you. We're not really all put together yet."

"It doesn't matter to us. Does it, Jake?"

"Are we going to get to play?" the boy asks.

My dad looks down at him. "Well, I'm going to let you play, but only if you promise me one thing. I want you to let your mother win. Okay?"

The boy looks up at him, waiting to understand if this is good news or bad. And then my dad smiles.

The boy jumps again. And his mother mouths, "Thank you." And so it is true. We are open. And that's when our scrambling really begins.

Mom rushes down the path waving. "Girls, get going!" She leaps up the porch steps. "I'll get the money. Bring the clubs out. Where's that cooler full of golf balls you saw?"

The previous owner had piled all the putters in our bedrooms for the winter; my sisters and I race up the stairs to get them. With three or four apiece we rush back down the stairs, the clubs banging across our arms like an assortment of long-stem chrome roses. "I'll arrange them later," Dad says, when we drop them with a clang in the ticket booth. We race back for another load of putters, as he raises the plywood flaps revealing the screen windows for the first time.

We lug out tee-off pads we discover under a bench on the porch. As our first two customers approach hole #1 with their balls and clubs, we drop a tee-off pad on the first fairway. As they finish up the first hole, we plop a tee-off pad at hole #2. There is an animated cartoon where people are laying train tracks just ahead of the barreling steam train they are riding. It is like that for us. As the mother writes their scores down for hole #3, we affix the sign to the front of hole #4. We find the circuit box switch to turn on the motor for #8, as they complete playing hole #7. We lead our first customers around the course, finishing a hazard and clearing away our tools just as they are about to tee off. When the sun begins hanging low and the course looks dark, we find a basket of colored lightbulbs that we screw into sockets under the eaves of the ticket booth. We light them, as if to announce, "Open for business."

It is about this time that our first customers lose their golf balls. "They just disappeared," the mother says, pointing to hole #16. Her son is poking the handle of his club up the eight-foot pipe where the balls should have come out.

"Girls," Mom says to Carla and me, "go see if you can help them. Take a few balls with you."

I am only ten and my sister is seven, but we swagger like cowboys, golf balls stuffed in our jacket pockets like six-shooters. It is not the exact moment we become grown-ups, but it is the first time we have ever felt the weight of a mission of our own. We have responsibilities now. We are coming to the rescue of an adult, a customer, someone trying to enjoy her brief vacation. This is only the first day, and already we are learning our purpose.

I throw a ball into the eight-foot pipe of hole #16. It does not come out on the green. "That's what happened to me," the boy says. We throw in a second golf ball, then a third. Each bounces around inside, but then there is silence. It is the sound of stuckness, which is, of course, no sound at all. We find a garden hose and run back to the hole like crazed dogs, the hose dragging behind us. We push one end in, but it won't go past the elbow. We consider connecting the hose and flushing the pipe with water. We consider reaching in with pliers to try to grab the source of the plug. Leaves? Twigs? Forgotten golf balls from previous years?

"Let me try one more," one of us says, I don't remember who, leveraging a golf ball into the hole with an extra push. This ball sounds different. This one has oomph. It rattles down through the first section; we hear it clear the bend, then it rolls a bit farther, much farther than the ones before . . . And then there is silence.

"Well, darn it," I say. We have no more balls to throw. A toad appears at the end of the pipe. He is dark green and fat, and he jumps onto the green followed by a rolling red golf ball. A green ball rolls out next. Then a yellow ball. A blue one. Four balls in a row roll out behind the toad, like ducklings after their mother. "That's my ball!" the boy says, picking up the red one.

The toad hops over the two-by-four and into the tall grass and weeds and disappears. Carla and I look at each other, eyes wide.

I think the phrase people use is *scream with delight*, but that sounds very Victorian, like something that might happen at an ice cream social when the caramel topping is discovered. For us, it was the scream of finding an amphibian, a living green creature, where a stone or dead leaf was expected. This was our discovery that life is like that: the startling recognition that you are not alone. In this case there was also a toad.

CHAPTER 2

THE CASTLE

Generations pass while some trees stand, and old families last not three oaks.

—SIR THOMAS BROWNE

If you are in the middle of a fairy tale, sooner or later you're going to encounter a castle. So, without further ado, I present you hole #2: Behold! The majesty. The turrets. White flags flapping from each tower! The Castle. La!

The walls are thick and painted royal blue. Three small gothic windows are cut into the sides. Above it all, a roof of silver shingles gleams in the sun. The castle walls are notched with battlements—places where a knight can crouch behind to discharge his sharpened arrows if he is four inches tall. (You don't have to notice that the flagpoles bear a striking resemblance to TV antennas, because we're not going to notice this ourselves for a year or two.)

You grip the putter with both hands, the fingers slightly overlapping. You look down at your dimpled yellow ball, and up at the fairway; down at the ball, and up again at the hazard.

Then you hear the can-opener drone of a motor. You notice for the first time that The Castle has dark brown doors. And right now they are closed; you can't get through. You lean over your ball, staring at the arch where the doors come together. You study the seam between them, and it is agony, sweet agony, waiting, waiting.

Hole #2, The Castle, is about Time.

In the land of lumberjacks there lived a girl who grew too tall to see her shoes. She looked over the heads of her younger brother and sister, and over the wavy hair of her classmates at school. She stooped low to enter the doorway of the bank where her father worked. The only people she didn't tower over were her older brother and sisters, who in turn, and in a way, towered over her. She was sad. Her middle name was Olive. When the chance came to graduate from high school early, she said yes. And that's how it happened that she was working at the bank one late summer when the new schoolteacher arrived in town.

Like the wind that rolls up one side of a mountain, his dark hair parted on the side to swoop over the top and plunge again. She was going to fall in love with his perfect small nose and the way his eyes crinkled when he smiled, but they hadn't been introduced yet. Let me tell you how that happened.

The town was too small to have more than one rooming house where a bachelor could stay, so he lived under the roof of Mrs. Bernhardt. She kept pansies and red begonias, but Mrs. Bernhardt wasn't a cook and she didn't offer meals. The new schoolteacher walked the three blocks to the café every day—breakfast, lunch, and dinner. Three times each day he passed the windows of the bank. The girl, now seventeen, watched him as if he were a sun that somehow rose in the north and traveled south on Main Street, a sun that determined the time of day she would step outside to make walks of her own, contrived errands to the bakery, or around the corner to the mill.

He smiled. She smiled back as she glanced down, searching again for her feet and the sidewalk that must be below. As he passed by her shoulder she would sneak another look at him as he opened the door to the Crystal Café, ringing the bell that hung over the entrance.

Leaves began turning yellow and brown, and sometimes she dared to look at his face, the center of the sun, which would make her flush red, and she would wonder if other people on the street had noticed.

They met in church. "You must be the new agriculture teacher," the girl's mother said, leaning back across the pew to shake hands with the man. Yes, he must have said, like he had seven hundred times already, as he met the residents of the town one by one. And then the woman—the mother—said the six words that the girl and the sun had both been waiting to hear: "Have you met my daughter, Jeanette?"

The man and the girl clasped hands briefly over the top of the pew—curved oak wood, a polished circular top, turned on the ends, a smooth wall, then planks joined for the seat. It was the remnant of a tree that had been growing in Wisconsin for 125 years before it was hewn with an axe by a strong Norwegian man who could have been the grandfather of the girl or the grandfather of the man, an ancestor lured to the north woods carrying one small suitcase and the knowledge that lumber equals potential. And this oak pew, made dense from layers and lines measuring the years of its agony through long Wisconsin winters, was shaped into seams to run your fingers along as you waited for the blessing to be over, for life to resume. Then they exited the church past the gray marble recesses and met again on the front steps and blushed in unison at the remarkable nature of daylight. Glory, it's called, and it reflected off everything, the grass, the pavement, the clouds in the sky. He towered over her by one or two inches, and this was a reason for her to begin her years of looking up. The beginning. The opening. Agony and then calm. The way the future curls into a ball on your palm to sleep in the comfort of you and you in the comfort of its throbbing heart, so small, so fragile, the furry tail wrapped around itself as it arches its back, then lies back down again, to sleep and dream up the life that lies ahead of you.

"He was so blame handsome; I could hardly stand it," my mother says now. "Your father would walk down the street—*Brrmmp!*—every day. He was so handsome I couldn't even look at him sometimes. I wish you could have seen him. I don't know if you girls are aware of this, but your father was a very handsome man. Is! Is a very handsome man!"

They wed two and a half years later. It has been forty-seven years and they are still married. I am forty years old and egregiously single. My mother says: "But I think it's okay you are still single, June. I am just so grateful that I didn't marry right after high school like the other girls in town. I'm so glad I had a chance to be on my own for a while. I'm glad I waited until I was twenty."

Finally a crack appears between the castle doors. With a groan the two sides separate and creak out to the fairway. As light rushes in, you can peek at the secret inner workings: skeletal metal arms hang low from the rafters. They push out the doors with their thin metallic wrists. For a brief moment you see that inside the castle the walls are not blue but the color of unpainted plywood, a psychedelic swirl of dark-colored swirls from pine cut in the direction of the grain and allowed to absorb the moisture over the years.

Then remembering where you are, you look back at your ball. Just before the doors reach the top of their arc, you putt. Ah, the timing is perfect. Your ball floats down the runway towards the castle doors, then drifts to the side. It plonks with a dull thud against the wall on the right. The doors are closing, and now you'll have to wait again.

* * *

This is the story of my great-grandfather.

There once was a man in Norway with no last name. He was poor and owned no land. He gave himself the name of the farm where he worked—Melby—and sailed away to a new country. He arrived in Wisconsin. There he bought fifty acres from a man named Pegleg who lived in a hole in the ground, a cavelike dwelling dug into the hillside. My great-grandfather lived in the hole while he built the Melby homestead up around him. Then he gave up bachelorhood at the age of forty-two and married a young woman, also recently arrived from Norway. They began a brood of many children. His wife—my great-grandmother—had three sets of twins, but it was too much: she died just a few days after the third set was born. This is all I know about her. As for him, he ran the farm and then died from bee stings after stepping on a hive.

Of his parents or hers, I know nothing.

Here is another fairy tale. This one is about my father, and this one's also true.

Once upon a time there was a coin toss. I don't know if the coin was a quarter or a dime or a nickel, or if there was a breeze coming through the window of the army recruitment office that day to catch the coin on its edge, making it swoop before it landed. I do not know if it fell onto a desk or was caught in the air by one of the two men in the room, local officials in the rural town who knew my grandfather and his family—after all, there were only several hundred people in the entire town of Blair. My father won the toss; that is the point. It was 1945, and World War II was just ending. A birth date had been drawn, one shared by my father and his fraternal twin. In those days there was a deferment available for farmers, determined by the acreage of the farm and the number of men in the family who could work it. One of the two brothers would be drafted. My uncle, my father's twin brother, lost the toss—that is, he had to stay home. It was his job, therefore, to take over when his father died. So he lived his entire life, seventy-six years, on the same land where he was born, working as hard as any farmer does, milking the herd twice a day, making little profit from his labor, as the farm fell down around his feet, like work clothes around the ankles at the end of a long day. Eighty years after it was established, all the buildings of the family farm—the barn, the milkhouse, and the granary—had collapsed, the animals sold off cheap. My father's share, which had been handed over in the interest of helping cash flow, had been sold off with the rest. The house where my grandparents lived and died rotted from the center and fell into the earth. My father's brother lost the coin toss. Only he was not interested in fixing roofs or protecting wood from the rain. He wasn't suited to be a farmer—an occupation that comes with responsibilities he never would have picked had he chosen a life for himself.

But I'm jumping ahead here. Let's start this story again.

Once in a land where there were woods and farms, a one-room schoolhouse, and more farms, there grew a boy in oversized work jeans. His name was George. His job was to help with the milking, stop pestering the horses, and raise himself to adulthood, seeing as how his parents, a farm couple, were already busy raising livestock. There were chickens for eggs, cats to chase mice, two horses, and forty milk cows, which were more than enough, especially when the cows stood at the ready, hoping to be milked. The horses could drag the fields, cultivate, and pull the binder in August, but they were no help at all in getting the milk from the herd. The milking had to be done by hand, twice a day, three hours from start of herd to finish, all the years of their lives.

To say that life was hard would be like saying that there was dirt: in the fields, out the windows of the farmhouse, and around the ends of the fingers of the boy, his mother and father, and also his twin brother. Of dirt there was plenty, of other things there were not. Clothing came from other farmers, who passed around any extra. Electricity had reached the cities, but not the villages and valleys, so for them there was a hand pump, an outhouse in the back, a stove that burned wood, and a drought that was coming on its tenth year. The dirt was hard as the unpaved highway out front, baked by the sun, offering no relief for the unemployed men who streamed past, hoping to find work in the next town.

One day the boys' father bought two new horses. They came in a team—just like the twins—a duo for pulling. It was important for the horses' temperaments to match; the people who broke them took great pride in their teams. Draft horses they were called, broad-backed beasts. They were not pets or good for riding, but they were given names, Rocky and Rudy. "Oh, Rocky," my father and his brother would say, "he is a smart cookie." If you left the top of the barn door open, he would reach in and lift the latch. The other horse, Rudy, wasn't lazy, but of the two he was less interested in getting in the harness in the morning. He was less engrossed by cultivating or threshing. The team was there to work, but they had wills of their own. Personalities. Like people.

One day when George was about twelve, his father, George Senior, asked him to step up onto the grain binder. There were five levers, but he only showed him two. After he sat him down on the seat, he rode off with the horses pulling George Junior behind on the binder. "You'll figure it out," his father yelled, and the boy, bewildered, learned how the other three levers were used to bundle the oats. He learned self-reliance, trial and error, and that his father thought him smarter than his twin brother, Jerry. And Jerry watched the procession down the fields and all the fields that followed, but was never taught this or the other difficult tasks on the farm. The father, a private man, like many of the Norwegian farmers of that valley, never explained things to either boy. But one son learned more by simply being relied upon. *He's just bigger than me*, the neglected one thought, as he watched his brother become more and more trusted by his father. The twins, like the horses, had come in a team. And just like the horses, one was more suited to farming.

But it was a coin toss that decided who, of the two, would be the farmer for life.

My father spent eighteen months in the army, and then returned to the farm where he had been the favored son, but now was a hero as well. His father sat him at the table and asked for stories about Japan. His mother baked him his favorite cakes and bragged about him to the neighbors. He took advantage of the GI Bill and attended college, the first person in his family to do so. Just three months after he graduated, he was hired by a high school to teach agriculture. He moved five counties north, and there he met the banker's daughter. He married her and bought a house with down-payment help from his in-laws.

When he was forty-six he invested in a business of his own: a miniature golf course located on a clear blue lake, where customers laughed on the lawn and hazards sparkled in the sun. His brother, Jerry, had to stay on the farm. He and his wife, Helen, moved into the house where he had grown up. His parents moved into a smaller house on the yard just down the hill from them and proceeded to complain about how Jerry did his farming. "I don't think it was easy for Jerry, not for Helen either," my mom has said. "Your grandmother didn't think she did anything right."

This is why my father worries. He may have all this here, this summer business, this beautiful land, but he wonders if somehow he could have saved the family farm. Could it have been possible to do both, run Tom Thumb and also keep the barn from collapsing? Why did his brother get the farm when he was never cut out for the job? Was it fair that his brother never had a choice?

"Well, I could have enlisted," Jerry said, one evening after Thanksgiving dinner, "but I would have felt very guilty because I would be leaving my father—"

"He couldn't handle the farm all alone, you see," my father said, explaining it to me.

"It probably would have been beneficial to everybody if I had enlisted."

"Looking back on it," my father said to him. "But at the time you certainly—"

"No."

"—at the time there was no way to think that way."

"Did a lot of the farms in your area get passed down to their families?" I asked.

"I think so, basically they did," Jerry answered.

"They were family farms," Mom said from the kitchen.

"You see, you just did. You just did what you were told," Jerry said. "I could have done a lot better, but then that's second-guessing too. But nowadays if I was farming and I had a son to take my farm, I'd say, 'Forget it! Don't even come near it!'" And then he laughed. Jerry always ended with a laugh.

When Greg, the previous owner of Tom Thumb Miniature Golf, moved out of the cottage, he left behind all his furniture, dishes, and a shelf of forgettable books. *Readings for Children*, a dreary collection of eleven volumes, offered illustrations in orange ink and bad poetry about seasons. Two volumes were somewhat tolerable, however—dedicated entirely to fairy tales. I spent the first two summers reading them in the ticket booth and feeling sorry for myself. I likened my plight to Cinderella's. I stared out the ticket booth window and imagined that I might as well have been locked inside the tiny castle turrets.

I don't have a favorite hazard at Tom Thumb; none of us in our family do. If you asked, we would say: "Do you mean favorite hole to play? Or favorite hole to paint? Easiest to clean up? Or least likely to break down?" After thirty years we can't think that way at all. We look at The Castle and remember the time we

discovered that the towers were made from coffee cans. How we
left the doors closed sometimes just to mess with people. There's
a memory imbedded not just in each hazard but in each corner
of a hazard. After thirty years, these eighteen holes are like an
elaborate diary.

Does that sound crazy? They say there was once a group of
prisoners who, wanting to keep a record of the time they spent
incarcerated, tied a small series of knots in string they had available, threads from their mattresses or the ends of their shirts. The
knots somehow acted like memories and later reminded them of
events. (Actually, they weren't prisoners; they were Jews suffering
in Nazi concentration camps, but that is too depressing. We are
talking about miniature golf here.)

Here at #2, the maple tree has an electrical cord attached to
the trunk. It carries current from the ground to a connector overhead, powering the ticket booth and pop machine since 1959. As
the years have passed the bark has grown over the cord. I remember
how when I was ten during our first summer at Tom Thumb, you
could still see the metal clips that held the cord to the tree. Now
they are completely hidden, but you can tell where the clips once
were. The cord plunges in and out of the tree like a white sewing
thread.

The tree keeps growing and so the bark keeps growing, and
each summer when I come home for a visit from California, I run
my finger along the cord while waiting for the castle doors to
open. The cord is still visible—maybe just for a few more years—
still carrying 110 volts to the ceramic connector above, which is
almost completely invisible.

By the way, hole #2 is not always The Castle. One year in the
1970s, none of us remember which, Dad built an alternate hazard
in his woodshop back in Iowa. We listened to him banging on
it in the basement all winter. He made a miniature building with

low red walls, a gambrel roof, and three plexiglass windows on each side—a secret, he told us, so we pretended not to know all along that it was a barn. The windows were trimmed with wooden strips so thin and intricate that he cut them by hand, pinned them into *x*'s with tiny tacks, and dabbed on white paint with a brush he confessed he had stolen from one of our paint-by-number kits. And the next spring he wheeled it out for us to marvel at: "A barn!" we said, feigning surprise. It looked exactly like the one that his father had built back in the 1910s, on the farm where my father grew up.

He wired a small yellow bulb inside, which made the windows glow at night when one of us remembered to feel under the eave for the switch. One year he added a *moo* horn he could turn on from the ticket booth to startle people when they were putting. "Like if someone were bending down because their ball got stuck underneath, and they were trying to push it out with their putter. That's when I'd use the horn."

"When their heads were inside the barn?" I asked him.

"Yeah. It was a car horn. Twelve volts. You can buy them from a surplus catalog."

"Was it loud?"

"Not too loud. I wonder where that went to. It's someplace around here."

The Castle is in storage this year. My parents alternate them every couple of years: barn, castle, barn, castle. Every farmer has a barn, and every man's home is his castle. My dad has had both, and they get painted every year.

The Castle was about Time, and now The Barn is about Time, and both open and close at about four revolutions per minute, because my father geared it down from six which would have been too fast when you are aiming. But you can't make time move more slowly, because time doesn't move at all. We are the ones in motion. And most of the time, we are moving away.

CHAPTER 3

THE ONE WITH THE HILL
IN THE MIDDLE

*The best way to keep children at home is to make the home
atmosphere pleasant, and let the air out of the tires.*

—DOROTHY PARKER

Hole #3 is called by many names. Dad refers to it as "The Mole
Hole," tourists call it "The One With The Hill In The Middle," but
the rest of us just call it hole #3. What everyone agrees, however,
is that #3 is the most difficult hole on the course. When customers need a tiebreaker, Dad sends them for a "playoff" to hole #3.
They groan at the news.

There are two zigzags in the fairway, so it is pointless to aim.
The best strategy is to whack your ball at the first angled board
and hope for the best. Your ball will bang around the corners
and then stumble upon three bowling pins dangling across the
fairway. They were painted years ago—what color is difficult to
tell. Above them is a flower box holding a piece of green foam
jammed with faded roses and plastic daisies that may have been
stolen from a gravesite on the neglected side of town, or so they
appear.

Hole #3 isn't trying to be pretty. The two-by-fours themselves
always look ragged and chipped just days after they've been
painted. They have the misfortune of forming the border of the

most frustrating hole on the course, and so receive a beating each day from balls slamming against them and from customers who, expressing their displeasure, flail their putters and their shoes against its sides.

The cup is on the top of a molehill in the center of the green. To sink your ball you need to putt with perfect speed as well as aim: too slow and your golf ball will roll back towards you; too hard and your ball will skip over the hill completely, rebound against the two-by-fours, and roll to a stop in the corner. Your next shot, from the farthest reaches of the green, will be almost impossible to sink. Sisyphus was cursed by Zeus to roll a huge boulder up a hill, only to watch it roll down again, and to repeat this throughout eternity. But at least his hill was symmetrical. The problem with hole #3, and the reason it is so difficult, is that the hole isn't quite centered on the hill. It's slightly off to one side. I mean, the course was built by a schoolteacher with a seventy-nine-cent trowel in his hand, so you know, things like this were bound to happen. Human beings aren't known for exactness, and most of the time I would contend that is as it should be. Symmetry is overrated. Predictability gets dull. But the truth is hole #3 is not necessarily fun.

After the relative *ha-ha* and *ho-ho* of the first two holes, the third one carries a message: Life ain't going to be easy. You can forget the idea that this game is going to make you look good. Hole #3, The One With The Hill In The Middle, is about Despair.

It was the first week of June. We had survived opening weekend: sixty hours of panic and wide-eyed thrill. We learned how to make change, select putters for differing heights, and, generally speaking, deal with tourists, both friendly and otherwise. We took turns at the counter. I waited on my first customers. Over the three days we had taken in $260, which to my parents seemed like a lot. *Wow, isn't this wonderful?*

And then all was quiet. The vacationers had left us. Their cottages were shuttered, the campers loaded up, as people returned to their permanent homes in Madison, Milwaukee, and Chicago for another week or two of school. There were no boats on the lake, except for a couple of old fishermen who floated motionless in a rowboat, as if they had forgotten the reason they were there. The road was empty except for an extraordinary number of flattened squirrels. When a car passed by, there was only one person, the driver. A local going to work, we said to each other. Or maybe someone getting groceries, we said, reassuring each other that there were perfectly good reasons that no one was stopping.

Our new territory—including the golf course, parking lot, cottage, and lawn—was a peninsula, a piece of land shaped rather like a tongue. It jutted out between two small connected lakes (Bass and Beasley) with ankle-deep Beasley Creek along one side. These were our borders. The road ran along the base of the peninsula stretching left to right. It defined the limits of our land, a boundary between Tom Thumb and the rest of the world. Like a lid used to seal a container, there was only one way out.

On the other side of the road was a steep slope of dark pines that formed something like a wall, but to reach it you'd first need to cross a four-foot moat of poison ivy. Beyond and above was a hill of even darker woods. Like the death knell from a forgotten church, a bell clanged twice a day from that direction. "Must be time to eat at Camp Tamarack," we'd say, referring to the Bible camp that was invisible to us, existing only as a bell, and the source of occasional screams from teenage girls, when the wind was just right, it was the end of the week, and relay races, presumably, were well under way.

Mom announced that she was going into town to start a new bank account for Tom Thumb. "You girls can come along if you like."

Our road was called Whispering Pines—a name I particularly liked. There were no other businesses on these three miles of road. There were no gas stations, no handi-marts, no souvenir shops, no fast-food joints. There were no boat rentals, no ice cream stands, no batting cages or bait shops. All these were miles away because the city had never approved the existence of Tom Thumb in the first place. It sprang up before the word *zoning* had ever passed the lips of the local elected officials. The course sat like a backyard hobby next to a cottage on a lonely quiet road. Which in fact it was.

The road was bordered with oaks and elms that joined their hands overhead, Norway pines taller than they needed to be, the floor an orange carpet of last year's needles. The maple trees reserved a lower branch of fingers and twigs for making an expert grab at your car as you passed. Dark and twisting, and with no intersecting roads, Whispering Pines was, in fact, more like a tunnel than a road. The ground was always dark, the cottages beneath in the spell of a permanent eclipse.

We stared out the car windows at the hand-lettered signs attached to garages or the tops of rural mailboxes: ROGERS ROOST, PINE HAVEN, and HENDERSON'S HIDEAWAY. Each cottage had been named by the family that owned it. One sign had a row of bunnies to indicate their many children; another sign on a mailbox was shaped like a tooth. "Must be a dentist," Mom said.

"Can we get a name for our cottage?" we asked.

"We already have a name," Mom answered. "Tom Thumb!"

The town, Waupaca, was six miles away and held 4,500 people if you counted only year-rounders. It seemed small and backward to us, less than half the size of our hometown in Iowa. Waupaca was the kind of town where there was one of each: one hardware store, one shoe store, one insurance company, one clothing store, one courthouse square with one bandstand, and one travel agency. While Mom and LeAnn did the errands, my sister Carla and I went into the five-and-dime. Like the rest of town, the store was empty of people except for us. We ogled the shelves of candy—so many more choices than we stocked at Tom Thumb. "School's not out," one clerk whispered to the other. "I don't think it is," the other clerk replied. "It makes me just sick when I see kids skipping school," the first one complained. The other one frowned and gripped the countertop tightly.

"They think we're playing hooky," I said to Carla, excited.

"School's done."

"I know, but they don't know that." Thrilled to be causing unrest, we went next door to Campbell's to see if by studying displays of nylon panties, we could distress the clerks there too.

Back home we were known as teachers' kids, obedient children. But here we were anonymous and could imagine we were outlaws. Rebels. Delinquents. Knowing we didn't have it in us to actually defy anyone or anything, we pretended as much as possible that it could be otherwise.

"Can you drive us back into town tomorrow?" we begged Mom, on the way home.

"Too far," she said. "Next week!"

LeAnn looked away from us and scowled.

During that first week, the Chain O' Lakes had two days of cool rain followed by a day so clear that the sunlight reflecting off the lake blinded you like a camera flashbulb. Canadian geese flew north over our heads in squadrons of twelve to twenty, honking loudly to get our attention, for what purpose I was never sure.

It was our first rain-free morning, and my sisters and I were gathered around the 18th hole. Mom stood nearby gripping a paper bag. "Let's just wait for Dad," she said, looking towards the garage.

"What's going on?" LeAnn asked.

"We have some things we want to talk over with you girls," Mom said. I took this as a bad sign. My parents did speak to us on occasion, but they relied, like generations of parents before them, on their children's ability to read the creases in their faces for clues as to what they were trying to communicate, the way ancient mariners, lacking compass or maps, stared up at the stars in hopes of guidance. *They are going to talk to us about work.*

All winter long I had waited for this summer. While the snow piled up outside the windows of our house in Iowa, I thought about mini golf. *Play for free, play for free!* From September through May. *Cotton candy, cotton candy!* We all thought about mini golf that winter and even *played* mini golf by hitting balls at plastic cups we scattered across the living room, using putters we had swiped from the ticket booth last fall. It never occurred to me that summer at Tom Thumb might have a downside.

From the shore of Bass Lake came the sound of one rubber band—"Thrig."

"What was that?"

"Bullfrog," my dad said, joining us.

"Thrig."

"Weird."

"Okay, now. There's one for each of you girls," Mom said, removing three spiral notebooks from the bag and handing one to each of us. LeAnn got the red one. Carla, who was always lucky, got the blue one. My notebook was the color of a brown paper bag.

I stared with shock at the front cover. "Steno?" I said.

"Just ignore that," Mom told me.

"We have to do steno?!"

"Forget about that! It's for secretaries. Girls, now listen. You can use these to keep track of your work. What jobs you do, what time you start and stop. In this column you can write in the total

hours, and at the bottom you can add it up. Then we'll pay you."
She told us how we would take turns in the ticket booth. My shift
would be from noon to two each day. LeAnn's would be from two
to four.

"When is Carla's shift?" I asked.

"Carla?" Dad said, his forehead wrinkled in a semaphore for
angry.

Carla was only seven. She wasn't expected to do much, in part
because Carla was the youngest, and in part because she was
always treated delicately, and in part because she was, in fact,
delicate. Pale skinned and frightfully thin, she was sick with a
cold or flu or *something*—the doctors didn't always know what—
most weeks of the year. She also had a tendency to fall, tumbling
off her highchair at regular intervals during the first five years of
her life. This gave her amazingly exotic black eyes, which turned
green against her white skin, and made her appear, somehow,
even more delicate. Carla was like a fragile kitten that wandered
over from the neighbors one day and then never left.

"LeAnn will get seventy-five cents an hour. June will get fifty
cents an hour. And Carla will get thirty-five cents," Mom said.

"How come LeAnn gets more?" I asked.

"Because she's older."

LeAnn nodded at her notebook, and then she sniffed in agreement.

LeAnn was less a sister than a threat. She had a way of
sniffling—two short, deliberate intakes—that let you know she
had leadership abilities. A brigadier general could do the same—
sniff, sniff—and an entire battalion would snap to attention, flip
their rifles in the air, and vow to re-enlist.

Her eyes were brown and focused, like Dad's. Her dark hair
was long and thick and brushed once in the morning, parted in
the center, and usually pushed back behind her ears. When the
weather was humid, it expanded and thickened. Her eyebrows

threatened to take over the world. Sweat gathered on her lip. The slightest exertion, like getting ice cream from the kitchen, was enough to make a mustache of pearls. I don't know why we came out so different. I liked reading humor books, while she preferred reading mysteries. I liked wearing ribbons in my hair and sewing clothes for Barbie dolls; she preferred pinning me to the floor with wrestling holds.

"I'd rather have a brother" was all she said when she let me get up off the floor. Her earliest memories, she admitted, were of reaching over the walls of my playpen to push me down. And then doing it again.

A second bullfrog, lower in pitch, commented from the shore by #12. "Blub." Like the plastic burp from a Tupperware lid.

"This is a great opportunity for you girls. You can save up for college."

Mom nodded in agreement, then she looked at Dad. "Go ahead," she said.

"No, you explain."

"Are you sure? Okay, well. Girls—"

Then Dad said, "Girls, the main thing is that your mom and I don't want to tell you what to do every day. We have a lot of work to do, and we don't want you interrupting us. You should be able to look around and see what kinds of chores—"

"On the mini golf or in the yard—"

"—that you can do. You should be able to find work for yourselves," Dad said.

"We'll do the tough jobs," Mom said.

"Just look around and see what needs to be done."

"We can help you open up cans if you want to paint, and Dad can start the mower if you want to mow."

"There are brooms here by the ticket booth, and rags and buckets in the garage for cleaning up."

White floss from a cottonwood tree flew down the road, across the parking lot, and up our nostrils. I looked down at my brown steno book. "Does it count if we're washing dishes in the kitchen?"

"No, only work you do for Tom Thumb."

"Making our beds?"

"Does that help Tom Thumb?"

"You girls," she said, looking at LeAnn and me, "should be able to do most of it. And Carla," Mom said in her most gentle voice, "you can empty the little buckets." Carla smiled and swung her arms back and forth like a happy toy.

The cooler on the Pepsi machine clicked on. A mosquito landed on my thigh, and I slapped it, ending its sad, sad life.

I wasn't sure if they were serious. For one, I had just finished fifth grade. College seemed farther away than the bottom of the ocean. Second, we weren't the kind of kids who helped very much around the house. In my case it was due to the fact that my father felt sorry for old televisions. He saw them languishing at garage sales and local repair shops and brought one home, as a form of adoption, at a rate of about one per month. Lacking storage space, he plopped a black-and-white TV—sometimes two—in the corner of each of our bedrooms. They worked, more or less, and so I watched a lot of television, out of duty, I could reason, to the poor abandoned set.

We were the kind of kids who were pretty well convinced that Mom and Dad would take care of all the household chores, because generally, that's what they did. Except for one dreadful winter evening. "I'm fed up with doing all the work around this house!" Mom said one evening, startling all of us. The next day a chart appeared taped to the fridge that listed jobs nobody liked, like emptying the trash and cooking dinner on weekends. At first we folded some laundry and took turns washing dishes, but that was that. The chart was ignored until one day it disappeared for good.

*   *   *

I spent the next several hours at hole #5, pressing my knees into the carpet and dragging a scraper across the peeling paint on the two-by-fours. The carpet was damp and so my shorts got damp, and they sagged around my waist like diapers. The sun was cooking my forehead into a piece of toast. Scraping wasn't easy, and the sound it made was shocking. When I finally finished, I skipped to the garage to lose the scraper. Mom said next I would *get to* wipe off the dirt along the boards I just scraped using an old rag. *Get to.* Those were her words.

People complain a lot about the world. How it isn't fair. Many of these people are children. That's because children have intricate internal measuring devices. They can eyeball an entire tray of birthday cake and instantly detect which piece to avoid: too small, not enough frosting, drooping on the top, et cetera. To a child, justice is palpable, obvious, another of the senses like hearing, taste, or smell. If you put a group of children together in a room along with a thing that needs dividing, minutes later you will discover surprisingly equal portions. Perhaps the reason there are rich countries and poor countries, rich people and poor people, is that the dividing up is done by grown-ups. Adults have weird ways of measuring fairness. Children would never allow such inequity to happen.

Carla disappeared into the cottage, playing with toys we presume, though none of us ever bothered to actually check. LeAnn had been out on the golf course like me, painting at times, helping Dad other times, and putting away his tools at the picnic table. She hadn't talked to me all day, but now we had something in common.

As I was heading towards the house to get lemonade, I paused by the picnic table and threw down my chewed-up rag with great flourish and disgust. "This working is for the birds, huh?" I said.

LeAnn looked up from the can of paint she was stirring.

"You know," I said. "All this work. What are Mom and Dad thinking?"

Her hand still posed on the stir stick, she focused on my face for the first time in days.

I nodded as if to add, *You know what I mean.*

She started the stirring again, slowly rotating the oily paint into the center. And then she focused on me with her dark eyes, squinting those immense eyebrows. She appeared to be analyzing the chemical makeup of my body: *What are you made of? Doughnut batter? Seashells?* And with a look of great pity, the kind that small mice probably receive just prior to being eaten by the great hawk above them, she sniffed. "Go back and help."

Each morning before 10 am we swept the greens, checked pencils, and scraped paint. We cleared cobwebs off the ticket booth and pulled weeds along the fence. We scrubbed rubber putter grips with a sponge to make them less sticky. We drilled holes in long pencils so they could be attached with string at the tee-offs. We studied the brooms, ranking them least to best. When it rained, we closed up—when the rain stopped, we opened again, after mopping up puddles, vacuuming greens, and sponging water from the holes.

But mostly, that first summer, we painted.

There were eighteen hazards with chipped or missing paint. It looked like the previous owner hadn't painted in five years. He was probably just too busy running the mini golf all on his own, we considered. And his wife was older. She might have been sick. So even though the course was in rough shape, we decided, as a group, not to judge him.

Each morning we would gather at the door of the garage.

"I'll do the red on The Windmill."

"I'll take the green on The Paddle Wheel Boat."

Dad reached up to the plywood shelf where the one-quart cans were stored, and we passed the cans around like hymnals.

With a brush in one hand and a rag in the other, we crawled along the fairways on our hands and knees. We painted two-by-fours mostly, because every hole had them. They formed the border around every green, and most were gouged and worn. Some were rotting. When you ran a paint scraper along the sides, pieces of wood would fall off and then you could get yelled at. It was tricky business.

At lunchtime, we squeezed our brushes into a jam jar of gasoline. In the evening we passed around paint samples and discussed which red was the prettiest. We dabbed ourselves with gasoline to remove smears of red and blue from our arms and legs

There was no shower in the cottage, just an old porcelain bathtub with a spigot no bigger than your finger. It drooled out water so slowly that by the time there was enough for bathing, the water had gotten cold or more often was simply forgotten. We sponged ourselves off on Saturday nights if Mom happened to notice dirt on our necks and remembered that we had church the next day.

The month of June dragged on.

When a child is bored or doesn't know what to do with herself, she stands in proximity to her mom and tries to be distracting, usually with well-chosen stares or sighs of discontent. My mom was sweeping the leaves off #3. I stood nearby with my hands in the pockets of my shorts. It was my birthday. I was turning eleven.

"Well, what do you want to do today?" she said, picking a twig up off the carpet.

"I dunno." Back in Iowa, birthdays meant birthday *parties*. Your best friends came to your house with armfuls of gifts, sleeping bags, and pajamas.

"I know. Why don't you take the day off. You don't have to work. All day. That would make it special," she said, walking over to the white fence to drop a twig into the swamp. "So many twigs today. I know what else, you can have a bag of chips. Pick out any kind you want. This lead is broken," she said, holding up the pencil tied to the stand at #4. "May be time to replace it."

"Why not take Carla on a bike ride or something," she added, noticing I was still standing there.

"*Carla*?"

"*Carla*?" I said again. My younger sister was only seven, nearly four years younger than me, and just recently out of second grade, and therefore a member of a lower socioeconomic class.

"If you take your younger sister along, you can each have a candy bar."

With my bike, and my candy bar, and my towel and flip-flops, and a couple of sandwiches, a bag of chips, and my sister in tow, I aimed my bike up the hill to the state park. It was two miles away, and it had a small beach, Mom told us.

"How about here?" I said to Carla, dropping my backpack on the sand. We tested the water and then ate our chips while two other families showed up at the beach. They carried chairs and tote bags and coolers of pop. Eight people crowded together, laughing and throwing fancy beach towels into the air.

"Other people," I said. And we ate our peanut butter sandwiches as the large family ran together into the water, splashing. The dad lifted up the girls one by one so they could dive off his hands. Then they'd surface like baby mermaids, palm the water from their eyes, and he would smile at them as if they were newly invented children just born at that moment from the depths of the water. "Me next!" the girls said, and one by one they climbed up on Daddy and dove.

"Do you want to share your Snickers?" I asked Carla.

Then the family came to shore, and the mother handed out lovely cupcakes, one to each one.

When we felt good and sunburned, we scrunched up our belongings, and all the sand that came with them, and climbed back on our bikes. "I think it's around here," I said, pedaling down a trail. There was a large campground in the park, I recalled, because we had camped there once before. We might have even played mini golf that day at what is now our own Tom Thumb. "Let's go take a look," I called to Carla over my shoulder.

"That's like ours," Carla said, pointing to a trailer.

"Yup," I said, waving at a pop-up. "Just like ours."

We straddled our bikes and stared. Trailers strung with clotheslines. Beach towels and life jackets draped on them like Christmas ornaments.

Dinnertime was approaching, and families were returning to their sites. Older kids played cards; younger ones in swimsuit bottoms ran in circles around a picnic table, hands in the air, giggling. Their flip-flops fell off as a mom called out, "Be careful now, kids," but they were not careful; they were delighted and uncontainable. A mother shooed her children away from the Coleman stove. Paper plates and hot dogs, ketchup and mustard, and cans of Orange Crush scattered around the ground. A dad threw a Frisbee and a dog leaped, his hind legs overtaking the front. Near the road was a post with the number of the campsite painted on it, and a collection of pretty stones gathered at the base—a shrine to the god of family fun.

"Let's go," I said.

Farther into the campground we came upon a square stone building. "Let's have a peek at the restroom," I said, parking my bike. "Look," I said, "showers!" It had been a week and a half since I had bathed, I figured, sometime during the last week of school. "They're dripping. They must work," I said, hanging up my backpack.

"If someone sees our bikes parked outside, won't they know we aren't really camping here?" Carla asked.

"Ssshhh! Sssshhh!" I said, taking off my clothes.

"What? What!"

"Don't—"

"I didn't say anything!"

"—say that! We're pretending that we're *supposed* to be here."

"You mean, we're *not* supposed to be here? But what if we're caught?" she whispered.

"Someone's going to catch us *taking a shower*? What are they going to do? Throw us in jail?"

"Well, if we're not worried about being caught, then why are we pretending?!" she said, removing her swimsuit.

"Ahh!" I said, looking into each shower stall to see if anyone had left soap behind. "I wonder if we should have hidden our bikes."

"Where?"

"In the bushes or something."

A large woman in sandals pushed the door open and padded into the restroom.

I got a cork-screwing feeling in my upper tummy; we were caught. "So," I said a bit loudly to Carla, "what do you want to do when we get back to our *campsite*?"

"Our campsite?"

"Yes, at our *campsite*."

"Maybe roast marshmallows in our *campfire*."

"Yes," I said, in a singsong voice. "Roasted marshmallows are *good*."

"Or take a nap in our *camper trailer*."

The woman washed her hands and went back outside. We laughed, exploding like a sneeze kept too long inside the nose. Then we took showers.

We dried off using our beach towels, carefully avoiding the parts coated with sand, also potato chips, and a smidge of peanut butter from a sandwich. We felt clean.

Then, straddling our bikes, we wrapped the long towels around our bodies like Greek diplomats and kicked up the kickstands. "Time to go," I said.

Once we returned from the park, the party was over. "Are you finally back?" Mom said. "Hang up your wet things. Ginny and Joe will be here soon."

The way that every church service contains a sermon which drags on far too long and is supposed to be inspiring but is mostly to be endured, quietly and with no small amount of boredom or grief, my grandparents, and my aunt and uncle who lived down the road, came over in the evening of my birthday, mostly out of obligation, and Carla and I sat and tipped cake into our mouths from the end of metal forks, while the grown-ups talked about all things tedious.

The water level looks low . . . Sure does . . . Rain is low . . . Sure is . . .

Gas prices are high . . . Sure are . . .

Several hours later, someone remembered that it was my birthday, and I pretended to be enthralled, bent my cheeks into a smile of beatific gratitude, and, in that state, opened a few meager presents.

As we lay in bed that night, Carla and I began plotting the next year's trip to the state park, the next time I could get a whole day off. "We should get up super early, eight am, or even seven!"

"Then we could spend all day there!"

For the remainder of the summer Carla and I would "bathe" like the rest of the family: swim in the lake for a bit and consider ourselves clean.

* * *

I accosted Mom the next morning, while she swept #17. "Let's go camping."

"What are you talking about?"

"In the pop-up."

"This fall maybe," she said. "Well, actually. I better not promise. We might have to come up here to rake."

"How about tomorrow?" I said. "Let's go camping tomorrow."

"June, you know we have to stay *open*."

"No one is coming! No one would notice! We could just close up for a couple of days."

"That's ridiculous."

"Well, when are we going back home?"

"To Decorah?" She laughed. "Not until August."

I said "yip." Or something like "yip."

"I told you to pack for three months because we weren't coming back if you forgot something," she said.

"But I didn't know we weren't coming back *at all*."

"When school starts."

"That's crazy," I mumbled, because it was. I asked if she could at least drive Carla and me into town so we could pretend to play hooky.

"Next week!" she said, smashing the broom up against the edges, forcing the maple seeds up and over the sides.

It was at this point in the game, hole #3, where people sometimes gave up aiming completely. This is called Miniature Golf Despair. We'd see both grown-ups and kids just swipe at the ball like it was tall grass that needed to be chopped. "Twelve. Thirteen!" They want to give up and leave, but it's early in the game, and so they keep trying, as their summer vacation seems more and more a time of trial. With great anguish, they would finally look up at the ticket booth, wordlessly asking, *Is there some point where I can quit?*

It doesn't happen during every game at Tom Thumb, but it will happen to you sometime. You might be on #3 or #14 or even at the long fairway of hole #10—this course was designed to be difficult. But when it does happen to you the first time—and my family would agree—you will most likely be at hole #3. And your ball simply will not go in.

Like gods on Mount Olympus hidden in clouds—only in our case shadowed by ticket booth screens—the moment would come when we could no longer bear to hear them, or watch their suffering. "You don't have to keep trying. You can STOP AT SIX," one of us would say, loudly enough they could hear us three holes away.

And the people would sigh with relief. Some would say "Thank God." And then they'd pick up their ball, look up to the future, and move on.

Only, as I was learning, this is exactly what we, in my family, could not do.

I walked behind the cottage to stare out at the lake. On the other side there was a man in a red shirt driving his lawn mower in circles around the lawn, like a lone bumper car in a green bumper-car arena. In the lake I could see the reflection of his red shirt, also going around, turning stupid circles. I walked to the other side of the cottage, to the far corner of our land, up to the bridge over the creek, looking left up the road. Our horizon was so artificially low here, the sky so limited because of the trees . . . imagine what we would see without these encroaching trees. From the girls' camp in the woods came the sound of the afternoon bell. It tolled five times, the last two peals becoming increasingly dim, more difficult to hear, as the enthusiasm of the person ringing it became more faint.

The sign at hole #3 said:

Until my parents had the sign repainted because they felt it was misleading people (especially the children):

We kept a list of names tacked on the wall of the ticket booth of people who had gotten a hole-in-one on #3, because it was that rare. "John Ernst, Milwaukee; Sheila Weinslas, Fort Wayne, Indiana; Tracy Johnson, Waupaca . . ." My dad had a siren he would blow from the window of the ticket booth when it happened so that everyone would know—presumably even the people who lived across the lake. In all my years of working, I actually never saw it happen, never saw *anyone* get a hole-in-one on The Mole Hill in all those years, though the names are there to prove it. My sister Carla, who is lucky, has gotten three holes-in-one there herself—the first when she was only seven. One of those times, I was actually playing with her and standing only a few feet away, but I happened to look away at the moment and miss it.

Take a break for a delicious SNO-CONE!

How to make sno-cones:

First, don't kill anyone. Don't make them choke on small bits of plastic, which might happen if you push the ice chunks into the grinder with the plastic scoop—something everyone in my family does on a regular basis. The ice clogs when you dump it in; usually the chunks are too big. Also the chute is metal—ice can stick like a wet tongue on a swing set. You're going to have to shove it a little, but not so hard that the plastic scoop gets mauled. The shaved ice is white and shiny. By some strange happpenstance, the plastic is also. It's really hard to know if you've ground up the scoop or not. If you think you *might* have chewed plastic into the shaved ice, while the customer looks in eagerly through the front window of the Snack Shack, just calmly scoop out the snow from the plexi bin and dump it into the yellow bucket below. Say, "I want to start over; I didn't like that bunch," and put more ice chunks into the machine. The customer will not know of his proximity to death by choking and in fact may actually be *flattered* that you took the time to chop more ice— better ice—for his long-awaited sno-cone. One truism about tourists: they like to feel important. A delay, when it's a delay *for* them and not a delay for someone *else*, can be interpreted as evidence of your personal interest and a wish to deliver them perfection.

Second, the grape flavor tastes watery. Don't push the grape.

Say, "Cherry, blue-raspberry, grape, or a combo?" The cherry is the best single flavor, and you will say so if asked, but generally you don't volunteer the information.

Mom says to give one squirt into the ice at the bottom of the cone, then two squirts into the dome on top. Do it slow so the ice doesn't dent. Add a straw.

The best ice is the cold ice, but customers rarely get that. We grind up ice for sno-cones one at a time because we don't get enough orders to shave up a mountain of ice and leave it to melt there all day. Dad would have a fit. Wasteful, wasteful. For one sno-cone, we chop one sno-cone's worth of ice. For four sno-cones, four sno-cones' worth. But the best ice comes after five or six sno-cones. The whirling blades get good and cold. The ice chopped for the seventh or eighth will be so light and fluffy that it may not even pack into a ball. If that happens, just dig into the mound with your scoop until you're at the bottom, then add some wet (bad) ice to your ball. People like their ice in a ball. It's how they imagine it should be. But we know better. We have become sno-cone snobs.

Mom and Dad let us have one free sno-cone a day. But we don't bother if it's made from wet ice. Even on the hottest day of July when we are dying. We wait until the blades are cold from serving up ice for other people, and only then add a few chunks for ourselves. The fluffy ice won't form into domes so it doesn't look picture-perfect, but it is the kind my sisters and I eat at any chance. The ice chopped last is like the snow that falls on your mitten in winter, and you can stare at it, so tiny, so cold, and so tight.

If the ice is wet, the cone may overflow before you get the third squirt on there. If so, stop. Hand the cone slowly to the customer. Say, "Be careful. This one is pretty full. You'd better take a sip right away." You know—and will never reveal—that if the cone is overflowing, it means the ice was not great. It will be gritty between the teeth, and the flavor will taste diluted. But the customer always feels privileged that his cone is overflowing with syrup, which, he thinks, is like getting front-row seats in the world of sno-cones.

What the customer wants is what he imagines a sno-cone

should look like. This is his vacation after all. Party, party, party. This is his week at the lake, and he has brought along his family, and they have played mini golf, and he is wearing his favorite red-and-orange shirt, and the kids have matching Brewers baseball caps, and they are getting along better this year—none of them fussed when no one got a free game by hitting their ball in the clown's nose—and the sun is hanging low, and it's getting time to head back, and this is the last day before the long drive home. And the little girl looks up at her father and, in her most delicate voice, asks, "Daddy, can we get sno-cones?"

He smiles, and then he says to me, "Do you have rainbow?"

"Sure, I can do that." And I drape perfect stripes of color over the perfect dome of snow. I make their change, and I say thank you. Then they stroll across the parking lot together, sipping cones and leaning towards each other.

If you see a bug inside the machine where the ice comes out, you can wipe it out with a paper towel even while the customer stares at you from less than two feet away. They won't see that you are removing an insect.

After you have successfully made eight or more sno-cones, run into the yard to find one of your sisters. Hold up your hand, spread your thumb away from your fingers, and say, "Look at my terrible rash!" Make the joke about dying from a terrible disease. Show off the tiny dots of cherry, blue, and grape that sprayed from the dispenser as you pushed down on the plunger. The stains will stay for hours, even after washing with soap and water. You are not unusual if you think it's cool.

One day your dad will say, "I remember the time I chewed up a whole metal screw with a batch of ice—that time the screw came out of the blades."

"What did you do?"

"I just avoided that spot in the ice and scooped from the other side. I made only one sno-cone, fortunately. I don't know what I would have done if they had ordered a whole bunch."

The sno-cone machine rarely breaks down, maybe once every three or four years. This is something of a miracle. It was purchased when you were young enough not to question whether your parents understood the idea of food product safety or lawsuits. And the sno-cone machine has been working every day, Memorial Day to Labor Day. And nothing bad has ever happened. This too is a miracle. Sometimes, if people come early—it's before 10 am, but Mom and Dad let them buy snacks anyway—the sound of sno-cone motor tearing into ice is the first thing you hear in the morning. The roar of hungry blades wafts through the house and wakes you in your bed. It grinds and grinds and grinds.

CHAPTER 4

THE COLORED LIGHT THING

And Heaven have mercy on us all—Presbyterians and Pagans alike—for we are all somehow dreadfully cracked about the head, and sadly need mending.

—HERMAN MELVILLE, *Moby-Dick*

There is a book called *The Swiss Family Robinson*, and they are stranded on an island, and their clever dad and patient mother are very inventive in their bizarre situation; they make weapons out of clam shells, they turn sea turtles into dinner plates and evening gowns, and they invent the television, and I may be making some of this up. But they do happily fend off tigers and lions, and penguins and ostriches, all from their living room tree house, so they had that kind of magic already going for them.

Officially, Tom Thumb Miniature Golf was not located on an island. A good number of customers did come by boat, but that was just for fun. We were on a *peninsula*; water was only on *three* sides. However, most of our problems, like those of the Swiss Family Robinson, were not solved the usual way.

For example, the Swiss Family Robinson had an ingenious series of buckets strung from ropes and pulleys that lifted their food high into the tree house. We used our canoe as a wheelbarrow. Life jackets were used as knee pads. The Robinsons developed an impressive irrigation system using bamboo pipes. We filled one-gallon ice cream pails with water, placed them in the freezer, then used an ice pick to laboriously chop the blocks into ice-cube-sized chunks—a process that took at least an hour each evening—just to feed the sno-cone machine.

"Don't most people just get an ice maker?"

"We aren't doing that."

The previous owner left behind a few plastic toy putters for the youngest children to use. When they broke my dad made replacements, painstakingly, by hand, carving each head out of pine using a pocket knife. Then he brushed on several coats of silver paint, attached a plastic handle, and even though each took several days to make, my dad produced nearly a dozen. This would have been admirable, because they did look so cute, except that they were given to the youngest children. To use for free. They grabbed the putters like turkey legs and banged them on the pavement until they cracked.

The father in the Swiss Family Robinson took great pains to simplify their lives on their tropical island. As we adjusted to our second year together at Tom Thumb, it became apparent that my father worked equally hard to make Tom Thumb as complicated as possible.

Which brings us to the next hole. Oh, hole #4 . . . the site of gizmos and gadgets and mother-knows-whatsits and motors that purr, and motors that roar, and motors that explode with a Bang. There have been many different hazards at hole #4. For some reason, the obstacles here all seem to develop problems. It's like the restaurant near my home in Hollywood that goes out of business every year; a new owner moves in—GRAND OPENING, THAI RESTAURANT—and then a year later that restaurant fails too.

Hole #4, The Colored Light Thing (and all the other hazards in its place), is about Complexity.

When we first arrived, hole #4 was The Outhouse, a small

building with two holes just like a regular outhouse. We noticed a slight problem: people were nearly getting killed. They thought the fairway looked long, and the ramp mighty steep, and imitating professional golfers, they'd take a big swing. *Clomp!* The balls went soaring over the green into the parking lot like so many escaped birds. People chased madly after—bent from the waist to scoop up the ball as it rolled, their eyes focused on the ground—nearly braining themselves on the front bumpers of cars pulling into the lot.

"Perhaps this isn't a safe place for this hazard," we considered. My dad moved The Outhouse to hole #10, where it has remained ever since.[1]

Next at #4 was The Loop de Loop. We discovered this strange object in the garage and believed it to be some kind of farm implement. But one day out of boredom we dragged it out into the sunshine and realized with a shock that we owned another hazard. It took four to six hours of labor to scrape off the rust, then two hours to paint it with primer, and then another four hours to coat it with two colors of enamel. But it was a free hazard. We were thrilled! The Loop de Loop lasted one and a half summers. "I hated that darn thing. It chip-chipped up the balls," my dad says, still so upset about it he can barely get out the words. "Remember that? The front edge was metal, and every time a ball went over that lip, it cut into it. Oh, that was a terrible thing."

"It wrecked I don't know how many balls," Mom agrees, and nods.

---

[1] And now for the exciting story of the biggest crime my father ever committed: he "borrowed" a cart from the high school after "noticing it" through the window of the industrial arts classroom across the hall. He strapped it to the roof of the car and drove two hundred miles to get it here. He hauled The Outhouse to the other side of the course with the help of the cart, and a handful of neighbor boys. "Did the high school know about this?" I ask him.

"One thing I learned in the army," he says, tapping his finger on his nose, and with no small amount of pride, "if you don't ask, they can't say no."

One reason there were so many hazards at #4 is that it was here that my father, a teacher of physics and chemistry, began carrying out what you could call his "experiments."

He created a device we called The Colored Light Thing. If the Nobel committee, in addition to awards for literature and medicine, voted to acknowledge "The Most Complicated Gizmo on the Planet Designed to Hinder the Path of Miniature Golf Balls," The Colored Light Thing would win the prize. And my father would dress in a tuxedo and step up to the podium, and everyone in Sweden would lean forward in their seats to learn from the expert how it worked. And my father would look into the microphone and say, "Well, uh . . . ," and then chuckle a bit. Because even though he was the one who *built* it, the one to *design* it, the one who thought it was a *good idea* in the first place, he finds it a very difficult contraption to explain.

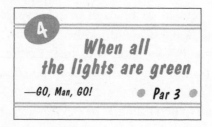

I do too. From the outside The Colored Light Thing looked like a white plywood box about the size of an ottoman. On the top there protruded a two-foot "tower." It had four red lights on one side, four green lights on the other. The lights would click over from red to green. When all four lights were green, a flap like a doggie door would lift up from underneath, and people would madly putt their ball. And then with a click, the lights all went back to red, and the door would close again.

According to Dad, The Colored Light Thing was supposed to resemble the starting lights at a drag-strip race. "It's called a

Christmas tree," he said. We never knew what he was talking about, and no one who came to play did either. In thirty years we never heard anyone refer to #4 as a drag-racing tree. People called it "that white box" or "that thing with the lights," while others simply called it "that one where my ball is stuck underneath."[2]

Eventually he replaced The Colored Light Thing, not because the mechanism broke down, but because he almost had a nervous breakdown whenever tourists shoved their putters underneath to push out their balls. In the end it was his love for the invention, and his need to protect it from people, that finished the hazard's life.

I haven't always questioned the judgment of my parents, just as I haven't always known to check that both metal tabs are firmly in place before pulling up a zipper. But during our first years at Tom Thumb I began to wonder about my parents and their fitness for duty. Of the five of us—Mom, Dad, LeAnn, myself, and Carla— were they really the right ones to be left in charge?

My parents had never run a business before. They didn't

---

[2] And now, without further ado, my father will try to explain his grand invention, The Colored Light Thing: "The first version I made I used two solenoids, and when that door opened, it went 'Booom!'" He claps his hands to demonstrate the explosion. "The voltage was too high. Noisy, and not really safe around people. Boom!" He claps again and laughs. "So I had to change the whole shebang." He tells me that the next version used roller skate wheels.

Why roller skate wheels? I ask.

"I don't know. Maybe I just had them around." He tells me how he carved four circles out of oak "—cams, one for each light—and the roller skate wheel rides along the cam. Then there was a flat spot. When the wheel hit that, there was single pole/double throw switch that moved one by an eighth of an inch—"

I nod as if I understand completely. I do not understand completely.

"—to turn the light to green. I varied the positioning so they turned one at a time. Then there was one more cam to trigger the door and a bracket on the door and a piece of metal that led up to the cam that changed the rotary motion into up and down, basically from vertical motion to horizontal motion in an arc," he says, and I have no idea what he is talking about.

"I might have drawn plans," he says, "but mostly I think I did it in my head."

realize it would be okay to ask the previous owner how much income to expect. Or ask how much expenses might be. Or how many people came to play. Or if there would be enough profit to cover the loan that the previous owner himself extended to them in the form of a land contract. (There wasn't.)

At the end of our first summer we had taken in $9,039. The total expenses came to $8,678. There was actually only $361 remaining, which, as you might assume, was not enough to make the first payment, which was $4,800. So my father took money from his teacher's salary, which couldn't have been much more than $15,000 a year. It doesn't really all add up. All I know is that my sisters and I wore secondhand clothes our neighbors handed us in paper grocery-store bags. And every Sunday evening Mom and Dad would team up in the kitchen to "mix milk," measuring Carnation instant powder into the blender and pressing WHIP. They poured it into jars, enough to last the week. As long as you were willing to wait a day or two, it tasted okay, once the initial layers of froth had died down.

The next obstacle Dad built for #4 was a motorized railroad crossing. This included a light that flashed on and off, and a bar that raised and lowered every minute or so. The Railroad Crossing has been at #4 for the last ten years, even though it works well only three days out of four and requires almost an hour of tuning and balancing every morning. But it has been a great improvement in the category "Well-At-Least-People-Can-Recognize-What-the-Hazard-Is-Supposed-To-Be-And-All-That."[3]

---

[3] The Railroad Crossing took two winters to make, longer than any other hazard, because my father enjoys a bit of "trial and error" the way other people might enjoy a cookie. To find the right counterweight for the crossing bar, he stole bags of sugar from the kitchen and carried them into his basement workshop. We probably had the only railroad crossing in the world that ran on roller skate wheels. These traveled on cams like The Colored Light Thing but were cut with ridges so that the red lights flickered on and off like a real railroad sign. He never

My mother didn't try to complicate matters, but she did, let's just say, *improvise.*

The money was kept in a rusted fishing tackle box. It was made in the 1950s, and we carried it by its wobbly metal handle into the ticket booth each morning, then back into Mom and Dad's bedroom at night. We placed it on the floor next to their bed like a thick dented book.

It wasn't a cash register. A tackle box doesn't make change. When we couldn't total the costs in our head from five sno-cones, three cotton candies, two bags of chips, and a candy bar, we used a white popcorn bag as scratch paper and added them up with a pencil.

The fishing tackle box had just the right number of compart-ments for coins, plus two trays we could use for bills, which is why we kept it despite its age, the chipped golden paint, and the faded decal of a leaping fish on the lid. The hinges were loose and threatened to come off at any time. Because the previous owner had used the cash box for fifteen years, my parents dutifully did the same. The only modification was to purchase a *new* tackle box to collect money in the Snack Shack.

Instead of counting every night, Mom just took out excess bills—*skimming* was what she called it. Then she tallied up the totals once a week. On Sunday after 10:30 pm, when all the cus-tomers had gone home and while my sisters and I spooned ice cream into bowls, she plopped the cash box on the dining room table. "Do you suppose we should close the curtains?" she'd ask, skipping around the table to look out into the darkness of our dock and the water of Beasley.

---

stopped tinkering with this one. "I bought a car horn for #4 that gives a railroad crossing sound, but I never got it installed," Dad says. "I also got a death-ray horn."

"A what?"

"I just thought it would be fun to put out there sometime."

"Do you think there's anyone on the lake who could look in?" LeAnn would say.

"Someone wants to steal all sixty dollars?" I'd add.

Mom sat at the table and lined up the bills in the same direction, padding through the stack twice. She'd write the total in her ledger along with her thoughts on the weather: "Slow day. Rained on and off." Once she was done, Dad would wander into the house and pull some wadded fives and tens from his pockets. "I almost forgot. Here's more from the weekend sometime," he'd say, dropping them on the table.

"Oh, good. I thought our total looked a bit small."

"I wonder if I have some in my other pockets. Maybe more will turn up later," he'd say.

Mom put our week's earnings into a satiny pouch from the bank, zipped it up, and then put it in a safe place, which is to say, she hid it. Sometimes she hid the money in the left-hand compartment of the buffet, between Sears catalogs, summer and winter. Sometimes she hid it in the top drawer above the pencils and rulers. And sometimes she hid the money bag in secret locations while we sat in front of our ice cream bowls, covering our eyes with our hands to keep from watching, and giggling.

"You girls are getting silly," Mom would say.

We whispered to each other, "I know where she puts it."

"I'm not hiding it from *you girls*!"

"It must be getting late," Dad would say. "Is it your bedtime?"

"That must be it," she'd reply.

Weekends were our busiest times, and so we always looked forward to Mondays. Mom would drive to town to make a deposit at the bank, get the week's supplies, and return in time for lunch. "Who's coming with me?" Mom asked.

"It's my turn," LeAnn said, jumping into the front seat.

"That's not fair. Why can't we all go along?" I said.

"Because Dad doesn't like waiting on customers by himself,"

Mom said. "You can go to town later in the week. Now let's get going. Oh"—she turned around and ran toward the laundry room—"I almost forgot."

There were a lot of wild animals in the vicinity of Tom Thumb. We saw beavers and barred owls, woodchucks and bull-frogs. At night we heard *barrumps* along the shoreline and "who-cooks-for-you" screeching from the trees; splashes in the dark water and screams from the woods that Dad said came from a raccoon. (I always suspected *raccoon* was a substitute for "I have no idea what animal. Now, you girls get to bed.") However, despite the wildness of our land, it was a scream from my mom that was so feral and unnerving, it proved beyond all other evidence that Wisconsin was, and always will be, a wild and untamed place.

"I washed the money!" Water dripped from the lower corner of the dark green money bag which hung heavily from her fin-gertips. "I've been hiding it in the washing machine."

"The washing machine?"

"Well, we've got to put it someplace, and I just thought a thief probably wasn't too interested in things like staying clean, so he probably wouldn't look in a place like a laundry room." She unzipped the bag and produced a dark green brick. "I guess the bills got washed when I put in a load this morning."

"Are they soapy?"

"No, they went through the rinse cycle."

"Are they ruined?" Dad asked.

"I think they held together. Paper is very strong."

We danced around the yard, flailing our arms with excite-ment. "Mom's a money launderer! A money launderer!" The term only had a vague meaning for us, but we knew it was a crime from watching *Mannix* on TV, Sunday evenings.

Now what? we wondered. Could we lay the wet bills on the grass to dry? No, they would blow away. Should we hang them on a string in the ticket booth? No, that would look odd. So we

followed Mom back inside the cottage and into my parents' bedroom. She held out the wet brick of money in her left palm, then
slowly peeled off a one-dollar bill. She laid it gently on the bed-
spread like a newly cut Christmas cookie. She patted the edges
slightly. "The chenille will help it dry, I suppose." Then she
peeled off another bill, handed it to Carla, and then held out the
stack to me. I made a row of fives, right to left, under the ridge of
pillows, and Carla made a column of ones, up to down, towards
the foot of the bed.

"The curtain's open," Mom said. "I hope nobody looks in and
thinks we're counterfeiting."

We made more rows and columns until the bed was covered
with wet green bills, the pink chenille transformed into a patch-
work of U.S. presidents. I ran upstairs and found my plastic camera. "Smile!" I said. Carla posed with a bill in her hand, grinning
like she had invented money. "Do you have to do that?" Mom
grimaced, but then she shrugged and let herself pose, caught in
the act, smiling as she laid out another wet bill.

CHAPTER 5

THE HORSE

It requires a certain type of mind to see beauty in a hamburger bun. Yet is it any more unusual to find grace in the texture and softly curved silhouette of a bun than to reflect lovingly on the arrangement of textures and colors on a butterfly's wing?

—RAY KROC

Miniature golf as we know it was invented in the 1920s, which is appropriate, I suppose. This decade was called the Roaring Twenties because it was, simply put, a truly crazy period. It was a time of extravagance and decadence, when women cut their long hair and threw out their corsets; a time that saw the invention of goldfish swallowing, dance marathons, and competitions for who could sit the longest on top of a pole; a time of giddiness as people regrouped from the horrors of the Great War, and the restrictions and austerity that the war effort required. People moved en masse from rural areas to large cities. One wild dance craze after another swept the country—the jitterbug and the Charleston, the shimmy and the tango. Alcohol was prohibited in the United States, but it did not go away, and there were bootleggers, speakeasies, and raids by the feds. Skirts were shortened, bustles abandoned, and women finally got the right to vote. (And I have to admit here that I'm a bit jealous of the Roaring Twenties, perhaps because the decade of my decadence, or what should have been my decadence because I turned eighteen, was known, quite blandly, as the Reagan Era.) It really shouldn't surprise us that another crazy fad hit the scene at this time: miniature golf.

But let's rewind a bit, because before there could be *mini golf*, there first needed to be regular golf—or *maxi golf*, as we call it in my family. Maxi golf began in Scotland way back in the 1400s. It was incredibly popular right from the start. In fact, in 1457 the Scottish Parliament banned golf altogether when they worried about an impending invasion from England. So many men and young boys were hitting pebbles around with golf clubs (sticks, actually) that they had abandoned their military training.

The first golf course on record was located at St. Andrews, Scotland. It had eighteen holes. Ever since, all golf courses (both mini and maxi) have had eighteen holes as well (or nine if space is limited), even though no one knows why the first one was built that way. Golf did not spread rapidly around the globe, not until the industrial revolution made it more accessible. When the railroads expanded, people could more easily get to golf courses on the outskirts of town. Also, golf equipment became less expensive because it didn't need to be made by hand.

By the beginning of the 1920s, golf had been in the United States for almost thirty years and was getting hugely popular. Because people were eager to play, some smaller-scale golf courses were built. These were sometimes referred to as *miniature golf*, but these courses weren't intended to be "fun." Instead they were built on the grounds of a regular golf course or at a hotel and were intended mostly as a place for golfers to practice.

At this time, golf was still considered a wealthy man's sport, and in the 1920s only a tiny portion of the population was wealthy. But the middle class was growing. It was a status-hungry time. By taking up golf, many people hoped to *emulate* the rich, if not actually be considered one of them. There was a need for a cheaper form of golf.

Which brings us to the place where miniature golf was about to be "born": on a hilltop resort in Tennessee. And let me introduce Garnet and Frieda Carter.

Garnet was a traveling salesman, peddling candy, souvenirs, and novelties. In 1924 he wanted to sell something bigger: real estate investments. With a partner, he bought three hundred acres of cheap rocky land on a semiaccessible hill known as Lookout Mountain. Then he divided the land into lots and, using his skill as a promoter, sold them quickly at great profit.

His wife, Frieda Utermoehlen Carter, loved fairy tales, so we can presume she's the one who chose the names for the new streets: Robin Hood Trail, Gnome Trail, Cinderella Road, and Tinker Bell Lane (all of which still exist today). Frieda, who was of German descent, ordered shipments of garden statues from Germany. She placed these elves and fairy-tale characters in prominent locations on the streets as decoration. In 1928, her husband, Garnet, started building a resort and a golf course there. They called their new development Fairyland.

At this point, however, there are conflicting stories as to how the first *miniature* golf course happened. One version says that the construction of the regular golf course was delayed for several years because the rocky land was difficult to smooth into greens. So while hotel visitors waited for the maxi course to be completed, the Carters erected a miniature version to keep them occupied. Voilà.

Another version says that the regular golf course was completed first, and then Frieda noticed a problem. Quite a few wives and children were spending afternoons draped on the resort furniture in misery and boredom. They had been abandoned by their husbands and fathers who were spending the day playing golf. Frieda took pity on the women and children, and built the whimsical miniature golf course explicitly for them.

It's possible that parts of both versions may have some truth to them, but in any case what we do know is this: Garnet built a small golf course. Frieda moved some of the fairy-tale statues off the streets to the grounds to decorate it. Together they designed obstacles, which added a randomness to the game that hadn't been there before. They used materials they found lying around such as hollow logs and car tires to make loops, et cetera. Frieda named every hole for a fairy story (elves, Snow White, etc.) based on which statue was placed at that hole. She planted flowers. Using drafting equipment, she designed a full-size gingerbread house to sell lemonade and gingerbread next door. Because they had called the resort itself the Fairyland Club, they picked an appropriate name for this smaller version of the game: Tom Thumb Miniature Golf.

It was a success. Actually, to say it was a success is a bit like saying that Ray Kroc sold a few hamburgers at McDonald's in his day.

People were thronging to play at Tom Thumb. In fact, adult golfers were crowding younger kids off the course. Visitors who came to the area were begging Garnet Carter to build an identical mini course in their own hometowns.

Garnet was a salesman by nature and certainly not the type to turn down an opportunity. Quite by accident he was about to start a Tom Thumb empire. But first, there was a problem that needed solving: grass.

The first miniature golf course on Lookout Mountain was planted with real grass, just like the full-size course. However, mown grass couldn't stand up to all the feet, let alone the heat of southern Tennessee. Once the greens were worn down to the dirt, the balls rolled too quickly and the game wasn't playable. At the time, felt carpet didn't exist, and the invention of AstroTurf was three decades away.

Meanwhile, in Mexico another invention and inventor were "paving the way," so to speak. A few years earlier, in 1922, an English cotton rancher named Thomas McCulloch Fairbairn wanted to make a golf course on his plantation near Tliahualilo. But grass wouldn't grow in the hot sun. One day while watching his workers haul in the cotton harvest, he noticed that the cottonseed hulls on the path where they walked back and forth had been ground into a fine meal. He took the ground hulls, added oil to bind them together, and spread the mixture on leveled ground. He dyed it green. The result was a surface that had friction like grass and even looked a bit like it. He registered the patent for his artificial turf.

Garnet Carter bought the cotton seed patent from Fairbairn. Then he applied for a patent for a complete mini golf course design, including the use of hollow logs for hazards. He began selling a packaged "Tom Thumb Golf" which could be shipped to your town and installed by the manufacturer for $2,000.

This was 1930, the beginning of the Great Depression. But more important (okay, perhaps only to me), it was the year of the Great Miniature Golf Boom. By July Carter had already sold about 5,000 Tom Thumb courses. If the sincerest form of flattery is imitation, then Carter should have considered himself very well admired. Copycat mini golf courses were being built with great fervor in all parts of the country by entrepreneurs who knew a good thing when they saw it.

Mini golf courses popped up in hotel lobbies, on the grounds of sanitariums, next door to movie theaters, and in empty lots around the country. There was a course built on a well-known European ocean liner, one at a prison, and one for airplane passengers at an airport near Chicago. Many celebrities built courses for themselves and their guests on their estates in Beverly Hills, including Mary Pickford and Douglas Fairbanks on the grounds of their 22-room mansion, Pickfair. Harold Lloyd had a difficult course with an artificial, pump-driven stream. President Herbert Hoover got a team of marines to build him a private course at his woodsy retreat in Maryland. In London the Prince of Wales had a miniature golf course built at St. James's Palace. A miniature golf course at Charing Cross station became so popular that guards were stationed to warn players when their trains were departing because people were forgetting to board.

In September of 1930 the Department of Commerce estimated there were 30,000 miniature golf courses in the United States, most of them hand-built. There were 60 in Kansas City, Missouri; 30 in Cleveland; and noise complaints about the mini golf courses in more than 25 cities across the United States. It was estimated that there were approximately 300 courses in Los Angeles and more than 1,000 in a thirty-mile radius around New York City. Roy Rogers pronounced to his audiences that in miniature golf the country had found a really good way to fill otherwise vacant lots. *Harper's Magazine* declared in December of 1930, "The rise of the miniature golf industry is a romance of American business in the old and grand manner—about the only success story that has lightened this year of gloom."

Hard times are traditionally good times for inexpensive amusements, and the early years of the Depression were definitely hard times. But mini golf generally cost fifty cents a round. (For comparison: admission to a baseball game was one dollar; a movie ticket cost twenty-five cents.) Before Prohibition, a glass of beer cost about five cents; during Prohibition (yes, it was still available) the cost of a beer rose to fifty cents. Miniature golf became an affordable alternative to imbibing. In fact, at the time some theorized that mini golf owed a great deal of its success to the fact that alcohol was just too dang expensive, thanks to the Eighteenth Amendment.

Another reason miniature golf became popular was that men and women could play it equally well. Whereas maxi golf required physical strength and endurance, good scores on the miniature courses depended on aim, skill, and luck. As a result, both men and women could play round after round as they tried to improve their personal scores, just as they could on the regular links. Only here they didn't tire out. Stamina was not an issue on the mini-links.

Dubbed "The Madness of 1930," miniature golf was sweeping the nation. Courses stayed open until 1 am or 2 am. Some were open all night, until proprietors were dragged into court and ordered to close by midnight. Young enterprising boys built courses for their low-income neighborhoods by digging tin cans into weedy vacant lots and charging their customers a nickel a game. Sheet music was published so people could play and sing songs at home, including "I've Gone Goofy Over Miniature Golf." And "Since My Wife Took Up Miniature Golf," which begins with this lament: "Look at me and you will see a most unhappy man . . ." The sheet music for another song, "I'm Put-Put-Puttin' on the Dinky Links All Day," included the following note on the back cover: "This song is dedicated by the composers to the new and fascinating game of miniature golf, and to those who have been instrumental in making this clean and healthful sport universally popular."

Commercial enterprises burst onto the scene to capitalize on the fad. Magazines featured advice on what fashions were appropriate for an evening of miniature golf. Major department stores offered clothing for both men and women that was specifically designed for the game.

The biggest fear at the time was not that the boom wouldn't last, but that miniature golf would bring the ruin of other forms of entertainment. Owners of baseball teams fretted about falling attendance. Young men were playing mini golf instead of developing a good pitch or swing, and baseball fans worried this would threaten the future of the national sport. Movie theaters were losing money. The night that a new mini golf course opened in Chicago, nearby cinemas found their ticket sales dropped to less than half of those the night before. Some movie studios in Hollywood began requiring their stars to sign a statement that they would not play miniature golf or be photographed on a Tom Thumb course. Other theater owners jumped on the bandwagon and installed mini golf courses in the lobbies of their theater buildings. A well-established speakeasy in New York offered mini golf in addition to expensive drinks, and stayed open all night—that is, until it was raided several months later.

The game of miniature golf, and the people who played it, seemed out of control. Mayors and city supervisors bemoaned the lack of existing ordinances to regulate the game. In Manhattan a new statute was proposed to ban courses from being built close to schools for fear that its presence was too distracting to the kids. In New Jersey a minister tried to prevent a mini golf course going up near his church, pleading that he did not want to hear people yelling profanity in the area. But the number of small golf courses continued to grow, as did the number of players. By then the country was realizing the severity and depth of the Depression, and people needed to be cheered up. Men, women, and children continued to eagerly line up for a cheap one-hour escape from grim reality.

The demand for cotton-seed hulls became so great, the market for cotton so increased, that there was hope that miniature golf might pull the entire country out of the Depression.

In early 1931, when the game had been around for more than a year, it became apparent that the popularity of each course seemed to grow in direct proportion to the difficulty involved. The most challenging set of holes attracted the most business. Owners noticed their customers trying to "master the course," or at least return night after night to better their scores. Proprietors began competing with each other to design more complicated hazards; some of the results were not only tricky, but downright bizarre. Guy Lombardo, for example, built a course where every hazard was a discarded musical instrument. One course featured a metal xylophone that required a player to tap his ball up the graduated rods before driving into the wide-open mouth of a sousaphone. At the Los Angeles Miniature Golf Course, a bear was chained on a green in front of a replica of the White House. Similarly, in London, a course featured a live monkey kept in a cage. Players needed to putt their balls past him as he grabbed at the balls, stealing quite a few. Surprisingly, there was not just one, but several courses in England that featured reminders of the First World War: miniature howitzer holes and machine guns and trenches that teemed with miniature soldiers. Thirteen years after its end, images of the horrific conditions from the Great War attracted families out for an afternoon of fun.

As the Depression deepened, more people lost their jobs. In 1933 the unemployed in the United States made up 33 percent of the population; the rate was more than 50 percent in Chicago alone. While miniature golf was one of the least expensive amusements, *any* form of amusement became out of reach for many. Attendance at mini golf, not unexpectedly, declined, as did the number of miniature golf courses. There was also new competition. In 1937 and 1938, swing dancing hit the scene. Music became the big draw. Given a choice of any two options, teenage boys would choose dancing with teenage girls—and vice versa. This decade also began the Golden Age of Cinema, when movie studios turned out some of the most successful films in history. Back at the Fairyland Inn, Garnet Carter, sensing that any craze must have a limited life, had sold off his Tom Thumb Golf franchise for $200,000 before 1931.

In the coming years, miniature golf continued to draw

increasing crowds in Europe, while interest dwindled in the United States. But it did not disappear completely. During World War II, when Americans were stationed abroad, military men built miniature golf courses on their bases, marking out fairways using logs and stone outside their barracks. These low-tech courses offered a reminder of home and perhaps a reprieve from homesickness.

These servicemen had an even greater impact on the resurgence of mini golf once the war was over. They came home. They got married. And then they made babies.

The Baby Boom began in 1946. There were suddenly throngs of children running around who needed to be entertained.

During the decade that followed, automobile companies promoted car sales with the idea that driving your family around the country was the American Thing to Do. And in a spirit of patriotism, perhaps, people did. It was the birth of what is now commonly called *car culture* and roadside attractions. Miniature golf courses were built along busy roads rather than in vacant lots. They featured taller hazards like windmills and dinosaurs to make them visible and enticing as families cruised past.

Because of the increase in population, new houses were being constructed at rates never seen before. Suburbs were spreading out from the cities. Developments gobbled up land that formerly had been available for full-size golf courses. The courses that did survive were now located farther from city centers. Golf course managers and owners bemoaned a startling drop in attendance. Which brings us to another reason why miniature golf boomed in the 1950s: regular golfers actively encouraged it. The National Golf Foundation sent out instructions to owners of maxi golf courses on how to build a whimsical mini golf. It was a responsibility, they said, to attract children to golf by encouraging them to play the mini game.

There were a couple of influential folks who prodded the business in their own ways.

Don Clayton, of Fayetteville, North Carolina, hated the gimmickry of miniature golf. So in 1953 he drew out a plan for a "superior" version that left out motors and gadgets. With his spartan design, he hoped miniature golf could gain respect as a competitive sport. He franchised and sold his plan under the name Putt-Putt. (You may insert your favorite registered trademark symbol here, because the Putt-Putt people require it.) And indeed Putt-Putt tournaments did follow, and his simplified game did spread. In 1960 Putt-Putt opened locations in Australia, Japan, and South Africa. They created "fun centers" in later years by adding arcades, batting cages, and go-karts. Putt-Putt became an international operation with $100 million in annual revenues.

Others took the opposite stance and designed courses with more moving hazards and stunts. Two of these major proponents were Al and Ralph Lomma. Under the name Lomma Enterprises, they began producing prefabricated courses and eventually sold more than five thousand.

However, not all the mini golf courses that popped up like daisies during the 1950s were prefabricated or franchised. Just as in the 1920s, many courses built during this time were handmade by their owners. They were creations of love, "folk art," made from available materials like concrete, tin cans, and imagination. Each was designed according to the builder's vision. They were expressions of each one's idea of perfection, or, in this case, the idea of the Perfect Game.

Just like our own Tom Thumb.

The hazard at hole #5 is a black-and-white pinto pony. He is about three and a half feet long from the tip of his ears to his ceramic tail, and is posed mid-leap over a white hurdle. The pony doesn't move or anything. He's just there to look good.

Underneath him are two long boards that extend out into the fairway. Your goal is to putt your ball between them. The boards narrow to a V and can guide your ball right up to the hole. If you get your ball down the middle, with just the right speed—and I'm not saying this is easy—you can get a hole-in-one.

But this hazard is not called The Two-by-Fours because, well, who would get excited about that? Instead, it's called The Horse.

It's a rocking horse. Well, it *was* a rocking horse. It is not a replica; it truly used to be a children's toy. "Greg's grandkids used to play on it." That is the story some of our first customers told us. "He had a playroom for the grandchildren, you know, at his house in New London. He had all these toys for when they came to visit." Twenty or thirty grandchildren bounced up and down on this thing.

In 1959, when Greg built Tom Thumb, his grandchildren were too big for a little rocking horse, so he took it off its springs, gave it a coat of glossy paint, and bolted it here at hole #5, where it has stood in mid-leap, a look of fierce determination in its painted eyes, ever since.

Duct tape holds the horse together. Also, fiberglass, paint, and cement on the back where the outline of the saddle is still somewhat discernible.

Toddlers see the horse and immediately run to it, lift up one leg, and try to climb onto its back, probably because it still resembles what it used to be, that is, a horse for children. So we keep an eye on that one.

"No, no, no!" my mom screams out as she flies over the ticket booth door to pull the child off. "This isn't strong enough to hold them," she'll say to the parents. To us she says later, "I wish people would watch their children better."

A forty-pound toddler would crack the thing now. It is an artifact, perhaps, something for a museum. Or a dumpster.

It doesn't look its age, but it doesn't look new either. Occasionally a customer will ask us directly, "Have you ever considered replacing that horse?"

This is how we know they are new to Tom Thumb; the regulars would never suggest such a thing. And then we tell them the story: "It's a rocking horse, you know. The former owner had it in a playroom, something for his grandchildren . . ."

"Really?!" they say, and then give the horse a second look. Admire it now. Notice how it is held in place, barely, by two four-inch bolts: one through a front hoof, one through a back hoof.

Once they hear the story, they never question it again. The next time they come, you can hear them say, "Oh, look! There's that horse!" pointing it out to their own children. "This used to be a real rocking horse!" they'll say, then tell them about the playroom. We know that most "normal" owners would probably replace the horse with something newer. Or shinier. Or at least less likely to fall apart. But we keep it anyway. The horse may not be perfect, but in its own way it's kind of beautiful. Also, it's always been here. The Horse is part of the history of this place.

And that is why hole #5, The Horse, and this chapter, are about History.

Which is to say, this entire place is frozen in time. On the back wall of the ticket booth is that same phone we've always had, with a round dial, for crying out loud. Underneath it, penciled on the wood, are the phone numbers we discovered when we first bought the place thirty years ago: "Pepsi man 258-xxxx." "B & A Candy 258-xxxx." Posted on the side wall is a piece of yellowed typing paper: "Extended Rules for each hole—if anyone asks." My mother's handwriting. My father's specifics. The thumbtacks are rusted, and there are streaks down the page from rain that must have leaked through the roof more than once, and many years ago.

When I'm in Los Angeles, it is the 21st century. We wear slick leather jackets, and we know what's what. We drive, drive, drive. We talk endlessly on cell phones. We discuss TV shows, which ones are popular; who is "in," and who is on the way "out." We keep up on trends and fads in case of an audition, or in case we meet a producer at a party, and because you don't want to be caught saying, "Uh, I've never heard of that. Can you fill me in?" There is pressure to keep *up*. There is pressure to be *hip*.

Then I come back here to Tom Thumb, and it's the other way around. *Not* hip. *Not* current. Sometimes I get confused as to what year it actually is. Not only are things unchanged from when I was a child—this is probably true of anyone who visits their parents' home—but the whole place seems stuck in another era. Flying back here is like traveling in time.

It is a little discombobulating.

Okay, it's also comforting. Sometimes I like the fact that things haven't changed. Even though that makes me sound crazy sentimental.

So, okay, I admit it, I'm crazy sentimental.

In 1937 a young couple built a two-story summer cottage on the shores of Beasley Lake on the west end of the Chain O' Lakes. Then the couple left on a trip, were killed in a car wreck, and never had the chance to move in. The floor was still sticky with newness when the cottage was bought later that year by a successful bootlegger. He had earned enough money from alcohol sales to buy the acre and a half at a time when most of the country was still aching from the Depression. He and his wife owned the cottage for twenty years, and when they died it was passed down to their nephew, Greg. It was 1959.

Greg was a schoolteacher. A terribly likeable man. He had a scar on his cheek that gave him a permanent smile. Like my father, fourteen years later, Greg was looking for a good summer job. He liked tourism, which he had worked in for several previous years. So when he inherited this cottage and the large yard around it, he decided to build himself a miniature golf course.

Before he began, Greg spent two summers traveling the Midwest, playing every miniature golf he could find. He carried a small notebook, and he sketched out his favorite holes. He preferred the most difficult hazards, that's what we've been told. And we have the evidence here. More than anything, Greg wanted this place to be *challenging*.

We don't know if he had ever heard of Garnet Carter or the course at Lookout Mountain, but in any case, like others before him, he named his golf course Tom Thumb.

And being thrifty with money—Greg grew up during the Depression, of course—he used whatever materials were handy. Like an antique buggy seat to act as a bench near #16, and here at #5, this old rocking horse.

Oh, horse. Symbol of our fragility. Relic from Greg. Tempter of small children. A snapshot from someone else's photo album plopped out on the course. A survivor, like the rest of the place. The early 1970s were not a boom for mini golf. By the time we bought Tom Thumb it was already a bit of a relic. It was built in 1959. And the novelty had worn off: people knew about this course, but they weren't coming to play.

"Don't worry," Greg told my parents. "Business will pick up." But it didn't.

When the third summer began, we still acted as if they were

coming. Mom and Dad replaced worn carpet and had several signs repainted. We planted flowers. We fixed the fence. We worked outside each beautiful day as if we were preparing for a party and still waiting for the invitees to arrive.

Each spring the horse was carried out in my father's arms like a baby, and it was laid on the wooden rests carved just right for its curves, in mid-jump! over a white-painted hurdle. Each spring the bolts were tightened, and each spring a prayer was muttered, *One more year, maybe the horse will last one more year.* And like the end of a prayer, like the sign of the cross, or touching one's fingers to the lips, as Dad set it on the wooden rests, we reached out to gently touch the flank. It was a kiss. Encouragement. *Hang in there, horse.*

"Don't hurt it!" Dad would say.

"We're not!" we would say.

"Do you think it's going to make it another year?" Mom would ask. She's the practical one and wonders if this year she should find a replacement.

But my father, who was born in 1927 and, like Greg, survived the poverty of the Great Depression, would smooth his hand over the spot he fiberglassed, that time he asked my uncle to teach him how, just so he could keep the horse together. He always replied, "I hope so, Jean. Still hanging in there."

Like the horse, we did too.

CHAPTER 6

THE SWINGING POLE

We will now discuss in a little more detail the Struggle for Existence.

—CHARLES DARWIN

Hole #6 is a pendulum.

Now, a pendulum is technically a weight suspended from a string. It's a famous thing, as far as the world of science is concerned. You give it a push, just one push, and then it's off. It goes one way. And then the other. Back. And forth. Teeter. Totter.

That's all that pendulums do. You can't make them go faster; you can't make them go slower. It's all very sciencey to explain—and I'm not sure I could—but pushing them higher actually doesn't change their speed. The rotation of the earth will change their path eventually, but you'd have to wait a long time to notice, and you know I'm not that patient.

Our pendulum is a log. It hangs directly over the hole. It is seven feet long, covered with thick globs of brown paint, and suspended from a rusted loop about the thickness of your finger.

This pole is not quite as big as a telephone pole, but it's probably big enough to clobber you, so you stand aside as someone in your group gives the pole a push. As it swings, the pole creaks and groans ominously. The wooden supports are swaying and creaking too. The sound reminds you of the ancient swing set you thought would collapse on you at recess on the playground of the elementary school. And you notice how much it resembles a hangman's platform.

But hey, it's mini golf. You put your ball in the tee-off. Then wait for your moment when the pole is off to one side. *Thunt*— you aim perfectly at the center of the ball. It rolls down the fairway directly towards the hole. "Looking good," you say, "looking good—"

But there's a problem. This is a long fairway, and on the way to the green, someone in your group decides to help you out. "Here," they say, giving the pole an extra push.

"No! Don't do that! Don't change it!" you say. But it's too late.

The pole has a different rhythm now. And your ball is heading right for it. *Thwack!* The pole slams your ball to the side of the green—*thud!*—the ball rebounds painfully to the opposite wall—*thud!*—and then again—*thwick*—from one wall to the next, like a baseball that should have been hit out of the park but instead was sent mercilessly into a nine-by-nine-foot room. You grimace at the person in your group who thought they were helping, but doesn't understand that magic thing about pendulums: you can't make them swing *faster*.

Is this a law of the universe? Or just a law of gravity? Did Newton speak on this, or was it Plato? Galileo? It's hard to know whom to thank. In any case, you are at hole #6, The Swinging Pole. This one is about the Law of Nature.

* * *

It was our third summer, and we were starting to get the hang of things. Business was actually beginning to pick up.

"Just like Greg said."

"He was right."

"Of course he was right."

My older sister was seventeen and was making great progress on her suntan. I had just turned fourteen, wore large plastic-rimmed glasses, and was fanatically reading every science fiction book at the library. Carla was ten and pretty much left to herself, as usual. She may have played with dolls, but to be honest, no one knew where she was except at mealtimes.

We had relaxed into a pattern. Things were going smoothly. The season had even started with a record-breaking holiday weekend. And then, the second week of summer, they shut down our road.

"I picked up the new sign at Florence's," Dad said, opening the tailgate of the station wagon and sliding out a three-by-five-foot plank of plywood. TOM THUMB MINI GOLF—*STILL OPEN DURING CON-STRUCTION!* At the bottom of the sign was an arrow. "We'll go put it up after dinner," he said, nodding to LeAnn, "at the end of the road." He leaned the sign against the car. "They've already started digging."

"Oh, I didn't think that would happen until next week," Mom said.

"Nope. I had to go the long way around to get home."

The previous year, the local homeowners association had voted to put in a massive sewer system around the lakes for all the cottages and homes. No more outhouses and septic tanks. This summer they were going to bury a series of huge pipes, and for lack of a better place, they were placing them down the middle of the road.

We were only a few minutes away from the major tourist hub,

but with the road closed people would have to drive twenty minutes through the boondocks to get to us.

"So, how long are we going to have the detour, you think?"
Mom asked. "Not all summer?"

"I hope not."

Dad grabbed a brochure from the ticket booth and unfolded it
to reveal the map inside. With a red pen in hand, he traced out
the new route.

*Go north, pass a cornfield, turn left, pass another cornfield, some
dying hay, an old one-room schoolhouse, and irrigation equipment;
take a left, left again, then drive through the desolate countryside until
you're completely lost, turn left, and wander down another mile and a
half of featureless road . . . And you're here!*

Of course, you couldn't say that to people. If anyone called for
directions, I planned to run around the yard in a hysterical panic
until I found Mom or Dad to explain it for me.

The detour looked bad. If you squinted your eyes and looked
at the map, the red line became a spiral, circling around and
around like the effect in a movie where someone is going insane.
With Tom Thumb at the center.

The next morning, we meticulously swept the greens and
fairways, raised the window flaps, sharpened pencils, and waited.
It was very peaceful, you could say, morguelike. Lacking any true
entertainment, we took turns biking up the road. "My turn," we
said, heading off, to stand on the lip of the hole, and stare into
the big dark crevasse of nothingness.

All afternoon the blades of The Windmill turned in the sun;
they were turning for no one. "That's so nice that customers all
left by 5 pm. So we can eat supper together tonight!" Mom said,
with cheeriness that made me shiver.

I remember the first time the world came to an end. I was eleven.
It was November, and I was late getting home from school. I had

lingered too long at the dime store, staring at the birthstone rings and candy. Then at the library I examined the arts and crafts books, which I considered my private collection. By the time I got home I was two hours late, but the house was empty.

"Mom? LeAnn?" Mom was usually in the kitchen by this time, and Dad asleep on the couch after a long day of teaching, his white socks removed and draped like flags of surrender on the armrests. Instead, the house was perfectly quiet.

That's it then, I thought. It is the Rapture, and I have been left behind.

Well, okay, I thought, locusts? Are there going to be locusts? Isn't there something about blood that rains down from the heavens?

Luckily, a few weeks earlier, my parents had taken us to a movie about the End Times showing at the local college, so I knew what to expect. There would be plagues and computer chips imbedded in our foreheads, and when the police came to arrest you for not having a bar code in your skin, you were supposed to run off and live in the woods like a caveman. I opened the fridge and helped myself to tatertot hotdish.

God had reached down to snatch up the true believers and carry them off to heaven. If you had even just a teeny-tiny bit of doubt, you would be left to suffer tribulations and then maybe hell—I couldn't remember the details after that. But there would be no warning. Cars would crash, and planes would plummet. I was probably walking up Washington Street at the time, a street so boring you'd never notice. For dessert I ate ice cream directly out of the container as I stood in front of the fridge.

Sure I'd had a few doubts. Church took a long time. "The Lord bless you and keep you, the Lord make his face shine upon you . . ." That was my favorite part, the part at the very end.

And I did believe in God, probably just as much as anyone else in my family. But it hadn't been easy. They cut Bible characters out of felt and pressed them on a felt board in Sunday School. That was really dumb. Felt doesn't stick, and grown-ups should realize. I had a problem with a lot of things like that: the way my mother washed plastic bags and clipped them onto the clothesline behind the house, the way my father sharpened pencils that were already sharp. If God was going to leave anyone out, it would definitely be me. My sisters were happier. They didn't ask as many questions. My younger sister even looked like my mom, my older one like my father.

I was a grumpy kid. And maybe, I thought, that's enough for God. If it's Judgment Day and you're God and you get to pick your roommates for eternity, I can't say I'd blame you if you leave behind the grumpy.

A few minutes later Mom walked in the door with Carla and two bags of groceries. "We stopped at the co-op. I hope you weren't worried." LeAnn plopped a couple of bags on the floor behind her and frowned.

July was upon us, and the sewer construction had dragged on. Their progress had slowed down further when they hit water while digging. "They didn't expect that? Water? Digging next to a lake?" I said.

We looked up hopefully every time we heard the crunch of gravel. But then we'd see it was the postman rolling over the edge of the parking lot as he headed down the road to the next mailbox.

At Tom Thumb we got a smattering of customers during what were usually our busiest times, mid-afternoons and evenings. But the numbers were down one third from the previous year, and that hadn't been a good year to begin with.

It was a stressful time.

Dad went to town and brought home a bag of wooden clothespins, took them apart, and spent his afternoons cutting them in half with a hand saw. "Clips!" he said, so excited that he couldn't get the words out fast enough. "I'm ma-ma-ma-king clips! For the pads! Writing pads!" We had no idea what he was talking about, and thought it best not to ask.

LeAnn began wearing a bikini from morning until night. There were boys in the neighborhood. She knew what she was doing. She stood out there by a sawhorse, caressing two-by-fours with her paintbrush. The boys would bike in. Moths. Flames. She had that "sweaty mechanic with oil stains on his face thing" going on; kinda sexy, arms and thighs smeared with red, yellow, and blue.

"Hey," the boys would say, popping quarters into the Pepsi machine.

"Hey," she'd reply. She knew what she was doing.

I filled an afternoon by playing a game of mini golf backwards, placing my ball on each green and chipping it over the hazard to the tee-off, starting from hole #18.

Carla went out for a bike ride and came home with a gashed lip and a sprained wrist or broken arm (we were never sure). She sat alone in the cottage staring out at the lake, her arm in a sling made from a knotted dishtowel. She couldn't do anything, not even eat, so Mom gave her milk shakes and a straw so she wouldn't starve to death.

Mom began singing loudly in the mornings. "This is the day! This is the day! That the Lord hath made, that the Lord hath made!" She aimed her voice up to our bedrooms to wake us up, cheerfully. And sometimes, much to my dismay, she would be clapping. "We shall rejoice! We shall rejoice! And be glad in it, and be glad in it . . ."

One day Mom and Dad made an announcement: "We've decided that from now on you can't get paid for sitting in the ticket booth if there aren't any customers—"

"There have to be people playing—"

"—we don't need anyone in there—"

"Unless it's a bunch of rowdy teenagers!" Dad said. "Then I want you in there watching! I don't want you reading books when there is 'a crew' out there! You should keep your eye on them and make sure they don't . . ." We waited while he continued with what we referred to as Lecture B.

"Anyway," Mom said when he was finished, "if you're supposed to be working, you can only count your hours if you're doing something else, like sweeping or painting. You need to find something else to do."

"Find work to do," Dad said.

I wasn't sure I understood exactly what this meant, but even so, I knew this change wasn't going to be good.

Before we came to Tom Thumb we were not a competitive family exactly, but we did play more board games than any other family I had ever met, or heard of, or may have existed in the wildest dreams of the Parker Brothers. But now, the activity we shared was the running of Tom Thumb. And unlike a game, there were no dice or game pieces. There was no system for keeping score.

I'm lying. We kept score on our steno pads—or at least I did. For the past three years my sisters and I had been writing down the hours we worked each day, and each evening we compared our status—or at least I did—by peeking into LeAnn's.

The goal was not to make money. We never went anyplace, so we had no place to spend it. The goal, as far as I was concerned, was to beat LeAnn. And up to this point I was doing well. Mostly because I had developed great tolerance for reading library books in the ticket booth.

Any new policy was not going to be good news.

When you are a middle child and there is a change—a change in family policy, rules, or standard operating procedure—often it just makes sense to go ahead and feel cheated. Much of the time it will be true, you are being cheated. Some of the times it will not be true. But if you just go ahead and complain, it does save time overall. And it just might take into account all the other occasions when you were being cheated, but you were too busy (or young, or trying to sneak a last piece of cake) to notice.

Our cottage had a porch. This was a good thing. If we hadn't had a porch we might have forgotten we had a house at all. For three months of the year we never went inside, except when the mosquitoes were bad, or it was finally time to sleep, or we were wondering whatever happened to Carla.

But every meal we gathered in the porch. It was raised off the ground and had windows on three sides, so it was like a lookout tower. It faced the parking lot and ticket booth, but you could also see the channel to know if people were coming from there. We sat on built-in benches around a table at one end. Dad claimed the head of the table to get the best view of everything. "I'm removing the spring from each clothespin, and then making a bevel in the writing pad, and drilling holes in each one—"

"By hand?" Mom said.

"Not by hand. I use a drill!" He said something about slots and then little screws for the bottom half, and then reattaching the spring and top piece. "For when it's windy! So their scorecards don't blow away!" It was here, over supper, we talked about our day, and Dad was trying to explain these little clips, one for each writing pad, and why it was important. And Mom was wondering why he didn't just fix the fence that had been broken.

Then LeAnn spoke up, still in her bikini. "I worked almost four hours today. Painting."

Dad came out of his little-clip coma to look at her. "Did you?" Dad said. "Good for you."

"I also started cleaning out that old fountain," she said, rather nonchalantly, adding ketchup to her burger. "It's not bad-looking under all those leaves. I'm going to see if I can get it running."

"That old fountain!" Dad said.

"That's wonderful!" Mom said.

"That would be great if you could fix that old fountain!"

"Wow!" Mom said.

The rest of supper Mom and Dad talked to LeAnn about the fountain, and they could barely chew their food, they were so impressed and excited.

LeAnn tilted her head. "Can I have more fruit salad?"

"Sure!" Mom answered. "Here you are."

"I worked more than an hour," I said, "in the ticket booth." But I would have to admit I sounded desperate.

As we cleared the table after supper, I sidled up to LeAnn. "What's this about a fountain?"

"By hole #16. What did you think that was?"

"Just a pile of rocks."

She sniffed and ignored me, returning to clear more things from the table.

What she called "the fountain" really did look like a pile of limestone with three aluminum saucers on one side. They drooped, and the rock pile sagged, and it looked like a drawing in a book by Dr. Seuss.

The next day I played four games of mini golf simultaneously by filling in the scorecard with names ME 1, ME 2, ME 3, and ME 4 and playing each hole four times before moving on.

That evening at supper, Dad starting talking about my older sister again. "LeAnn was a big help today," he said. "She held boards for me while I sawed. And weren't you painting the fence by #14?"

She nodded. "And I found a pump in the garage today. I think it's meant for running that fountain."

"Oh!" Dad said.

"Really?" Mom added.

"No kidding!" Dad said. My father had eyebrows that he could raise like flags to commemorate a good deed done. And it was at this moment, in addition to fruit salad, that LeAnn was given the ultimate prize: the Eyebrow.

"Where did you find it?" he asked.

"Under the work bench," she said, tilting her head. "Can I have more fruit salad?"

"Sure!" Mom answered. "Here you are."

I was shoveling mixed vegetables on my fork. *Are you kidding me? A pump? What the heck is a pump? How does she even know what a pump even looks like?* I had grown up on Barbies, and none of them came with plumbing.

While they raved on about her, I came to a startling realization: my parents didn't just want us to *work*; they wanted us to be *good workers*. To be a good worker is not to complain about the sun or the wind or the bugs that crawl into the wet paint and die there. They wanted us to feel a personal concern about Tom Thumb, that is, to want to work for our own private reasons.

"In the garage I also found a gallon of stain, and tomorrow, if it's sunny, I'm going to stain the dock," LeAnn said.

"Great idea!" Mom said.

"Wonderful!" Dad said.

What's stain? Is that like paint?

It became apparent to me that this was not a new belief of my parents; instead, it must have been held inside each of them for many years, like genetic code, waiting for the chance to break out, or a herpes virus that appears as cold sores around the lips. My parents were becoming the people they had secretly been all along.

I went ahead and felt a strong sense of betrayal.

What they say about middle children, that they get lost in the shuffle, that they are mostly ignored, tends to be true. This is fate. Or luck. Darwin said that animals tend to adapt to their surroundings. As a middle child, you adapt by feeling a pinch in your gut when you sense people are clamoring for something. As a middle child, you may start clamoring for it too, sometimes without even knowing what "it" is. This is what I call the Clamor Law of Nature.

The next morning, I ate breakfast quickly and showed up at the garage early. LeAnn was already sashaying towards the dock in her blue bikini, paintbrush and stain in hand. "Hey!" I called. "Hey, LeAnn."

She seemed not to hear me.

"Hey!" I said again. She finally stopped near the clothesline, which had drooping vinyl cords stretched almost to the ground.

"Hey," I asked, "do you want help with that? With the stain?"

She hooked one finger under the bikini bottom to hitch it higher on her hip.

"You know," I continued, "I could do one end of the dock, and you could do the other. It'll go faster that way. We can do it together. I can get another paintbrush."

She looked at me, frowning her thick eyebrows. Sweat formed on her lip like clouds gathering before a storm.

It was like the time we had played the game Risk, just the two of us. A few minutes in, and she was already ahead of me. But then things got even worse. "I don't know if I mentioned it," she said, "but you know the rule where I get to add extra armies?"

"What?"

"Oh, it's in the rules somewhere. I forget where," she said, pulling armies out of the box and piling them up onto her countries.

"What?! What?!"

She kept adding more. "Oh, it's in the rules. Okay. Now I'm going to attack you. I rolled a six," she said, happier than a puppy just before you throw the stick. "Now you have to roll."

To this day, I do not know if she invented a rule, or if she intentionally withheld one from me until it was to her advantage to reveal it. Either way, I wasn't going to win.

"Go! You roll!"

"But, wait!" I said. I ran my fingers along the edge of the board and lifted them up towards the ceiling. *Whoop.* Hundreds of blue and yellow armies flew into airspace over our card table. Casualties fell onto the table, on the floor, and into our popcorn bowls.

"Why did you do that!" she said. "I'm never playing that with you again." She slammed the kitchen door and stomped down the stairs. It was a vow that she kept.

"Help me? With the stain? Go find your own job." And then with a left-foot pivot, she turned her beautiful blue butt away from me and towards the horizon.

I tried to think of something I could do for everyone's betterment, to help in the task we shared, called Tom Thumb.

I went to the garage to talk to Dad. "Can I paint #11?"

"I did that yesterday," Dad said.

"How about #10?"

"LeAnn finished that last week. The good news is that I think we're done with painting for a while."

"Okay."

"I'm rewiring the boat. Go ask your mother if she needs help."

"Anything for me to do?" I asked her. "Do the pencils need sharpening?"

"No. I did it already," Mom said, filling out a candy order. "See if you can find some other job to do."

"What about that pile of old rocks by #12? Maybe I'll clean that up."

"The other fountain?"

"That's a *fountain*? There's another *fountain*?" It looked more or less like a construction site after the workmen give up for the day and go home to their families. "Well, if that's a fountain, maybe I'll clean it up and see if I can get it going!"

"I think LeAnn already claimed that."

I walked diagonally across the course, looking for wrongs I could right. On the pond of #7 there were two brown leaves and a twig. I picked them out. Okay, that took about fifteen seconds. The buckets that hang from The Wishing Well on #8 were tangled slightly on their ropes. I twisted them around. Much better. So I guessed I had worked about three and a half minutes total.

I was an out-of-work, Depression-era hobo at age fourteen in my own backyard. It was time to take a brave step. I was going to have to explore the garage.

From the outside our garage appeared normal. Two lawn mowers, gas cans, and rusted gardening tools. But the inside was unexplored territory. Like the Northwest Passage, there were corners that had yet to be seen by human eyes. You couldn't count on finding anything specific, but you were sure to find something. It was like going on an archaeological dig at an abandoned amusement park.

I stepped past a hazard that looked like a gingerbread house, and a concrete donkey about the size of a small dog. Lengths of painted two-by-fours were heaped on the floor like multicolored spaghetti noodles. I tiptoed between them, spreading my arms for balance. There were signs for hazards that no longer existed; cardboard Tom Thumb advertisements from 1959; boxes of pulleys, motors, and shims; and several squat machines that might be vacuum cleaners or digging equipment left behind by gold miners. To find a "job to do," I needed to excavate one of the dark corners, a land untouched by the single naked lightbulb.

I brought out a wire cage with a door on a little hinge, suspended on a rope. "Look at this, Mom!" I said. "Maybe it's part of a hazard!"

"Well, let's have a look. Hmm. I think it's what fishermen use after they catch fish. To keep them from dying. They put them in the water inside it. That looks like the remains of a dried fish stuck in there."

"Yuck," I said, dropping it. I ventured back in.

"What's this?" I asked, returning with a wooden square painted green, an old-fashioned latch on one side.

"Looks like a trapdoor," Mom said.

"A trapdoor?"

"For something that no longer exists, I suppose," she said.

"What can I do with this?"

"No idea."

"Huhhmmm."

That night at dinner LeAnn announced that she had discovered what looked like a rotating disk the size of a dinner plate. "I think it goes in front of a light and then spins. With these colored plastic sections it will make a colored light show on the fountain."

Mom and Dad almost dropped their hot dogs in admiration.

After a few years of watching people push the pole higher and higher at hole #6, my dad, the physics teacher, wrote a note on a white index card and thumbtacked it to one of the supports of the swinging pole:

> According to the Law of Physics, if you swing the pole higher it will not change the interval of time your ball is safe from getting hit.

The words *will not change* were underlined, but people didn't believe it. Every day they were at it again, grappling with gravity. Not giving up. Which is, perhaps, one of the laws of being human.

Meanwhile Carla sat on the couch inside the cottage, alone. She should have gotten stitches on her lip, we realized at this point, but despite the fact she was frail and the color of your average ghost, she was stubborn. "No doctors." She sat staring out at the lake, her arm in the dishcloth sling.

A calico kitten had been coming out of the woods every few days to beg for food. A stray, we figured. Today, she had shown up again. I put my arms into one of the lost-and-found jackets, and then I zipped the cat inside. I smuggled her into the house, opened up the zipper, and plopped the cat onto Carla's lap.

"The kitty!" Carla said. And she was so happy that she smiled, and this brought on a new wave of pain on her upper lip, which was split into two or three pieces, we weren't sure. So she put her index fingers on each side of her bloody mustache to hold the skin together.

"*Sssh*. Don't tell Mom," I said. "Okay. Also, I have a joke. How many tourists does it take to change a lightbulb?"

She shook her head. *I don't know.*

"None. They want us to do it *for* them."

She held her fingers more tightly and tried hard not to smile.

"I have another joke," I said to her. "How many old-men-tourists does it take to change a lightbulb?"

I answered in a funny voice. "Did you know you have a burned-out light up there? It might need a new bulb."

She grimaced, trying not to laugh. Shook her head, *No, no!*

"How many tourists does it take to change a lightbulb?" I asked again.

I knew I shouldn't make her laugh. *She'll probably get scars.*

And then came the day that LeAnn Dropped the Paint. It was green, and by her account only one quart, even if I recall it being a full gallon. In any case, you could call this day the Ultimate Moment of My Defeat.

Like other mornings, it began with LeAnn announcing the job she was about to do, just so you would be sure to notice. "Today, I'm going to paint the trim on the porch."

"There's trim on the porch?!" I said. "What's trim?!" Apparently there was dark green that ran around the windows, but it was not something I felt a need to notice.

Anyway, she was in her blue shiny bikini. Her hair pulled back into a ponytail with a guitar capo. She opened the can and grabbed a brush and headed across the yard, the gallon can between her hands.

Then she dropped it. The entire can. Maybe there was a root she didn't see in the long grass, or her hands were already damp from sweat, but whatever, the can hit squarely on the ground. One gallon of oil-based semi-gloss paint flew up into the air like some kind of physics experiment gone wrong, and green splattered on her all over. At her chest, face, and hair. There was a scream. Mom came running.

We spent most of the afternoon watching Mom dab a soft cloth dipped in gasoline on her cheeks and eyelids as if LeAnn were a baby still in arms.

"Impressive," Dad said, that night.

"You've been so brave," Mom added. Everyone felt sorry for her, and LeAnn just smiled. At supper she got the biggest portion of the lemon cake.

For that entire week there was nothing I could do to get a raised eyebrow at the end of the day, no amount of work or creative finding things to do could compete with LeAnn's sacrifice. "She was just covered in green paint!" Mom told our aunt and uncle over the phone. "My older daughter was painting the house when the paint exploded all over her," Dad said to customers who had asked, "So how's it going this week?" "I still have green pores," LeAnn said three days after the accident, pulling down her eyebrow to show. She was milking it.

She knew what she was doing.

CHAPTER 7

THE WATER HOLE

Thousands have lived without love, not one without water.

—W. H. AUDEN

Ahead of you is a quiet pool. Six inches deep and perfectly oval, it is painted a bright glowy blue, the color of a Tahitian lagoon in *National Geographic.* The pool is slightly longer than you are tall, and along it bloom a bed of wild roses behind a miniature white fence. One green leaf falls from the tree and flutters to the lip of the pool. A breeze nudges it into the water, where it floats and turns in the sun, like a sunbather. "Look," a seven-year-old boy screams, running up to the pool, and swamping the leaf with the handle of his putter. "A water hole!"

You'll notice there are two paths around it to get to the green: one to the left and one to the right. One path looks safe, the other more risky. You'll need to make a choice, but we'll get to that in a moment.

1

You may shoot either way

—*on this hole* • *Par 3* •

Hole #7, The Water Hole, is about that wet thing that covers the earth, Water (you know you can't live without it).

This is what people like to do in the water: wade. Also: dive, gurgle, swim. One of the deepest pleasures in life is dipping one's cupped hand into the water, bringing it up to the surface, and flinging it at a nearby sister. Just see if you can live an entire life without splashing someone once in a while. Consider that there are nuns and monks who vow to lead a life of celibacy. But can they get through seventy years without splashing someone? Perhaps one day at the kitchen sink, while washing up? I think not.

Once upon a time, the state now known as Wisconsin was completely covered in water. In fact, there was a huge body of water over most of North America. It sounds so exciting. You could travel by boat from Maine to Oklahoma. Then suddenly the land under the water bubbled up due to something called *gastric pressure*. (This is according to an article about the area I found in an old newspaper from 1936. Maybe they have a better name for it these days, but if so, I don't want to know about it.) Anyway, the earth was like a giant stomach full of gas, and it pushed up and up on the land under the inland sea, and it created hills and valleys, and the water splashed out every which way. Some of it ran off the edge of North America as if it were a giant picnic table. Some of the water was trapped and remains here today. We call the trapped water Lake Michigan, Lake Heron, Lake Erie, and the other Great Lakes. I like to think of them as giant souvenirs from a great boating vacation (that is, if you had a boat millions of years ago).

After this era came the *Jungle Era*, when Wisconsin turned into a tropical wonderland—giant ferns, maybe coconut trees, and weird ferny plants the size of a barn. I would love to see Wisconsin as a jungle, but it was millions and millions of years ago, so I'm sorry we all missed it. But we can enjoy the souvenirs: fossils, and fossilized prints of corals and exotic plants.

Next came the *Glacier Era*, and these giant ice bullies pushed everything around, the dirt, the rocks, everything. When they couldn't push any farther, they stopped. Then they got a little melty. You can see where the glaciers quit because there is a steep ridge of dirt and rocks, like you see around these Chain O' Lakes—one of the souvenirs from *that* era. Another is the sandy soil all over the state. The glaciers were like giant rock tumblers. When they were gone, they left a lot of gravel. Also sand, sand, sand. Along our property is Beasley Creek, and from a distance it looks muddy. But that's golden sand under clear water. You can walk in bare feet and pick up pretty rocks. And we do.

And now, here, these lakes. This beautiful, overpriced, looping chain of lakes. Another souvenir left behind by the glaciers. Crevasses and valleys that filled with water after the melt. So clear. So deep. When you are swimming your toes are always colder than your shoulders because of the springs underneath. You can say, "I found a spring!" and then try to hover over it so your cousin, who is visiting, can swim over. She wants to feel the cold on her toes too. But it's not easy to hover when you are treading water on a lake. There are no landmarks. But you try, and the cold will make you giggle.

This lake, Beasley, they say, goes fifty feet down or more. There once were giant muskies living in the deep, some more than twenty feet long. My uncle says he saw them swim under the boat launch he drove years ago, and maybe they are still down there, but you try not to think about this while you swim.

One day when we were eating lunch on the porch, we saw something disturbing out on the lake. Like sharpened arrows, forty canoes were flying in slow motion through the channel from

Long Lake. Forty canoes were flashing in the sun; the lake was filled with silver. It looked like target practice, and we were the bull's-eye.

"Something weird going on," LeAnn said.

"What is it?" we said, running to the windows.

"It's all boys. Young ones. Looks like they're coming here."

"Oh, yeah," Dad said. "We had a phone call last night."

"You knew about this?"

"I may have forgotten to tell you," he said, with a shrug. He stepped outside to wave at a man who arrived in the first canoe and was now wandering across the yard half-naked, carrying a grill. "Hello, there!"

Of course, water is the usual way for invaders to approach, I mean, historically speaking. Water silences your approach, and invaders really like sneaking up on people. Some of my ancestors were Vikings, or so it seems likely, so I should probably be accepting of these things.

In one of the bigger of the lakes on this chain there was a small heap of forested land, Onaway Island. It had been purchased and turned into a boys' camp almost a century before. Kids from Appleton and Neenah took a boat to the island and then spent a week there at Camp Onaway in a tent-cabin. They were members of the Boys' Brigade, which was like Boy Scouts, they said, but different.

"They're going to eat first," Dad told us, coming back in the porch. So we returned to our sandwiches as their grills went up. They knocked on our door to borrow matches; then the smoke from their lighter fluid blew in our open windows.

"Someone needs to be out there," Mom yelled, as a group of ten-year-old boys formed a swarm and moved as one towards the mini golf course.

"I'll go," I said, and trotted down the path. I pulled open

the Dutch door at an angle to maximize the scrape of the wood against the threshold. There were other, gentler ways of opening the ticket booth door. But we in my family knew—like Eskimo words for snow—varying ways to pull the handle, each one making a slightly different scraping sound from the rest. This one announced: I AM HERE and I AM IN CHARGE.

Swarm. Troup. Pack. Herd. Colony. Army. Drove. Brigade. However you collect them, soon a scary quantity of ten-year-old boys ran barefoot across the grass, or stepped gingerly over the gravel parking lot as if they were walking on hot coals. They wore name tags on lanyards, which probably helped the leaders tell them apart, because the boys all looked the same—fifth and sixth graders, each with wet hair, and a white t-shirt that was either still on his back, or decorating one of our fence posts.

Boys pressed their faces as close as possible to the front screen. "I'd like a blue ball." Then another boy would grab his shoulder and still another punch his arm with his fist. "I wanted the blue ball." Dad appeared then and took charge of the ticket booth, much to my relief. Mom and LeAnn and Carla and I stood in the path, safe from the mayhem. Which sounded something like this:

"Do you have pop? Can I buy a pop?"

"How much does it cost to play?"

"Can I get a cotton candy?"

The boys ignored the troop leader who was fretfully waving his arms. "Boys. Okay. Boys. If you want to play golf—boys. Oh, boys."

"This is a mess," Mom said to us.

"How about groups of three boys each?" Dad said to the leader. "Tell them to form groups. Three or four. But not more than that." The man looked relieved at getting some kind of math-like instructions.

Mom said, "Girls, we're going to need all of you."

"I'll help Dad," LeAnn said, joining him in the ticket booth.

"I'll take the Snack Shack," Mom said. "June, why don't you take a scorecard and start a group ahead?"

Then Dad put on his charming face and turned to the front window. "Okay, who's the first group? Step on up. I'll size you up for clubs." LeAnn reached for golf balls behind him.

"Follow me," I said, leading the second group out onto the course. "You'll start here so you don't have to wait. Play all the way through #17, and then start back on hole #1. Whatever you do, play #18 last."

There was not room in the ticket booth for more than two people, unless you were people who knew each other well. Which we did. I slipped in along the side to get more scorecards, reaching around Dad's arm as he greeted the next group of boys. When I turned, LeAnn curved past me, moving to collect more balls from the bin. At the door, one of the leaders handed me a camera. "Can you keep this for me?" "Sure," I replied, slipping past LeAnn's knees, aiming the camera for the shelf as Dad made a pivot saying, "I've got a longer club over here." Graceful. Like a well-rehearsed troupe. This is how we move.

As the brigade finished their game and turned in their putters, they rushed to the Snack Shack where Mom and I were waiting.

And then she and I did a dance of our own, she whipping up the cotton candy while I took orders and made sno-cones, took in soggy wet bills and gave back change, until Mom called, "Next one's ready!" and handed me the newly made cotton candy cone. "Okay! Who's next?" I said loudly to the boys, doing a skip to the front window.

Forty cotton candies, fifteen sno-cones, and several bags of popcorn later, the boys hot-coal-stepped back to the shore. The leader nodded at Dad. "All right then, see you next week."

"Tuesday?"

"Just like today. Different boys, though."

"Thanks for the warning."

"Well, if you want to know ahead, we'll have boys' camps the next eight weeks until the middle of August, and then one week of girls."

And so once a week we would be attacked. You knew it was Tuesday because twenty to thirty canoes plowed into Beasley Lake coming our way. Forty to fifty half-naked boys ate hot dogs on our lawn. Forty to fifty boys carried their leftovers on paper plates to our dog, Bo. "Please don't feed the dog," we would say, but each week they were different boys, and each was away from home and his own beloved dog, and each felt a need to spoil our dog instead; to tickle his ears and tell him he was good-looking, and see if he liked to eat cotton candy (just a little) or popcorn (quite a lot).

Water is so strange. I am made of it, and you are too. Seventy percent if we believe the stories they tell us. Water is also a force. Like a giant magnet, every body of water will draw objects towards it. A memorial fountain in a city will attract spare change, pigeons, unattended children, dry leaves, and empty paper cups. Build a dam across a river, and you will attract motorboats, skiers, and trapped salmon. This pond at hole #7 attracts twigs, golf balls, putters, and bare toes.

Water even attracts itself, one water molecule grabbing on to the next one, the hydrogen pining for the hydrogen from the molecule next door, so that even a tiny droplet on the plastic tablecloth will form a raised dome of itself, as anyone knows who has fingertips and poked at the ring left behind when a pitcher of iced tea has been removed.

Like a campfire, water is irresistible. Not all of the four basic elements are this way. Air? Rock? But fire and water, they are magnetic attractors. Pulling us towards them. The way the Chain O' Lakes themselves have attracted these cottages and summer visitors who return to swarm the shores every year.

One year after construction began, our road was whole again, and then we began to notice a change: there were more people in the area. It was subtle at first. A few more bikes on the road. A few more Cris-Crafts in the water. A few more cars ogling for the good parking spots. More people asked if they could picnic on our lawn. None of us can say exactly when, but it was clear, more people were being drawn to these lakes, and, as a result, more were coming to play at Tom Thumb.

We called them customers.

They came in pickup trucks and school buses, station wagons and jeeps. They came in sexed-up passenger vans with airbrushed moonscapes on the side. They came on scooters, motorbikes; whole families on tricycles, mountain bikes, and tandems. They came on Harleys so large they buzzed the windows of the Snack Shack. They drove in Cadillacs from Milwaukee and Mustangs from Wild Rose. Volkswagen Beetles from Weyauwega and Chevy Novas up from Madison. They came in three cars at once, four or five at a time; a family reunion came in six matching Oldsmobiles.

They came in pontoon boats they had just rented for the day, without any training on how to make them stop. *Boom.* Our dock took a blow from a boat-size battering ram. *Revvv*—they reversed. They tried again. *Boom.*

They dragged canoes onto our shore. They padded across our lawn in their wet swimsuits and shorts. They stared in our living room windows and clomped past our front door. They set down picnic baskets on the long grass we had just been planning to mow. They unloaded grills and watercoolers and ice chests packed with wienies. They put their wet butts on the merry-go-round in the yard. They wore bikinis and baseball caps and hats made from beer cans. They carried bug spray and canoe paddles, maps and life preservers. Flip-flops that had snapped. Jackets for the wind. They dropped sunglasses, lip balm, baby bottles, and cotton candy cones; bags now empty of chips, smoldering briquettes. They left soda cans and beer cans, even though beer was not allowed; Cracker Jack boxes, candy wrappers, suntan lotion, and beach towels. T-shirts and sweatshirts and broken ankle bracelets. Cameras and diapers, pacifiers and a doll. Gloves and baseball caps, twenty-dollar bills.

We cleared a small shelf in the ticket booth to hold the lost-and-found. We draped jackets on the two kitchen stools hoping someone would reclaim them. More were added as the summer progressed, so we could measure the passage of time by the thickness of the layers of lost jackets behind our backs.

In fifty miles of shoreline, there was no public land along these lakes, no grassy bit of ground where people could pull their boat over. So my parents bought picnic tables, and my sisters and I painted them. We wheeled them to the shore. Set them down by the merry-go-round, which we painted too.

We posted an OPEN sign, but for the most part they came when they wanted. They came when we had just sat down to dinner. They came when we were shutting up for the rain. Sometimes they came to watch, not buying anything at all, just wanting to sit and watch other people play.

For reasons we could never explain, customers arrived in clumps, three cars at a time, four at a time, unrelated families and unsuspecting couples, all pulled in at the exact same moment. The way stars cluster in the sky.

What is the smell of the water? The lakes? It's faint but still so familiar, and when the wind picks up, it brings the lake to you. Slightly sweet. Not bitter. Not tart. Somewhat like leaves you rake up in the fall. A bit like the inside of a greenhouse: humid, moist, laden with other life.

One day a Jewish camp came, and we learned about the idea of keeping kosher and what candy was not allowed. A girl received a "laying on of hands" behind the Snack Shack after she ate the wrong candy bar. I watched.

Another week it was a different Jewish camp. They were fifty angry boys who argued within their groups or refused to play together at all. "Some are here for six weeks," the counselor said. "Some even longer. They've been sent away for the summer. They'd rather be home with their families."

There is no sound from a lake. It is stillness. You hear the things that are drawn to it, the red-winged blackbirds, outboard motors, the buzz of a fly. Or heavy equipment coming around the corner. Not one bulldozer, perhaps a few. Several bulldozers? No, the sound was moving too fast. Insistent like a jackhammer inside your head. Racing, roaring. Harley-Davidson motorcycles, about fifty of them, and they were coming our way.

The motorcycles pulled up to the split-rail fence in front of the ticket booth. Some had handlebars that came up near the riders' ears. It was a gang. Leather vests. Leather hats. Bandannas made entirely of leather. Tattoos of skulls—some with hearts, some with wings.

I tapped the red button on the intercom. "Call—call." This made a *beep-beep* in the house. It meant, "Please come! SOS! I need help out here!"

The men wore leather chaps, the women leather shorts. One of the women had a terrifying resemblance to my elementary-school gym teacher, Miss Vedvik.

Beep. Beep. "Please come."

They kicked at their bikes until they rose up on metal pedestals.

They raked their fingers through their mustaches. The women took off their mirrored sunglasses and pulled at their leather shorts.

My dad came trotting down the path, my mother behind, at a respectful (and possibly terrified) distance. He hurried inside the ticket booth.

One of the men came to the counter. "Can you tell me how I get to Clear Water Harbor?"

"Sure," my dad said.

My sisters and I stood in the gap between the ticket booth and Snack Shack, cowering like schoolgirls on the playground when worms were being thrown after a rain.

"Where you folks from?" my dad asked.

No, don't talk to them. Don't delay their getting out of here.

They started chatting with Dad, and you could forget for a moment that they were child killers and dog molesters. They seemed to be only dressed like murderers. But still, you could tell Dad was nervous. These guys could rip out everything with one sweep. His own arms were the size of small pipes. "Well, let me show you on a map," we heard him say.

No! No, Dad! Not a map! we mouthed to each other.

My dad, a schoolteacher, loved to point things out on maps. He could tell you where to find the new box of breakfast cereal in the cupboard if he could draw a map. He came around the front of the ticket booth. Now he was surrounded by them, all wearing leather, so much leather, where once he, as a farmer, had stood calmly among the herd of Guernsey cows, who were similarly clad, only their hide was still untanned.

Maybe everything would be fine, except for one thing: my father tended to give directions using the wrong finger. "Now you start out here on Q," he said, pointing with his middle finger. "Then take that north, oh, about a mile or two to here." He traced the path for them by dragging his middle finger along the road, then pointed to the men who stood around him.

The man in the leather head wrap looked at my father's face. *Is this guy threatening me?*

"Now, you don't want to get off on QQ," my father continued, still tracing with his middle finger.

Head Wrap looked over at Muttonchop Mustache, who looked over at GrayBeard and FlyingSkullTattoo. *Is this guy flipping us off?* They squinted at each other to signal, *Not sure.* And my father stood between them in his blue shorts and black knee socks which were tucked into his white tennis shoes.

"I think you should be able to find it." He folded the brochure. "Go ahead and take this."

"Okay, that'll help. Thanks," said Head Wrap. "But first—"

We cowered behind the ticket booth.

"—we've come for a fierce game of mini golf."

"Well, you came to the right place," Dad said. He smiled and handed them putters, pointing out all the advantages and disadvantages of the "elite" clubs, which usually only went out to his favorites. "We call this one Fat Sally," he said, and the leather men laughed. They showed the putter to their gym-teacher girlfriends. "Fat Sally!" the women said, laughing, taking off their bandannas and draping them on the bikes.

For the next forty-five minutes we were allowed to stare at bikers because they had come to our backyard. And even though we thought they looked really overdressed for the heat in all those chaps and vests, they seemed to be rather happy.

"Wow," we said to each other. "Bikers!"

"I know! And they're having so much fun," we said, marveling at the sight.

When they finished, Mom smiled and made them cotton candy. "That'll be seventy-five cents," she said. "Thanks! Take care now!"

Then they roared off down the road, screaming from the tops of their mufflers that they had had a good time at Tom Thumb.

Back to hole #7. As I mentioned, you're going to have to make a choice. There are two fairways: the safe one and the risky one.

One path is banked at a gentle angle and follows the bend of the pool. It is lined with bricks most of the way, and they will guide your ball gently to the green. Except your ball will rebound off one side and then the next because the safe route does not direct your ball to the hole. You will land in a corner. The hazard is designed this way.

But the other path looks scary. It is only fourteen inches wide with no rims to keep your ball in. It skirts along the other side of the pool and is aimed directly at the hole. It's so narrow, you'd have to putt so straight. You wonder if it's even doable.

One path will get you there safely. But the other gives you a chance at a hole-in-one—greater success. So, which will you choose?

On the ground is a pole with a cup on the end. It looks like an ice cream scoop with an unexpected six-foot handle. It's a ball retriever. For those unfortunates who lose their ball in the pond. The cup is dripping wet. The sight of it stops you for a moment. You think: It could happen to me. This may be the hole where I embarrass myself. You begin to feel dread.

Three out of four people choose to take the safe path. I say three out of four with more confidence than you might think. Because, you see, I've been watching. There's psychology involved. There's the desire to be different. If the first three people in a group all choose the safe path, the fourth one will say, "Well, if no one else has the guts . . ." and go the other way. One of the four will rebel. Or simply try, in their small way, to stand out.

Others in the foursome may yell, "You're crazy!" Or more often they may say, "Do it! Do it!" Because people in a group really like seeing someone else in their group mess up; they would sure enjoy that splash. They anticipate the fun it might be to see what happens when someone takes the risk that they were not willing to take.

What I'm saying is that in any given family there's the desire of one of the group to be different. In my family, it was me.

CHAPTER 8

THE WISHING WELL

*I don't know much about being a millionaire, but I'll bet I'd be
a darling at it.*

—DOROTHY PARKER

They say that cockroaches will survive the next apocalypse and
be running around the earth after the rest of us are gone. So, too,
the next hazard, The Wishing Well. It's huge. And it's made of
rock held together with concrete. (Okay, so it won't actually be
running with the cockroaches, but you know what I mean.) Each
fall, before the rains of September, and the deep snows are upon
us, we move all the hazards indoors. Except this one. It will be
stuck out here forever and ever. The Wishing Well will never die—
which is too bad, because I don't really like it. From my perspec-
tive it's just a heap of local rocks with two small buckets hanging
over the center, and above it all a simple shingled roof. There are
two tunnels that pass underneath this hazard, and that's what
you will aim for.

The left-hand
opening

is in line with
the hole here   ● Par 3 ●

Our Wishing Well has a piece of plywood over the opening, so you know, it's not really a well at all. This keeps people from making their wishes here, which I've always considered unfortunate. I like when people make wishes, because I'm a dreamer too, and one of my dreams is to be the person who cleans up all the coins that others toss into a fountain. Wishing doesn't require coins, but if people want to throw their money away, I'd be happy to take it in. Hole #8, The Wishing Well, is about Dreams.

One time when I must have been about fifteen years old, a woman paid me extra for her cotton candy and chips. I had never heard of tipping, so I usually tossed the surplus into the money box. But this woman, in addition to more quarters, gave me a frown and what sounded like a scolding. "Your prices should be higher. You don't charge enough."

"Uh, thanks," I said.

I cornered my mom in the Snack Shack that afternoon. "I think maybe our prices are too low."

"They are low," she said, tipping oil into the popcorn kettle.

"I think we should raise them."

"Why?"

I told her about the woman, about how she gave me extra money.

"I've had people tell me that. They're used to paying more. I'm sure everything costs a *lot* more at Wisconsin Dells," she said, mentioning the resort area two hours south of us.

"That means we could charge more," I said.

"I suppose. But we aren't going to do that," she said, pouring in popcorn kernels.

"Why not? We could make more money!"

"Your dad and I talked about it. We're going to charge what we would want to pay for our family if we were on vacation."

"If *you* were on vacation? That's how you set your prices? But you're teachers! You don't have any money!"

She replied by gently closing the door of the popcorn machine and staring past it out the window, and I realized I had made a mistake. "I don't want to talk about it," she said quietly. "That kettle isn't warmed up enough yet. Have to wait a while."

All last winter Mom and Dad had borrowed from my babysitting earnings. Fifty cents here, a dollar there. We kept track on a blackboard by the kitchen sink. I shouldn't have reminded her. You can't take back your words, so instead I backed out of the Snack Shack. "People would still come," I mumbled. "It's embarrassing."

"No! No more talking about money! And that's final!" To make sure I'd leave, she began dragging a thick dull knife around the metal walls of the cotton candy machine. It was how we scraped off hardened pink sugar, but it sounded like the cries of the tormented in hell, or so I always thought.

I stomped out of the Snack Shack, letting the screen door slam.

She called out to me, "But you can keep the change if people give you extra. Sometimes people give me extra too!"

Inside the garage I yanked out the nearest bike and pedaled fiercely down the road. I pumped and pumped until I got to the top of an incline, then let the bike coast downhill. The camera crew appears on the side of the road, following me as I bike along. *Oh, there you are.* I smile at them. I am on a photo shoot. Like the famous model Cheryl Tiegs, my hair is swept gorgeously from my face by the wind. I pull my t-shirt down off one shoulder and tilt my head while the camera shutter clicks. I lower my eyelashes to flirt with the cameras. I emerge a mile and a half later at the intersection of county road Q—*Good job, guys.* I wave to the photographers as I turn.

At this corner is my uncle's canoe rental business. There are a cluster of white garage-shaped buildings, a hundred cars in the lot, and a dozen or so shirtless high school boys. Pale fiberglass canoes lie facedown in the sun as if sunbathing together, while the boys, sporting new muscles from lifting canoes, lean over them like lovers spreading suntan lotion, applying fiberglass squares and resin to patch the most recent holes. They are suntanned, bare-chested, and I try to keep my bike from spinning off the road. As I coast past, the one that looks like Luke Skywalker notices me and my Cheryl Tiegs hair. He sets down his brush and runs up the steep driveway, "Oh, June! You're here! I'm in love with you. I always have been. But I've been afraid to tell you!"

Then the other blonde employee, the one that looks the second-most like Luke Skywalker—only he is a bit too tall and has slightly darker hair—runs up and elbows First Luke to the side. "No! I'm the one who should be June's boyfriend! Look how good we look together!" He stands next to me, and I straighten my shoulders and look askance; I have become accustomed to this competing, and I have learned, like all celebrities, how to tolerate the attention. *Now, boys . . .*

The parents of the First Luke fall in love with me too. "You can move in with us, June, and be a part of our family. We will treat you better than your own parents! We think you deserve the world!"

They give me a dazzling bedroom with windows in a circle, like a turret, that overlooks the lake. "You can stay here all winter and not go back to the school in Iowa where the other kids don't seem to appreciate your talent and beauty." The room is pink with carpet so soft that I go barefoot year-round.

"Well, that's awfully kind of you," I say, blushing.

"We will miss you," my parents say, "but we cannot give you the happiness that the Skywalker family can provide." And my dad hands me a wad of bills that I had no idea they even had.

I came to a stop sign just past the canoe rental, stepped off a pedal, when a car pulled up next to me. "Are you from the mini golf?" a woman said through the open window. I nodded. "I thought I recognized you." She poked the man next to her. "See? What did I tell you?" Then turning back to me, she said, "So how late are you open?"

"Uh. Ten o'clock."

"Great. See you there." Her window slid back up before I could add:

"But you have to start by nine thirty."

The real obstacle of #8 isn't The Wishing Well; it's the fairway; it slants wickedly. It was intended to lean, we are pretty sure, but we also know it's gotten worse over the years. To get your ball through the *left-hand* opening, you actually need to start your ball on the *right* side of the fairway. If you tee off from the center, you are doomed. The Wishing Well is not a straightforward hazard; you'll have to take my word on this one. My cousin Noel moved to New York City to become a pianist and played on the streets outside subway stations for a year. Then he switched plans and became an executive at Walgreens. When he came to visit, I remember how he kicked the tee-off pad to the far right side of the fairway. He started farther over than anyone else I had ever seen, correcting for the slant by putting across it at a sharp angle. Oh, how we laughed to see him do it. A joke! He must be kidding! But then he would follow through like someone who was not kidding, the putter pausing in the air like a duck when it pulls itself up out of the creek and into flight. The ball crossed over the slant, made a soundless journey through the opening, and came out safely on the green. Sometimes he got a hole-in-one this way. Miracle. Walgreens. You start from one corner, and then you end up someplace else. "Why did you give up piano?" people asked years later. "No, I still play," he would say. But I remember that summer he would sit at our piano after a game of golf, and he would improvise, and we felt like we were in the company of a genius. My mom still talks about it, how Noel would fill the house with music without looking at piano books at all.

If you're like most people—and let's face it, who isn't—you haven't thought about the tee-offs until now. You may not have even noticed where you've started, where you've come from at all. You put your ball into the center hole of the tee-off. There are three holes to choose from—you just went for the one in the middle. But perhaps it's an advantage to come to life from another direction.

Several years earlier, my parents had bought an old piano from a woman in town, knowing that during the summer we were missing our piano lessons and marching band practice and sports practice and, I might add, television. The piano sat in one end of the living room next to a box of books and sheet music we inherited from my grandparents' attic. Lacking anything better to do, I poured through that box the way I used to scroll through TV channels.

"I'm glad we decided to get that piano," Mom said. "Probably the best fifty bucks we've ever spent. You know, June, maybe you should take organ lessons. You could marry a minister someday. You could be the church organist!"

My reply was to play more from the Russians who wrote weird angry stuff: Scriabin, Kabalevsky, Tcherepnin. Where I used to enjoy sitcoms, now I pounded away in dissonance.

"Are those the right notes?" Dad would ask. I would wave the book as my reply. Oh, the power of the Russians. Discord really has so much in common with a good joke.

When there is something you are good at, you can gloat by doing it all the time in a conspicuous way. I was gloating through most afternoons. Chopin's "Funeral March" on a bright summer day was downright hilarious.

One day I heard a terrible sound. "Ju-wen," Mom called out. The two-syllable version of my name had never been used to announce good news, for example, a cake was coming out of the oven. "Have you been playing LeAnn's music?" Mom asked, rushing through the kitchen.

"LeAnn's music," I said, as if it were a composer with whom I was unfamiliar.

"From her lessons. Her piano books."

"Well, there are a lot of books."

"You know which ones are hers. From now on there is a new rule: you can only play your own piano music. Not LeAnn's."

"But that's not fa-a-a-a-i-i-r."

"It *is* fair. I've got to clean up the sno-cone machine," she said, going outside.

"But why not? I like George Gershwin. I'll play her books, and then she can play mine." I followed her like a whining bird.

She sighed. "It isn't fun for her to hear you play music that she is struggling with sometimes. Can you get that?"

"Because I play the songs better than her? Is that why?"

"Well, just think about it. She is three years older than you." Then she waited.

"Yeah. But—"

"From now on, LeAnn's is off-limits."

With a pout I took out Chopin again, a book that we had *both* been assigned the previous year. Yes, Chopin might be able to say a few words about my terrible plight. And also would sublimely express my Polish-variety sadness.

The last notes of the prelude are still vibrating the doors of the kitchen cabinets when there is an unexpected rap on the porch door. I lift my fingers from the keys and step gently through the kitchen, so as not to disturb the aura of "Chopinish" melancholy that still lingers in the air.

"Oh, excuse me. I am sorry to disturb you," says a gentleman standing on the top step. "But I was wondering who that was I heard playing the piano just a moment ago." He is tall, about six foot four, and a bit older than my parents. Salt-and-pepper hair.

"Why, that was me," I say, with a slight curtsy.

"You?!" he says, getting excited, and perhaps swooning slightly.

I tip my chin in a demure smile.

"Well, that was just . . ." He fingers the tweed cap in his hand. "I am a producer," he says, "in Hollywood. I can tell by your exquisite touch of the keyboard and by the exquisite feeling in all of your notes that you would be an excellent actress to star in my next movie. I need to speak to your parents!"

Luckily, that week I had read an article in the weekly *Picture Post* about a movie crew filming in the area. Warner Brothers Pictures. Big stars! I watch from the porch as the producer man talks to my parents outside, one foot perched on the bench of the picnic table like a pirate. "Your daughter is so talented and mature! How have you kept it a secret all these years?"

Mom and Dad pour him a lemonade, apologizing. "She has always just worked here," they say, "you know, painting and scraping."

The man winces. He explains his fantastic world, and the world that will soon be mine—filming in Italy, premieres in France. From there I don't listen too closely, because I don't want to embarrass Mom and Dad by witnessing how superbly naive they are about these things. I open the porch door and descend the unpainted porch steps, wearing a deep green Scarlet O'Hara gown that must have been hanging in the back of my closet. My fingers trail the edge of the faded banister. Carla runs to pick up the train of the dress and help me walk to the picnic table. LeAnn scowls from the door of the ticket booth, but they all forgive me for being so special.

And that is how it all begins.

"It's just a thrill for me to drive you around," says my new chauffeur.

I live in a glowing stucco home in Hollywood with three fountains in the yard, and every week receive complicated and doting letters from my fans—I try to answer them as best I can, but I am only fifteen—and I have generously offered my house as a refuge to my poor, underprivileged friends from school, and they move in where they adore me and are undyingly grateful for rescuing them from the terrible small town where they had been stuck until I rescued them all. "Can I get you another caramel apple?" Michelle says, bowing slightly even though she is my friend, because she is so grateful to live in Hollywood. "No, let me get it," Christy says, racing off to the kitchen because she knows she is the fastest runner in school. And all the people from my hometown of Decorah, Iowa, one day turn away from whatever they are doing and turn to face 714 Pine Street, like sunflowers in the sun, facing the house where I grew up. And I realize, Aha, that is why I was raised in a house on a hill, up, up from it all—

"What's wrong with you?" LeAnn yelled, leaning out the ticket booth door. "Can't you play something more cheerful?"

"What?"

"You've been pounding away for hours. It's miniature golf! People don't want to hear that Russian stuff."

"You could hear me on the golf course?"

"Are you done now? People can hear all the wrong notes too, you know."

"Are you sure? These people out here?"

A family of four stood staring from the fairway of #18. The boy, who was about to tee off, had stopped mid-aim. Apparently he had found it more interesting to find out who had been making that noise than it was to try to win a free game.

"I don't know why you have to play so loud all the time. Get their putters. I'm going inside," LeAnn said, and strode down the path.

"But, wait—" There were about twenty people spread out on the golf course, and they were all looking at me like I had just run over a deer.

The family who had been playing #18—the hole closest to the cottage—approached the ticket booth with their putters. The mom stood several feet away from the window and, using both hands, poked in her family's clubs from a safe distance.

"Thanks!" I said. "Thanks for coming!"

She said nothing in reply, but silently joined her family as they walked across the parking lot, every few steps looking over their shoulder to wince.

CHAPTER 9

THE WINDMILL

There is something curiously boring about somebody else's happiness.

—ALDOUS HUXLEY

"At three under par, Lee Trevino, the sexiest man alive, is about to become the next champion of the Bob Hope Classic."

"Sexiest man?"

"Ssh. If he can just sink this—"

"Shut up and putt already." A couple of teenage boys are whooping it up on #17.

"Here it comes. Oh! He chokes."

"Make way for Arnie Palmer. Git!"

"Choke."

"Shut up."

The other boy whispers again, "Choke."

Its suppertime, and we are seated around the picnic table by the last hole. We pass around a plate of semi-burned hot dogs. "Is there mustard?" I ask.

Beneath the table a severed chipmunk head is lying in the grass. We lean down to take a look. "The cat caught another one," LeAnn says. We move our feet a few inches to the side. Carla, who is shoeless, lifts her feet up to the bench and holds her knees like a bundle. "Again?" we say.

Dad mumbles, his eyes on the course.

"George, can you get that out of there so we can eat?"

"What's that?" he says, and he finally drops his eyes below the horizon of Tom Thumb. "Frankie got another one?" He grass-hoppers his skinny legs out from the picnic table and disappears into the laundry room. He returns carrying the bent-up tin shovel that Mom wishes he'd throw away. "Get it! Get it!" we say, holding up the ends of checkered tablecloth while he pokes the tall grass. Then he holds the shovel at his waist. "Wanna have a look?" he says, presenting the chipmunk head like an hors d'oeuvre on a tray. After we finish screaming, he carries the head to the area behind the garage. This is where we put all things we don't want to deal with: broken lawn mowers, the women's outhouse, and a collection of mildewing life preservers. He drops the chipmunk head into one of the garbage cans, or else he tosses it in the weeds along the lake, or else it just disappears, which is fine with us.

Then we eat.

"Where did you put it?"

"It's gone," Dad says.

"I hope so."

"Until she gets another one tomorrow."

"Why does she keep doing that?"

"Because it's easier than catching muskrats."

"But it's so cruel."

"It's in her nature."

"At least she eats most of them."

"Is that right? Is she really eating the rest of the animal?"

Ick.

"I suppose so," Mom says. "She seems to eat everything but the head and tail."

"Is there a tail down there too?" We lean over to look.

"That's disgusting."

We wonder out loud if we should feed her more.

"She would probably still catch them, only then she wouldn't eat them."

"She's definitely a hunter," Dad says, watching the boys, now on #18. "I'll get 'em," he says, and heads for the ticket booth, pausing on the way to rearrange a wet rag drying in the sun. As we eat our chips, the tail of the chipmunk is still there between our feet, but it's easier to ignore than the head.

"Is there mustard?" I ask.

The cat had come to us the way the customers do, with tentative steps across the parking lot, walking towards us, needing something. Mom set out food. The cat ate some, seemed to appreciate it, and then disappeared into the woods across the road, gone forever.

Two or three days later she appeared again, padding around the ticket booth. She was small, long-haired, and calico. "Hello there, Frank," I said, because I thought it was hilarious to call a delicate cat "Frank," the way my best friend's father back in Iowa used to call me Fred.

"If it's calico, it's a she," Dad said.

"So she should be Frankie, not Frank," LeAnn added.

"Frank-lin," Mom said.

And then the cat disappeared back into the woods.

One day she padded even more tentatively across the lot, side-stepping the cars that were backing up. Her jaw hung off her face.

"It's broken," said the vet in town. "I'm going to have to wire it."

"Must have picked a battle with a raccoon," Dad said.

"Something too big for her, that's for sure," the vet said.

But she survived, and she learned to eat food from a bowl instead of catching it live. For the most part, I mean, she couldn't stop hunting, even though she had only one fang left out of four, after that fight with the presumed raccoon. Now she hunted out of habit. Frogs and birds and baby muskrats, chipmunks, and baby squirrels. She carried them in her mouth towards us, sometimes eating them, more often dropping them at our feet.

"Uh, thanks, Frankie."

"What's she got?"

"Mouse head."

Ick.

When she wasn't hunting, she slept, often on the front counter of the ticket booth, where she ignored our need to pass out clubs. Or she napped on the carpet of whatever green was most bathed in sunlight. The customers just had to putt around her. Or freak out if she was blocking the hole. She was a menace, but she was ours.

So, too, were the customers.

"C'mon, princess."

"C'mon, sugar."

"You got two."

"No, yuh gotta tuuh."

The sound of the Wisconsin "two" has some extra vowels in it. They purse their lower lip to add the extra "uh." "Tuuuh for me tuuh."

"I wonder if we'd be breaking the law if we placed bets, you know, like gambling. Actually, we're just betting backrubs. Lowest score has to give a backrub. But you have to be careful, you know, they find out you've been gambling, and they'll come and arrest you . . ."

Which brings me to hole #9. The Windmill.

In California, when I am introduced to someone new—at a club or coffee house, for example—and the person learns that

I grew up on a mini golf, nine times out of ten they will blurt out: "A mini golf? So, do you have a windmill?"

That's your first question? I think. *About growing up on a mini golf course? About having tourists in your backyard?*

To answer your question: Yes, yes. We have a windmill.

When tourists (including me) go to Paris, they need to see the Eiffel Tower. When tourists go to the mini golf, they desperately need to see a windmill. The same way that the Eiffel Tower says, "Hey, you're in Paris!" The Windmill announces, "You're at the mini golf! Woohoo!" You can take a picture of yourself standing next to it, the Eiffel/Windmill, and show it to your friends later as evidence: "This is where *we were.*"

Almost every mini golf has one, and for the life of me, I don't know why that is. I mean, I admit that a windmill is a big, tall thingamabob, and big, tall thingamabobs catch people's attention. The rotating blades announce "WE ARE OPEN FOR BUSINESS" more loudly than the small plastic OPEN sign we wedge into the ticket booth window each morning. If The Windmill blades aren't turning, motorists will stop in the road and yell out in a panic, "Are you closed? Why are you closed?"

Our windmill is seven feet tall and painted cherry red. The shingled roof is white, and the rotating blades are yellow, green, orange, and blue. Cute, sure, but we don't like it. The Windmill's too easy. We find this hazard dull.

The Windmill blades turn slowly, which you should know is by necessity. When you have eight-foot beams spinning through the air, someone is going to put their head in there. Someone else will put in the head of their younger brother. Dad geared the motor down twice so that it turns like a slow-motion grandfather. The Windmill blades could *in theory* block your ball, but generally they're just a distraction. It would be much more difficult if instead of getting past, you actually *tried* to hit the blades.

Sometimes we sit around the dinner table coming up with

ideas for replacing The Windmill with some other waving thing, but then we come to our senses and just pass the salt. People are really picky, especially vacationers. After waiting all year for this week, they have hopes! They have dreams! Like children who wait all year for Santa Claus, you don't want to see them disappointed on Christmas morning. (Actually, this happened to my father. When he was about ten, he and his brother came down from their attic bedroom on Christmas morning to find that there were no presents under the tree. I'm not sure there was even a tree. "You're getting too old for presents," their parents said. But the truth is that there probably wasn't money to buy anything.)

This hazard is not for us; we understand that. The Windmill is for *them*, the customers.

And that's why hole #9, The Windmill, is about Them (the *Others*).

9

**WATCH OUT
for the BLADES**

—*Green leans slightly left* ● *Par 3* ●

"Can I have a white ball?" A man holds up his ball to his face, like a tube of toothpaste in a toothpaste commercial.

"All we have are colored balls," my dad answers.

"No white balls?"

"Sorry, no."

"I thought I had one last time I was here."

"Sorry."

The man starts to walk back to hole #5, but then turns back. "No white ones?"

"Sorry."

* * *

"Can I get a empty sno-cone cup, so I can get water for our dog?"

"Can I leave my canoe here all day?"

"Can I post my business card on your wall?"

"Can I borrow a coat hanger?" *Coat hanger?* "Keys are locked in my car."

When we began seeing the same faces again and again, we did what sensible business owners do: we gave them nicknames. This made it much easier for us to discuss them over lunch.

There were "The Victorian Ladies," "The Sit-Down-People," "The Cotton Candy Family," and "That Couple With That Korean Girl They Adopted." There was "The Family With The Crippled Boy" (who we liked very much) and "The Couple Who Can't Keep Their Hands Off Each Other" (who we didn't).

"It's The Bathroom Guys," Mom said once, as several young men approached the ticket booth. "Bathroom guys?" we asked. "Just watch," she said.

They were men in their twenties, who seemed healthy enough, but every ten minutes one of them would drop his putter and run off to the men's room.

"Fascinating."

There was "The Man Who Comes and Photographs Everything, and Measures When We're Not Looking."

"There he goes again," we'd say, watching from the porch, as he snuck around the course, looking over his shoulder, pocketing his measuring tape.

"Go ahead and build one!" we'd say.

"Yeah, tell us how it works!" I'd add, in hysterics. "He can't hear us, right?"

"You'd better keep it down just in case," Mom said.

There was Tom, the cook from Camp Tamarack just over the

hill from us, who wasn't really a customer because he didn't buy anything. But he came every weekend to sit and stare out at the golf course a couple of hours as a way to recover from the stress of camp. "I'm not much of a cook! I'm surprised no one's died!"

There was the family of normal size who wanted to use our smallest clubs. Like clowns on tiny bicycles at the circus, they had to reach down to hold the handles, which were somewhere near their toes.

Dad didn't like The Tiny Club Family. He thought they were showing off. "What if a bunch of young kids show up! We won't have any clubs to give them!"

"I guess they like bending over for some reason," we said, trying to make sense of the customers' behavior, which was one of our hobbies.

At one point we tried to find a new word for the customers. The local high school boys who patched canoes at Ding's Dock called them *tourons*, for *tourist + moron*. "There are some tourons walking towards the ticket booth," we said to each other for a day or two, but it didn't stick. They weren't morons for the most part. They were people from Oshkosh, Madison, and Elgin (Illinois). But that doesn't mean they weren't scientifically *interesting*.

Teenage girls twirled their putters like baton majorettes, or teeter-tottered them in the sun, the chrome making great flashes of light. Teenage boys shot their putters like rifles. Younger boys leaned on them like canes. Some kids, while waiting their turn, tried to twist the handle off.

Sometimes in mid-afternoon, a man—presumably with a little extra time on his hands—would walk down the road and appear in our parking lot. "Business a little slow today, huh?" he'd say, leaning on the front counter of the ticket booth.

"Uh . . . huh."

He might then comment on the dry weather, or the difficulty he'd been having with his battery, or the car parts he was unable to find anywhere in town, and about the time you had begun selecting one of the extra long clubs to slam into your skull, he'd say, "Well, I just wanted to see what was going on at Tom Thumb." Then he'd buy a can of pop and disappear back up the road.

It wasn't easy to have people come to your backyard to spend part of their vacation. For one thing, they are on vacation. You are not. So you do your best to have a good time about it.

One of the exciting things we did as kids was to take a piece of cheese and drop it into our soup. Then we could fish it out with a spoon and marvel how the cheese had melted.

"Okay, three kids," a woman at the front counter said to me. Then she leaned down to her kids. "Are you sure? You really want Mommy to play too?" She turned to me and sighed. "And one adult too. I suppose. Miniature golf. How dumb," she said, looking into her wallet.

They were hard to get away from. One day I pulled a chair to the creek and was reading *The Hobbit* when two canoers came up the channel. They were so friendly, these half-naked tourists, because tourists act friendlier than they probably do in real life, as if acting all friendly with the world will make their vacation a happy place. "Oh, I remember reading that," the wet woman said to me. "I could never finish it," and then she threw back her head and laughed, and the man with her laughed. And I smiled rather than saying something like, "Boy, you must be pretty dumb," because even though I was in our own backyard, you had to tiptoe around them. People on vacation, I realized, are like people in the hospital. They get special treatment. You had to talk to them nicely and sometimes very slowly.

*   *   *

"Excuse me. What happens if your ball goes in on the first try?"

"That's called a hole-in-one," I said.

"Oh, that's what that means! I have always wondered." He picked up his ball, and then called out again. "So you don't win? Not a free game or anything?"

"No. But you got a one. That's a good thing."

It was anthropology for all of us, watching them out there.

I could tell when a girl was flirting. She would take tiny steps in her little white sneakers, elbows at her side. Like a baby bird who hasn't yet learned it has wings. "Oh, oh! I can't find my ball!" she'd say. The high pitch of her voice would awaken the boy standing nearby, as if hearing a cry for rescue from a swamped riverboat. "I see it!" he'd say, spotting the ball on the grass, which was perfectly obvious to see (I mean, the ball was orange, for crying out loud). He'd proudly bend to pick it up. Hold it out in his hand like offering her a diamond ring. Her knees would bob as she reached out to receive it, the remains of a curtsy one century after the fact. You are so brave and strong, she'd say by tipping her chin towards her heart-shaped pendant. I would do anything for you, he'd say, by changing the rules of the game, which he had just spent ten minutes explaining to the rest of their group. "Why don't you just start over. We won't count this one."

The scene was more theatrical than the stage play by the high school, and the acting about as believable. An orange ball lost in green grass . . .

"You missed it completely!" a father yelled at his son who appeared to be about twelve.

"You're not even aiming," his mother complained.

"Take it back! Do it again!"

"Do it right this time!"

Their eight-year-old girl stood trembling, waiting for her turn, with a grimace she might have made before jumping out of an airplane.

"I saw that family!" my mom said at lunch. "It was too painful to watch. I yelled out from the ticket booth, 'Hey, just for fun!' I couldn't help myself."

"Do those parents think there are mini golf scholarships out there?" I asked.

Mom said, "I shouldn't have said anything. They'll never come back. But I just felt so bad for those kids!"

"They'll go to Harvard for free? If they can just get the ball in the clown's nose?"

"If they're miserable playing mini golf, how is the rest of their life?"

In the same way that each sailor at sea is said to have "his wave"—the one that will strike him down with great seasickness, despite his many years at sea—each of us developed a tender spot, a type of customer we hated to see on the course. For Mom, it was parents who bullied their kids.

Dad said: "It bothered me when the low-man-on-the-totempole was putting and everyone else in his group just ignored him and moved ahead. And he had to play all by himself while everyone else was already on the next hole!"

LeAnn: "I hate it when kids go to the Snack Shack for a snocone or cotton candy before they're done with their game. Their golf clubs get so sticky! But at least it's entertaining. When they try to putt one-handed."

Carla: "That group last night that just left their putters in a heap on the counter? Underneath they hid one they broke! I hate that."

As for me, I was bothered by the oversexed teenagers who sucked at each other's faces before they teed off at each hole. They took *forever* to play. Also, it looked gross.

* * *

"Your father and I pray together in the morning," Mom told me once, "that the families that come today will have a pleasant time and will be more bonded because they're playing a game together." After reading the Bible during breakfast, my parents thumbtacked favorite verses to the outside walls of the ticket booth hoping to inspire customers to ponder their faith, and possibly, my mother admitted, to inspire them not to club each other on the head.

Sometimes parents would teach their children how to cheat. They'd sneak up the fairway on the last hole and wedge their ball under the screen, encouraging their kids to do anything to get their ball in the clown's nose.

I waited in the ticket booth to see if they'd dare ask for the free game.

"Uh, I think my son got it in the nose," the father said.

"Well," I said. "Sorry, but you have to shoot from the tee-off to get a free game." *Like the sign says!* The parents skulked away like I was the school principal, and not just fifteen, and I had told them they weren't going to prom.

Dad thought it might create a happy, happy mood for the customers if we broadcast music on the course. There was a "radio" on the back shelf of the ticket booth which looked like a slab of plywood with holes cut in for dials, which, in fact, it was. Dad had soldered it together one winter from a kit that came in the mail, but it didn't come with a face, for a reason we never learned. He cut a slot across a piece of plywood so the "tuner" had a place to travel, with a ball of cotton taped to either end so you couldn't turn the dial off the face of the radio "earth."

After he wired it to the old speaker on the roof, he tuned it to the station that played mostly Beatles tunes. Which might actually have been nice, and might actually have been appropriate, if it hadn't been a swooning orchestra of Muzac.

"It's embarrassing," LeAnn said.

"It sounds like a grocery store," I said. "Like we should be shopping for dog food."

"This is a family place," he argued, and so we argued back, which is to say that we gave up after begging him once or twice to turn it off. Whenever he stepped away, of course, we changed the station, with a meaningful shrug towards the other teenagers on the course, in a conspicuous, eye-rolling way. *So sorry.*

"Girls! This rock music is too hard!" he said when he returned, reaching up to turn the dial back across the plywood to *"WROE, Beautiful music, all day long."*

"Your dad is right," Mom would say. "This is a family place." But actually, when no one was looking, she turned the radio off entirely. Mom's favorite station was silence.

When your parents are wrong and you are right, you bide your time until you can get, what you might call, a "tie-breaking vote." It came one day in the form of a family from Milwaukee. They appeared rather unassuming, neutral perhaps, like Switzerland— what you might want in "tie-breakers." A dad, a mom, and two teenage daughters, they all had dark curly hair. They smiled a lot.

"Oh, this is my favorite music," said one teenage daughter, reaching for her club.

"Me too," said the other daughter, looking up at the speaker.

Did they just say that? I ran to tell LeAnn. "Those girls who just came. They said they liked WROE."

"You're kidding," she said, running out to see for herself.

The four of them were wearing matching blue jackets: snap fronts, epaulets, and there might have been a label that said MEMBERS ONLY. The girls looked *too much* like their parents.

"I can't believe it," LeAnn said.

"WROE-fans," we said.

Dad was smug the rest of the night.

He was smug the next night when the family came again. And then again the next night. And the night after that. When Dad recognized their car pulling in on Friday, he ran ahead to make sure the radio was at WROE before they arrived, the volume up one notch.

"Hello, George!" the WROE-fans said on Saturday when my dad worked the ticket booth. "Grandpa's with us tonight. How's business?"

"Not bad, considering the mosquitoes. Nice to meet you, Grandpa," my dad said. "You like Fat Sally, right?" he said, handing WROE-fan-mom her favorite club. When they finished their round, my mom gave them a round on the house.

The WROE-fans were not cool. Those girls didn't wear tube tops. I wasn't sure if they were serious about listening to Muzac, but worse, they didn't seem to know that they should pout. They seemed to actually enjoy spending an evening with their parents. They had way too much fun together. And my parents simply adored them.

"I found out their name. The Ernsts! The mom is named Faith," Mom said, as we peered at them through the windows of the porch.

"We'll be here all week. We play Tom Thumb every night when we're at the cabin," we heard Faith proclaim the next night they arrived.

"Yes, we do," the daughters agreed. "You go first, Mom. Impress us."

"I will! Oh, I will!"

This family was just so gosh-darned happy. I was quite perturbed.

It bothered me that my parents seemed to prefer the non-cool customers. Not the wealthy folks with big boats but the humble people. The modest people. The ones that came in older cars, dressed in simple clothes. When a man wore a mesh farmer hat, my dad perked up like a talk show host. "You folks are from Neillsville? No kidding! What are you farming out there?" He enjoyed asking them questions, drawing them out, if they seemed like people who would never willingly draw attention to themselves.

Faith had a roundish face, big dark eyes, and short, practical hair. We learned eventually that she worked in the school cafeteria, and if you measure in laughter, she was the happiest customer we ever had on the course. "Oh, LINDA. You almost had a HOLE-IN-ONE," Faith called out from #6. "Just a bit HARDER, you would have HAD IT."

"You get bonus points if you can get your ball AROUND the hazard, instead of through the middle," she joked. We could hear her laughing from the kitchen. "HO! HO! NO! GRANDPA!" Faith laughed as if she'd been saving up all year.

One night at the end of the summer, Dad came running into the house. "The Ernsts. They are so loud out there," he said, letting the door slam.

"Some people just have to be loud to have fun," Mom said.

"I think it's starting to bother other people. That other group on #6 looks like they are about ready to quit."

"Well, George. It's a party atmosphere, you know."

Dad paced the porch. His model customers, his favorite family of all, was not acting modest. The Ernsts were having so much fun, and had gotten so loud, that they almost appeared to be "show-offs." And it was true, the other groups playing on the course did not look happy. The foursome near the Ernsts had stopped their game, and seemed to be discussing whether it was even worth continuing. My dad looked at my mom with the face, that meant *What can we do?*

Tourists are like children. And like sick people in the hospital. And also like feral animals. Which is to say, they aren't in charge, but the line is definitely blurry. There are limits as to what you can *say* to a customer. You can offer them bug spray. You can give them a hint on how to play #10. You can suggest they allow another group to go ahead if they are slow. But you can't scold people for laughing too hard.

"Wha!"

"OH NO!"

There was some commotion from the far corner of the course. "Ahh!" came a call from hole #12.

"Help" came a yip from hole #8.

Several customers on the back nine were running away from their holes.

"Now what's going on?" We ran outside the house.

Frankie was walking across the course, leaving a wake of screaming people behind her. "I think Frankie's got something," my father said, showing his mastery of the understatement.

There was a woman about to putt at #6. The cat walked right in front of the fairway, then stopped to turn her head, displaying the impressive animal-something hanging out her mouth.

"Oh my god!"

"What is that?"

Next the cat went to show off her fine catch to the folks on hole #4, who happened to be the Ernsts. Faith was teeing off. The cat walked directly towards her. Then it was time to hear an even louder version of a scream. "Aaaaaaahhhhhh!"

A pair of long green arms dangled out of one side of the cat's mouth. A pair of similar green legs stuck out of the other side. Both were twitching. The cat adjusted her grip to hold the frog more snugly, then pranced across the fairway with as much grace and purpose as if she had trained with the Bolshoi Kitty Ballet.

She paused to show off to the doting audience. "John! John!" Faith said. "Get that thing away from me!" She abandoned her red ball, which was still poised on the tee.

The daughters laughed. "Cool. Frankie's got a frog."

The Ernst dad (or John as we learned to call him) was laughing, but not so much he would be hit by his wife's club.

My dad apologized to them repeatedly, and when they finished their game, he insisted on giving them a handful of free-game cards.

"I thought it was great," the older daughter said. "I might major in biology."

"She likes dissecting frogs," her dad said.

Tourists are allowed to scream. They are allowed to be demanding. And they are also allowed to be loud. You are not allowed any of these things, but you are allowed to have a cat, and sometimes the cat will express these things for you.

The cat was also pregnant. Soon enough five kittens came forth, and she licked them clean despite her jaw. "She sure is a good mom," we said, admiring her pluck.

Next year, more kittens. The years after, more kittens kept coming.

The cat was ours, multiplying herself each summer, like the customers. Becoming part of our family. The WROE-fans sent Christmas cards, kept showing up in our parking lot, just like family, or perhaps like a stray cat, whom you adopt without ever knowing exactly when it happened. When their daughter got married, they invited my parents to the wedding. (They couldn't attend, of course, because they had to run Tom Thumb. But they sent a nice card with several free-game cards inside as a gift.)

Take a Break to SIT ON A BENCH!

You've finished the front nine! You're halfway. Time to add up your scores. Whew, thankfully, someone else in your group says, "I'll add 'em up." While your brother stands there chewing on the pencil, you say: "If it looks like you're winning, then we'll know you've added wrong." We've heard that joke a million times, but go ahead, it's just so tempting.

Here's a bench. How convenient. While you wait for the totals, you can sit and enjoy the view . . . Bass Lake . . . the seaweeds floating on the surface . . . the muck at the far end . . . the slightly swampy smell . . . ah, summer . . .

What you don't want to know: this bench where you are resting has been sat on by hundreds of naked bodies. Hundreds. Perhaps thousands. Sorry. But the butts of your neighbors and ancestors may have perched on this bench, back when it was an examining table used by my great-uncle Emlin, who was an osteopath, and who I know very little about, not even what an osteopath is. Sorry. Again. You might be less relaxed about sitting here now, just knowing about the naked butts, even though we have coated it with about a zillion gallons of paint since then, because people don't like to think about naked butts, that is, other people's butts. Other people's butts are objects of questionable toxicity. Of dubious hygiene. Of nakedness itself. People are much less critical about their own butt for reasons that aren't clear, but which I won't dwell on any further. Anyway, Great-Uncle Emlin was an osteopath; he had a practice near here, until one day in the 1960s he closed up shop and moved to California. He left this bench behind—so to speak!—and my grandfather moved it into his woodshop to use as a worktable. Years later, my grandfather handed it over to my dad, who sawed six inches off each leg, added a backrest, and now you have a bench, a place to rest, while your brother adds up the scores for the first half incorrectly, giving himself a four-point edge—something most people don't ever discover, like the origin of the bench itself.

And that is the Secret of the Bench. Now back to your game!

CHAPTER 10

THE OUTHOUSE

Remember, as far as anyone knows, we're a nice, normal family.

—HOMER SIMPSON

At eight o'clock in the evening the sky is a pale pillowcase blue, still holding on to the last of the daylight. But the lake has already turned black, reflecting the idea of upcoming night. Pontoon boats and flagpoles make white skeletal reflections across the dark surface. Our yard is completely hidden in shadow.

But Tom Thumb is ablaze with light. Lights above, lights inside the hazards, a white light inside the Snack Shack. Along the parking lot and the road, there is a string of colored lights: red, blue, green, and yellow. It looks like Christmas.

It is the middle of July, midweek, and we are medium-busy. There are two groups on the front nine and a large family on #16.

"I'm taking a mulligan. Don't hit me!"

"No gimmes!"

"Too late!"

My parents, Carla, and I are sitting around the firepit on metal garden chairs. This is where we spend our evenings. Facing the course. Watching. This is our summer living room, just outside the fringe of light. The fire is our television, the glowing coals, the actors. Above us, cicadas drone in the trees.

LeAnn skips down the porch stairs. "Look," she says, taking off her shirt. "You can see handprints on my shoulders. From suntan lotion." She turns to show us her bare back, bikini top, and the pale visible outlines of fingers.

"Wow," Mom says.

"Looks like you're working hard," Dad says.

Of the five of us, only LeAnn has found a way to "get away." She is working for my uncle Joe this summer. He bought a frontier village near town and renamed it Fort Waupaca. It's vintage 1950s, which is to say, no one goes there anymore. It's the kind of theme park that has exactly one ride: a small train, driven by a teenager, that goes in a circle through some woods. The Fort also has one general store, a saloon, some penny arcade games, and fun for the whole family, for, oh, about twenty-five minutes. To add one more attraction, my uncle decided to build a moat. He will fill it with water, add little boats, and then—well, jangle my spurs—a boat ride. Which might increase the fun by about fifteen to twenty minutes. He hired my sister to join his crew of workers, pouring cement.

"I'm glad you're finally using some suntan lotion," Mom says.

"I had Dale rub some on me this morning."

"Dale?" I say. "Those fingerprints are from Dale?"

LeAnn is the only girl working among a team of lean and muscular local teenage boys. Each day she comes home increasingly suntanned and popular.

"When I'm there, all the boys work harder. That's what everyone says."

"They're all trying to impress you."

"Seriously? Dale?" I stare at the outlines of the masculine fingers that must have touched her. Apparently you need to know how to pour cement to attract a boy in this town. And it's unlikely

I'll ever get hired to work at The Fort, unless my uncle needs someone to sew flowered blouses or play dirges on a piano.

My dad carries over an armload of brush and drops it on the fire. A shower of sparks shoots six feet into the air, and flames rocket towards the maple branch that hangs barely out of reach. "Hey!" We leap up. "Why did you do that?"

"The brush needs to be burned."

"I was about to roast marshmallows!"

"Well, I didn't know!" he says.

Like dead flies on a window ledge, Carla and I are stuck here at Tom Thumb. We don't get away much and haven't developed close friends here. A couple of years earlier we invited a girl from town to come play Monopoly, but by the middle of the game she had crawled under the table, put a popcorn bowl on her head, and refused to say anything except "beep" and, sometimes, "meep." It took us half an hour to get her out of there. The whole experience made us wary of letting strangers in the house.

There are kids in the neighborhood, but almost all of them are boys. Each summer I pick one to be the object of my affection, in the form of a mad crush. In past years there were some girls down the road whom I became friends with, but they weren't year-rounders. Their families had cottages, which meant they'd be your friend for a week and then disappear. Then they'd show up unexpectedly on a good-weather weekend. You'd be friends again, and you might even get a boat ride, but then they disappeared, and it'd be worse all over again.

Carla and I spend all our time with family, which is to say, *here*.

"I think I got sparks on my jeans."

"Keep that webbed chair away," Dad says.

We see the silhouette of a man walking towards us from the Snack Shack. "How are the Melbys doing tonight?"

"It's Phil!"

"We didn't see your car!"

"I'm on a bike."

"Join us, join us," we scream out, and offer him a chair because seeing our cousin is about the most exciting thing that's happened in days. "Popcorn?"

Phil is a college student. He works for my uncle at the frontier town. It is his job to strap on a holster, tie a handkerchief over his face, and rob the train twelve times a day.

"How's it going at The Fort?" Dad asks.

"Joe told us we only get fifty bullets a day," Phil says. "We are on a fifty-bullet-a-day limit."

"Which sounds like a lot—"

"Which does seem like a lot. But it isn't enough!" You can tell when Phil is about to say something funny because his Adam's apple—which looks big enough to choke a man—bobs up and down before the punch line. "We have shootouts on Main Street some days. I got my buddy Pete a job as the sheriff. We shoot a hundred to a hundred and fifty pretty regularly—"

"Wow!"

"I've been begging Joe for more. *'Please? Can I have another bullet?'* I feel like Barney Fife on *The Andy Griffith Show. 'You guys shouldn't be out of bullets for weeks yet!'*" he says, in a gruff voice, imitating my uncle. Then his Adam's apple leaps around, and we break out into hysterics.

From #18, the father of the family wanders hesitantly towards our fire. "Uh, is there something going on?"

"I'm Black Bart at Fort Waupaca," Phil says. "About seven miles from here."

"Oh, I heard you talking about bullets. I was wondering if we should be concerned." Reassured, he returns to his family.

Phil's life at Fort Waupaca sounds so much better than ours here; almost worth living even. "It's a weird job," he continues.

"You're getting ready to go to work in the morning, sittin' around with your friend cleaning your pistol, loading on your gun belt. *'Let's go hold up a TRAIN!'* " When the laughter and apple bobbing subside, Phil pushes his chair back to leave. "I almost forgot to tell you. My folks are coming out for a visit the end of next week—"

In a normal family, hearing that your aunt and uncle are coming to visit would only rate a 3 or 4 on the Good News Scale—there might be chocolate cake, more varieties of cookies, the cousins might be distracting—

"Good, good, good!" my mom says.

"There's a rumor Ann and Dave are driving out this way," he says, referring to my mom's sister and husband on the East Coast. "So that's the timing here—"

"Wow! Really?!" we say.

We ask if others are coming too. "Well, you know how this family is!" someone says. Yes, we know how this family is!

His Adam's apple is dancing up and down his neck, and we stay for the most part in our metal chairs, but we are dancing too. *Really, really, really?* I almost drop my marshmallow in happiness.

Hole #10 is an outhouse.

Not for real, I mean, don't get the idea that you can actually *use* it. (If you need a bathroom, you'll find them on the side of the garage. We've got flush toilets now! Since they put the sewer in.)

The hazard of #10 is a *model* of an old-fashioned outhouse. The roof is slanted and shingled, and the walls are layered in siding. It's a bit smaller than normal, like the buildings in Disneyland that are "built to scale," which means that they look strangely real, but also strangely like toys.

This pretend outhouse, just like the outhouse on my dad's old family farm, has two holes to go into. It's a "two-seater," as I believe they've been called.

You'll want to aim for the right one so your ball drops with a beautiful *thoop* onto the green behind. If your ball falls into the left-hand hole, it will *thiddle* in a shallow cavity, emerge from an opening in the ramp, and roll back down the fairway to rest at your feet like a lost dog. Arg. You'll have to try again.

The sign alerts you to GO IN THE RIGHT HAND HOLE—OR YOU'LL BE SORRY. GO is capitalized. It is a euphemism, which basically means a word or phrase that has two meanings: one honest and the other nefarious. Like a set of identical twins, one of whom is stealing your car, while the other one makes you a delicious cup of tea.

The word *go*, of course, can mean [word deleted for modesty's sake]. Most people don't like it when you mention things like [word deleted for modesty's sake]. Except, of course, people under the age of seven. People under the age of seven really, *really* like it when you say [word deleted for modesty's sake]. Also, perhaps, people who are *remembering* what it was like to be age seven. Which is, of course, one reason we like games like mini golf: they are good for reminding you of what it was like to be the age when you could admit that you liked the word *poop*. [Word not deleted, for rascality's sake.]

In any case, let's take a moment to ask the obvious question: why in the world would an outhouse—an actual outhouse—have two holes? If you went in there with someone else, would it keep you warm in winter? Would going two-at-at-time actually save you a lot of time? And more important, who in the world would you ever do that with?

And the answer, of course, is family.

Ah, yes.

We do weird things with family. Things we wouldn't do with anyone else. And we like it that way. That's just the way it should be.

And that's why hole #10, The Outhouse, is about Family (the extended kind) and The Weird Things We Do Together.

So the big day arrives, and it looks like the circus has come to town. A village of pup tents goes up under the oak trees. One cousin is juggling pins in the front yard. Two others are dueling with swords. One cousin plops a full-size harp in our living room. The cousins from the East Coast, who always seemed exotic, dive impressively off our dock, then wave with a smile, "We're going to swim across a couple of lakes and back."

My mother's family is the kind that your parents may have warned you about. "Stay away! Leave them alone!" Not because they are a bad influence, but because you're going to feel like poop standing next to them.

My mom's family is, quite simply, successful. At everything.

They started out life at the top of the hill in their small town, so people looked up to them to begin with. My grandfather was the town banker. He gave people loans and kept their money safe during the Depression. (No one in the town, they say, lost a cent in that bank.) The family were pillars in their church, et cetera, et cetera.

"Before I married Jean, a good friend of mine from back home, near the farm, talked to me about it," my dad once told me. "'Are you sure?' he said. 'Do you really want to marry into that family?'"

"What did he mean?"

"Well, just look at them! How do you keep up with that!"

My grandparents had seven children: one daughter, one set of twins (boy and girl), one daughter, a second set of twins (boy and girl), and then one daughter. My grandmother must have had a thing for symmetry. All of them were valedictorians until the school became so annoyed, they considered disallowing them. (Okay, that's not true, but you get the idea.)

This group had an incredible lack of problems. There was no alcoholism, no drug addiction, no mental illness. There was never even a divorce among all seven aunts and uncles and all nineteen cousins. (Okay, one cousin divorced thirty years later, long after this story takes place.)

The lack of problems might have encouraged the growth of another inborn trait: stubbornness. To say my mother's family was stubborn is like saying the lake sometimes feels wet. But I guess they got along, because they all "accidentally" showed up here at the same time. When one announced an intention to visit the lakes, the idea would spread like pinworm through a kindergarten. (Or some other less "poopy" comparison of your choice.) The family reunion, though unofficial, always took place here at Tom Thumb. It worked well for the purpose: our yard was large, we had a mini golf, extra bathrooms, and a lake for swimming or canoeing. Also, my family couldn't leave.

Just so you know, the big party will end in a fight. I'm getting ahead of things here, however, I will tip you off that the fight is going to be about money. It is always about money. But, to be honest, like my family itself, it's going to be a bit weird.

The seven contestants:

My mom's eldest sister, Aunt Elaine, has been known for being perfect, which might have been a burden if hadn't also been true.

Uncle Arch was Abraham Lincoln, or at least that's what I believed during most of my childhood. He was a college professor, tall and lanky, with overarching eyebrows; I admit he scared me a little. (His wife, Mary, was an elf. She had red hair, and her eyes twinkled, which is something I had only read about in books until the day I met her.)

Next was Aunt Ann. She had an advanced degree in who knows how many fields, and was the type who read Kierkegaard at the beach.

Aunt Connie had a PhD and a fantastic sense of style, and would stand around in a beautiful gauze swimsuit cover-up, analyzing just about anything for you.

Uncle Joe, who owned the canoe rental and now also the frontier town, was either six foot five or six foot ten—depending on whether you were measuring to the top of his hair. He wore cutoff shorts and clomped on thick cigars, and thought it entirely reasonable to build a boat out of concrete. Which he did. It held forty. Usually tourists. He had the voice of an angry giant who had lost his golden goose.

Aunt Darleen, the youngest, taught at a missionary school in the Philippines. She came back so skinny, she has looked like a hungry bird ever since.

And my mom? She was the middle child, born between two sets of adorable, high-achieving twins. Started out life stuck between a rock and a hard place. Or perhaps, you could say, between Kierkegaard and a concrete boat.

Our yard has transformed into a wonderland. There are cousins singing around the firepit: "Blue skies, shining on me, nothing but blue skies do I see. . . ." A group of seven or eight cousins and aunts are loading canoes with paddles and life jackets, pop and sandwiches. A volleyball game erupts under the oaks. "Later this evening, I can take whoever wants out for a spin in the concrete boat," my uncle bellows.

Of course, there is also a "fierce" game of mini golf. With my mom's family, everyone seems to forget they are supposed to try to win.

"Why don't you go first?" they say, and "Oh, no, after you."

"Good for you!" they chirp, each time someone does well.

Anyone who gets a hole-in-one is quick to apologize. "Oh, well. I just got lucky."

"You *are* lucky," someone will say.

"*Blessed,*" an aunt will correct.

People talk about luck all the time while they are playing mini golf. They come up with theories on why some people win or lose. Why some people get holes-in-one and others seem to struggle. My mom's family does this too, only instead of *luck* they prefer to use the word *blessed.*

"We are *all* blessed," one aunt will say.

"Because our parents' faith was so strong," says another.

"Wait, wait!" I say. "I want to be in this group." More than winning, I want to play with my cousin Noel. He also works for my uncle Joe, came all the way from New Jersey to drive the train at The Fort. Twelve times a day he pulls the tourists through the woods, and twelve times a day the train is robbed by Black Bart—as played by Cousin Phil. "I'm not much of an actor, but I try to fall over when they shoot me. They've gotten bored, I think, because they are making things up. Sometimes when I come around the gulch, the sheriff runs out, and he's the one that robs the train. It's to the point where the two of them are staging comedy routines.

"They put a log down on the tracks—that's the normal part— but then the sheriff comes out, and they both shoot me. So I am lying there in the dirt, but I don't know if I'm supposed to be dead or not. They're older than me, so I have to go along. And then Phil takes this book out of his pocket, *The Code of the West—*"

"Code of the West?"

"It's something they made up. And they have this serious discussion about the rules, and I'm lying there facedown—the tourists on the train just staring at me."

From #10 we hear cousins screaming, "Oh, you missed it! Why don't you take it over?" "We won't count that one!" Everyone is almost too nice.

There is only one group on the course who is not related to us. When the couple finishes, my dad goes to collect their clubs because he says he wants to talk to them. In an almost-whisper, his raises his eyebrows in an apology: "I'm sorry it got so loud out there for you. We're having something like a family reunion."

"Oh! We were wondering what was going on," they say, looking back at us, our mob of tall, bushy-haired Norwegians. And then the customers smile. And then my father doesn't feel so bad, and the customers don't feel so bad. How bad can you feel when people are having fun?

The relatives were like perfect weather that rushes into town, but never seems to linger long enough before it sweeps off to the next town, leaving you to feel the cold wind that blows in behind it.

It is the last day of this reunion and along the shore and beneath the oak trees the tents are coming down. The bags are being packed. "The time went by so fast." "I know! It feels like we just got here!"

Soon it will be time for the Big Fight. Every family has its traditions. As with most traditions, there's no telling when or how it got started. Our customers sometimes tell us about their own: "Oh, we always play mini golf on the first and last day of our reunion."

"And the losers buy the beer!"

"When we visit Grandma's cottage, we always wear blue. That was her color."

"And the men always have to cook!"

A tradition is a code that each family shares. And outsiders would probably not understand, but that is how it should be. When you think about it, the weirder your tradition, the more *special* it seems. The more *special* it seems, the more you feel like a member of a secret club. And who doesn't want to be in a secret club? Even if it is—sigh—a secret club of *family*.

But first: a lovely picnic . . .

"Shall we sing?" someone asks.

"Let's wait for George." My dad is in the ticket booth waiting on some customers.

We are thirty people, milling around the tables. It's like standing in a grove of trees, among my tall cousins. Finally there is the familiar squeak of the ticket booth door.

" 'Be Present?' " one aunt suggests, which is the name of the song we always sing.

"Feast in paradise?" another aunt says, clarifying which version of the words we always use.

Uncle Joe removes the cigar from his mouth, and with the great tuba of his voice, sings the first few notes . . .

Be present at our table, Lord . . .

And on these first notes, we all join in, because somehow the song is started at just the right pitch, as if the first note were written down on a piece of paper that my uncle kept in his pocket since one year ago, the last time we sang this together.

. . . be here and everywhere adored . . .

The song opens up like a fan, the way a baseball team spreads out on the bases, and somehow everyone knows which part is theirs to play: some take the alto, some the tenor; my aunt Ginny soars above us on soprano; Phil, who sings in his college choir, is our baritone; his three brothers, who juggle and swordfight, take the walking bass line. The music forms here, in this unlikely space behind the ticket booth, near #18, and the people on the golf course stop playing. They step towards us, still gripping their putters. What is happening? Is this a choir?

. . . these mercies bless and grant that we . . .

And here is where I admit that my voice gets very faint—I'm afraid I'll start to cry, the harmony is so beautiful, and the song is too short; with each final note comes a tremendous sense of loss; it will be another year or two before we do this again, and we never know when it will happen; the family reunions are never planned, and they come less often than before, as people scatter more each year across the country, one family in Washington State, another in New Jersey, another in Oregon, one in Ohio . . . We are so lucky. That we can do this. Sing like this together.

. . . may feast in paradise with thee . . .

"Not lucky," they would say, "blessed" . . . but this word has always bothered me. Just because my grandparents believed in God? We get to be lucky? What about those kids out there with miserable parents? Who get yelled at all the time? Are they just unlucky? It doesn't seem fair. Did they have bad grandparents? Are we just lucky our grandparents got it right? But I can't think any more about it because the song is coming to an end, and I am trying to sing, and also hang on to this moment . . . this moment . . . why can't we live forever in this moment . . . ?

And then . . .

. . . Amen.

We suspend the *amen,* out over the lawn, across the fairways and over the greens; it floats over the gravel, between the parked cars, up into the wooded hills beyond; it seeps out past the cottage and out onto the lake; it hovers there over the water, calm, like fog in winter, warmer than the water, like a heavenly mist . . .

We are singing in ten parts now, and why not? This is the moment, during the *amen*, that stops time. It holds itself and wraps around me like a warm beach towel after you climb up out of the lake.

The song ends. One of us whistles.

"Thank you, George," Joe says, and some people laugh. I am too far away to hear the joke, but with the laugh we are back at Tom Thumb. It is as if we briefly, for thirty-five seconds, were together in some other heavenly place, and now, with a joke, are back to the land of paper plates and: Do we need more lemonade? You kids go ahead. I'm starving. Oh, I've forgotten about the beans in the house. I'll get them. No, I'll go. I need to grab another spoon. Did you make this, Connie? I'm starting with a hot dog. Are there enough buns? Whoa, are you going to have some hot dog with that mustard? Does it look like there are going to be enough buns? We are short on knives so we'll have to share . . .

A car pulls in, and the crunch of gravel is like a dog whistle that only my family can hear. My mom, dad, my sisters, and I find each other's eyes among the aunts, uncles, and cousins. W*ho wants to go?* With a nod, one of us volunteers to take a turn in the ticket booth. When several cars pull in, we find each other again. *I'll take my plate with me,* one of us says with a silent nod.

The younger kids finish quickly so they can play more mini golf. The adults linger at the picnic tables, poking at the vegetables, sipping coffee. My mother starts the cleanup by loading a tray with mayo and pickles and other things for the fridge. Aunt Elaine, the perfect one, gathers up the extra cutlery and follows her up the steps and into the house.

"Take these extra buns," she says to my mother, holding out a package.

"What are you talking about, Elaine?"

"Jean. We've eaten all your food."

"You've hardly eaten anything. You need these to feed your boys."

"Well anyway," my aunt says, putting some folded bills into my mother's jacket pocket.

My mom pulls the money out and looks at it as if it's an old leftover sandwich she's discovered in a strange place. "I don't want this."

"Let me at least give you a ten."

"Don't be silly. I owe you for all these buns!" my mom says, thrusting the bills back into her chest. "And I want to add a few more." She grabs another couple of tens out of her other pocket and holds one out.

"But we didn't pay for golf yesterday."

"It doesn't cost us anything!"

"I need to pay for the cotton candy the kids have been eating."

"That sugar probably costs about five cents each! What about all this baking you did? All these cookies? That's a lot of work!"

"No, I enjoy it!" Elaine says, running out the door.

My mom tries to push bills into her sister's back pockets, but they fall onto the steps.

"No, no, no, Jeannie!"

"Elaine!"

"No!"

And while that battle simmers along, let's have a look around the picnic tables, where the violence seems to be spreading: "I want to pay for the potato salad," one aunt says to another. "I've already written out the check, so you have to take it."

"Can't you rip it up? Here hand it to me. I'll rip it up."

Aunt Ann jams a twenty into my father's jacket pocket as she speaks with the assurance of a philosopher. "George, in the interest of fairness, I have the right to pay for the golf game from last night—"

"Well, that's on the house," he says, blocking her with his hands on his chest.

My sister LeAnn is fending off my cousins Lore and Sharon as the mayhem seeps down to our generation. "Take the money!" "No!" "Take it!" "No!" One runs after her one way, while the other circles around the other, chasing her around the firepit and knocking a thermos of Kool-Aid onto the ground.

"I want to pay someone for the hot dogs!" an uncle yells.

There are only two or three people still seated. Everyone else is trying to insert bills into each other's waistbands. It looks like a chase scene at a strip club.

"That's too much!"

"Take it!"

"No, you take it!"

Aunt Connie, wearing a fabulous flowered blouse, gestures as if standing at a lectern, "There is something in the Scandinavian psyche that says you shouldn't just get things free. It could be connected to Christian guilt, but of course, the harsh winters required—"

Someone sticks a five-dollar bill into her pants.

She screams and runs.

My uncle Vern is a gentle, decent man, which is to say, an easy target. My mother leans towards him quietly, and gently pats money into his jacket pocket as if she were planting a sunflower seed in the garden. "Why don't you give this to your wife . . ."

"One time in our living room," LeAnn says, "I found money someone had stuck between the books."

"Last year I found some bills under a potted plant in our house," a cousin says. "They must have been there for months. I have no idea who might have left them."

Abe Lincoln and the Elf approach me. "So how is your summer

going, June?" they ask, and then intently study my face. "Do you get much chance to swim?" "Are you looking forward to high school?" They tip their heads so as to listen more intently. I'm not used to getting this kind of attention. "Uh—," I say. Behind them, their daughters are crawling like commandos up to the ticket booth, crouching low to keep their heads down, heading towards the front window—

"Hey!" I shout, running inside. Two sets of fingers are pushing dollar bills under the front window flap. They fall to the floor, I pick them up, then I feed the bills under the flap of the side window, one by one. It looks like some kind of money processing machine, as bills come in one way, then go out the other.

And this is the point in the weekend when you begin to wonder if it isn't best we live in separate towns after all.

Family reunions are like going out for all-you-can-eat pancakes. So warm, so sweet, so comforting, and so fun. Until you realize at some point that you have eaten too many pancakes. You're full, but they keep coming. You are starting to get a sick feeling in your stomach. It all started so well, but now you want to yell, "Hey, no more pancakes!"

Every family has its traditions, and I would say that is as it should be. Traditions are a comfort. As they are repeated, they remind us that all is well. All is familiar. Even if *all* is also *weird*. Each family invents its own; the Big Money Fight was one of ours. Perhaps this is how we made it easier for everyone to say good-bye.

Eventually the weak among us give up, or just become disgusted, and the money finds homes in pockets or purses. Hugs are exchanged, coolers are loaded, and cars are packed with suitcases and bags. "Have a safe trip!" "See you next summer!"

We wave as the circus leaves town, one car at a time.

"Don't get lost in Missouri!"

Abe Lincoln and the Elf back up their station wagon; my two

cousins wave and call out from the backseat. "Good-bye! Good-bye!" We see their windows close, and we start walking away. Then from across the lawn we hear, "You better come and get it before someone else does!" The back windows of their car are open just a crack, and there are dollar bills falling onto the parking lot. LeAnn runs after, grabbing money off the ground. "Crank them up!" the Elf yells. LeAnn tries to push the money back in the windows. The station wagon pulls ahead too fast, the tires of their car chewing up the gravel as they peal out of the lot. As the gravel falls back down to earth, it sounds to us like "Gotcha."

(By the way, back at The Outhouse. Remember that sign, GO IN THE RIGHT HAND HOLE? Well, each summer there are two or three bats living behind it. If you lean underneath, you can see them hanging there, yet another family. They nap together during the day behind this plywood sign, which hangs over a pretend outhouse, while golf balls bang around beneath them. That would be the weird thing *their* family does together.)

CHAPTER 11

THE COVERED BRIDGE

It is better to have loafed and lost than never to have loafed at all.

—JAMES THURBER

Which brings us to The Covered Bridge.

It leans.

It's dark.

It sits in the corner.

We made Carla crawl inside it.

Thankfully, she's forgiven us a lot of things.

Nine feet from front to end, the opening only about ten inches wide. The bridge is low, thin, and long. Skinny. So was Carla. So you can't blame us for seeing if she could fit inside. Which we did one time (okay, maybe two), to see if she was able, and presumably to shoo out leaves stuck inside from the winter.

It's a covered bridge, like ye olden days. The sides are brownish red. And the roof is layered with cedar shingles. On top is what used to be a weathervane, only now is just a weird piece of metal that spins if you turn it. The bridge is old. It is one of the original hazards.

There is a pool of water underneath the bridge, and so when your ball swerves off the fairway to splash in from either side, the people in your foursome can add to your misery (and one-stroke penalty) by saying things like "Aw, that's just water under the bridge." Then they'll enjoy a good laugh. If your ball rolls underneath, you'll have to reach in with your hand to find it by feel. There is time for more helpful comments: "Haven't you had enough swimming already today?"

"Be careful, your ball is going to get waterlogged."

"Your ball has been in the water so much that if it had lips, they'd be turning blue by now," they quip. Oh, how they quip.

This hazard is easy to ignore. For one thing, hole #11 is in the corner. The green is the farthest point on the mini golf course from anything else. But also, it's dark. We should put another bulb over there. People lose their balls in the grass all the time. It's isolated. But The Covered Bridge is not a dark secret. We have no dark secrets. Our lives are public. People come here. They lounge in our yard. We can't keep much from them and have mostly stopped trying.

The Covered Bridge is where an animal got stuck once, or that's what Mom thinks. (This was during a summer after I left, so I heard about it later.) One morning she and Dad found a torn circle of carpet around the cup. It looked like a long-clawed creature had spent the night desperately clawing at it.

"A raccoon?" I asked.

"Raccoons are too big."

"A baby raccoon?"

Mom cut a piece of new carpet and patched it with glue. The patch was a perfect circle with a hole, like a doughnut of green felt, or a giant version of one of those reinforcement stickers you adhere when a page rips from your three-ring binder. "I think we had just replaced that green that same year. It almost made me sick to see it. That was new carpet!"

But we never found out what animal it was, or more curiously, whether the animal was trying to claw its way *into* the cup or desperately trying to claw its way *out*.

That's why hole #11, The Covered Bridge, is about Escape.

On days when we would all rather have been anywhere else, but had nowhere else to go, we went to separate corners. Dad huddled in his workshop. LeAnn worked for my uncle at Ding's Dock or lay in the yard working on her tan. The dog hid under the porch steps. Carla hid under the porch with him, talking to him nicely. Mom didn't bother to hide because we never saw her anyway. She was running between buildings for so much of the day that for all intents and purposes, she was just a blur. As for me, I went to the lake.

We had two docks, the public one and the private one. A big one and a small one.

The big dock was for tourists; TOM THUMB MINIATURE GOLF said the box-shaped sign we screwed onto the pier. The box had an ugly cartoon man on top. Three feet tall and made of plywood, he had a big nose, and a putter made from a wooden dowel. With the saggy cap on his head, he looked a bit like the comic strip character Andy Capp.

"Good golly," LeAnn said, the summer we bought Tom Thumb, when she saw this box-shaped-cartoon-man sign strapped on the car of the previous owner.

"I'll leave it for you," he said with a smile. "You can put it on your own car now. Advertise as you drive around town."

"Over my dead body," LeAnn said, threatening many forms of Japanese suicide if she had to be seen in a car with that thing on top.

So the ugly box-shaped-cartoon-man-sign-that-would-have-driven-LeAnn-to-suicide found a new home: here, on the end of the public dock. It's for *them*. It's to attract *their* attention as they cruise around the lake.

The second dock, located on the side, we consider our private dock. It's a bit rickety. The paint is peeling, and you have to watch your step because the boards aren't all level. This dock is hidden behind the garage and gives access into Bass Lake, which is not much bigger than a pond. You wouldn't jump in unless you were on a dare—there are so many weeds knotting the water, you might never escape. The ground so mushy, if you tried wading in from shore you might sink up to your neck in muck.

When I needed some time alone, I snuck over to the women's outhouse—which we were now using as a shed—grabbed a life preserver and paddle, and heaved the canoe into the water. "You're taking the canoe out?" Mom or Dad would call. I acted like I couldn't hear them. It was a dumb question. Also, if you really want to escape, it's important to pretend no one knows where you are.

I'd sit in the back of the canoe, push off from land, and then . . . oh. That first gliding on the surface. When you first begin to float, the smooth lifting up of the canoe. That is the best part. There is this feeling of luxury. As if the water is letting you borrow it for a while, for an hour, or just a half hour, and imagine you are water too.

There was a spit of land on the opposite side of Beasley separating our lake from the next one over, just wide enough for some white pines and tamaracks to take hold. It wasn't far, you could still see our cottage from there, and not far from Bass where I started, but it felt like another land. That was where I headed.

Once there, I drifted in the shallows. The water was clear and still and lily pads floated like green vinyl dinner plates on the surface; small fish swam beneath them. Bees and wasps walked in circles on one dinner plate and then flew off to the next one, presumably to see if there was anything tasty there. Between the leaves, water lilies poked out of the water on pencil-thick stems. The flowers grew to the size of grapefruits, extravagant white pompoms with a bright yellow center.

I gave the paddle a gentle push as I peered over the side. There was an underwater cliff where the depth would drop from one or two feet beneath you to thirty feet or forty feet below. They say Beasley is one of the deepest lakes in the chain, fifty feet deep or even more. So I searched the shallows, until I nosed over the spot. And then, as if standing on the edge of a tall building, I would feel the air suck from my lungs. The drop-off. This was what I came for, the take-your-breath-away feeling looking down at the vastness. The depth beneath appeared endless. It was dark like a forest, with ten-foot weeds stretching up like trees, and creatures yet unseen living down below.

And so I hovered, staring into the water.

"Lose something?" a man called out. A pontoon boat was idling near me. Four people on board, and they were all looking at me. "Did you drop something into the lake?"

"No," I called out. "Um. I'm fine."

"Okay. We were wondering if there was a problem."

"No. There's no problem."

"Okay," said the man. "What a nice day, huh?"

I nodded but I didn't bother to smile. Time to paddle home.

The purpose of summer vacation is to eat bad food and argue with your family. Perhaps not, although most vacations seem to have a good deal of both.

But if you boil it all down, the summer vacation is this: a reason to go on.

Your vacation time isn't really to give you time to relax; it's to give you something to look forward to. You need something to picture during the fierce crossing of the Antarctic, which is what every family does, in effect, by trying to survive the six long months of winter without killing each other and chewing on each other's bones. Like a tulip bulb asleep under the frozen ground, there is a germ of hope inside your skull . . . Hold on, hold on. Just make it till summer!

It might surprise you to hear that summer vacations are rather a new invention. If you look around, there are trees in this yard that are older than the idea of "taking time off."

Vacations started in the early 1800s primarily as a way to improve one's health. Rich folks would visit towns with mineral springs, "take the waters" as it were. And while there they also did a lot of dancing and ate at lovely restaurants, and yes, often their health did improve.

It was not until after the Civil War that you could just make out the baby beginnings of a middle class—and ooh, look how cute you are—when office workers and teachers were first given one week's paid holiday. By this time employers were starting to believe that the human body could use a break. A week spent outdoors might prevent their workers from getting sick the rest of the year. Vacations were more about health than they were about travel, and days were granted to employees more from self-interest, perhaps, than compassion. But hey, I doubt anyone complained.

As we stand here at hole #11, The Covered Bridge, let me tell you that the men who built wooden bridges like this one a hundred years ago, say, working-class people, were not trusted with time off. The laborers, the housecleaners, the guys employed to build the roads, didn't get vacation time. Nada. People worked all year. That's all there was to it.

In the beginning of the twentieth century, businessmen started wondering if a vacation might help more of their workers, but they weren't sure the working class would do it right. Would they know they were supposed to leave the city and get outdoors? Would they just take a second job and become less healthy?

Would they just get drunk and stay that way, returning to the job less useful than before? A few companies even built summer camps for their employees for a supervised holiday. Imagine a vacation with your co-workers. Sponsored by your boss.

The working class got its biggest break—and this is ironic—during the Great Depression. Even though there was rampant unemployment, the number of companies offering paid vacation actually increased during the 1930s. One of the main reasons: unions. Even though the unions didn't really care about vacation time, businessmen started handing it out anyway. Employers would do anything to keep their workers from joining a union. Ergo, keep them happy; ergo, a paid vacation.

Finally, the working class was allowed to join the elite and actually dream about a week at the lake, lie in the sun, throw a tent in the car, drive to some other place, and then discover you forgot the tent poles.

Everyone loves The Covered Bridge. They are so happy to discover there's a second hazard with a pool. That's because the water is clean; it isn't a heaving pile of mud. One thing you should know about the pools is that keeping them clean is horrendous.

Cleaning the pools involves sucking all the old water out with hoses, sponging the remainder by hand, then lugging a couple of buckets with soapy water out there, and on your hands and knees cleaning out the dirt and broken leaves. Then it's time to drag hoses across the course so you can refill them with water. You have to start early in the day because the whole act takes hours. By *you*, of course, I mean *your mom*. It was her job to clean it. Because cleaning the pool is a terrible job. And like most other Mom-jobs on the planet, no one else will do it.

The day after she cleans it, there will be a thunderstorm and the rain will pour down so hard that sand will wash into the pool from the road, along with leaves and twigs and sediment from the flower bed, and you are back to where you started. And again by *you* I mean *your mom*. The person at Tom Thumb who never seemed to need to sit down.

"Whew!" my mom said as the porch door slammed behind her. "We sure got a lot done this morning." She had cleaned the pools, mowed the golf course, replaced one green, and cooked a hot dish to put in the freezer for a family event weeks later, all before I had brushed my morning teeth.

"Uh," I'd say. "Is this Friday? I think it might be my turn to open."

"Might be. But I did everything already. I swept all the greens. You can just carry out the money boxes."

That evening she would sit down to an empty plate.

"What's going on, Mom? Aren't you eating?"

"I'm fasting today," she said.

"Why?"

"It's not hard. And I've heard it's good for the body. Just to give it a break."

She did it again next Friday. "If you set the table," she said, "I'll start making dinner. Just leave off a plate for me. I'm not eating today."

"You're cooking but not eating anything?"

"Well, I might drink the water left in the saucepan after cooking up the broccoli. I've heard that's good for you. Vegetable water."

Well, hurray.

One's relationship with one's mother is never going to be easy. First of all, you deny you need each other. Second of all, you have the same nose. Third, eventually you realize she is not as dumb as you had been thinking, but by that time a lot of seeds have been sown and are screaming to be plucked, harvested, ground up, and thrown to starving children who are waiting at the back of the truck.

She did almost everything to keep the mini golf running. Like laying all the carpet. Dad did help, I suppose. His job was to remove the bolts from the two-by-fours and help pull back the old carpet. Then on her hands and knees, Mom would scrape off the old glue. Then she'd lug the old carpet to the driveway and, using a knife the size of an apple corer, cut out a new piece of carpet the same size. Then lug it to the green, spread out the glue, roll out the new piece, stretch it to the corners, push it down over the rusted bolts, and then with a deep breath and perhaps a prayer to heaven, she plunged the carpet knife into the middle, hoping to reveal the cup underneath, and not ruining the new carpet. It was a tough job; she had to start early in the day.

I would have *liked* to help, but, you know, I was just never usually around at that time.

I did try once. I set the alarm on "carpet day" and ran outside to assist. But then found myself standing on the side of the green watching. She was just so darn capable. She could work better without me. "You can hand me the spatula," she said, when it was time to spread the glue. "It looks like pudding, don't you think?"

Vikings. You've heard of them. My mother's ancestors—and mine—came from Norway. It's entirely possible that her genes come from those fierce people who crowded themselves into tiny boats and sailed off to conquer the world. On a diet of dried bread.

These days historians argue about the Vikings, and whether they could have successfully navigated to America four hundred years before Columbus and without a map. But spend one morning with my mom, and you could be reasonably convinced that Vikings crossed the Atlantic, felled trees, planted crops, and built homes for their families, and got back to Norway in time for lunch.

You never hear about Vikings "taking some time off," and my mother didn't seem to either.

* * *

Our "vacations" consisted of an hour or two when we would try to escape the pull of Tom Thumb. My family kept three bicycles in the garage which were all more or less the same size and second-hand quality, with the same tendency to have flat tires. When my sisters and I needed to get away, we'd grab the handles of the least entangled one and race for the road before Dad noticed us. "Going for a bike ride?" he'd say, if he spotted you. "Let me put some oil on that chain for you" or "Adjust that seat" or "Check those tires." He could make the bike fit you perfectly, and you would stand there watching him while kids your age fell in love, got married, bought houses, and sent their children off to college, then moved to Florida. All before he finished. "Here you go. Oh, I see it's getting dark."

We all worked, but it appeared to me that Dad had gotten the long end of the straw. His job was the motors, and Mom did everything else. Okay, he also repaired the hazards when pieces had rotted. But it was calm work. Leisure work. Jobs that seemed to be more or less optional. He stood over the picnic table next to the garage, which was his summer "workbench." "I'm replacing the motor on the barn," he said. "This one's getting noisy."

People waved at him as they walked by.

"Beautiful day," they said.

"Sure is!" and he smiled.

"Nice place you have."

"Thanks."

It was irritating.

One day when I was about fifteen or sixteen, I was unloading balls in the ticket booth when a man approached Mom, as she came out of the Snack Shack. "This is a really nice course," he said. "George Melby? He's the owner?" Mom nodded. "He does a really nice job."

"Yes, he does."

"He really keeps the place up nice."

"I agree."

"Please thank him for me."

"I will."

After he left, I confronted her. "Why did you do that?"

"Do what?"

"Give Dad all the credit."

"I don't know what you're talking about."

"That guy made it sound like Dad deserves all the credit. Dad doesn't do all the work. *You* do all the work. I mean, us girls do too, we paint and do stuff . . . But you do more than any of us do." It was the Teenage Manifesto, which is to say, my mother had no idea what I was talking about. I wasn't really making sense, yet I felt every word emphatically.

"It's not like the olden days, you know," I said, "when women gave all the credit to their husbands. You should stand up for yourself," I continued, because once I start talking I tend to go on a bit. "You should have told that man. How you do most of the painting? And cleaning the pools?"

"I've never thought about it," she replied. "Hold on, someone wants something in the Snack Shack." When she came out she said, "I've been thinking. About what you just said. You know, people see Dad all the time out here. He's working at the picnic table or fixing things on the course. Most of my jobs are done in the morning," she added. "I think that people just don't see me."

I looked out on the course to see a mother and daughter playing The Swinging Pole. They looked like the same person, first at age twenty and then at age fifty. The girl wore her blonde hair in a ponytail; but when she is fifty, she'll wear it frosted and cut to the shoulder. The girl was willowy with slender legs poking out of her shorts. Her mother was the same, only now she has a slight lean, like that of a tree that has adapted to the yard. The skin of the girl will someday match the skin of the mother, thickened by enjoying afternoons like this in the sun. They putt in, then smiled together. The girl's cheeks will form creases over time from smiling like this, just as her mother's have. It is a good day. It is the same smile. The girl reaches into the hole and retrieves both balls, hands the red one to her mother, keeps the pink. "You're up."

I couldn't understand why my mom and I weren't more like that. Which is to say, alike. It would have helped, I believed, if sometimes she'd complain.

During the winter she worked as an elementary school librarian. She also had lunch duty, patrolling the playground. Not an easy job. We'd come straight to Tom Thumb right after the last day of school. Run the mini golf seven days a week. Then we'd close up on the very last day before school started, drive back to Iowa, and the cycle would begin again. This had been going on for six years by this point, and she had never taken a day off. I tried to convince her.

"I'll work for you, Mom, if you want to go do something," I said.

"No. After lunch I'm going to go rake the lake."

"Don't you want to take a nap or something?" I'd say.

"No, I want to rake the weeds."

"That doesn't sound like fun."

"It is! It looks so good when I'm done!" My mother was the type of person who—for fun—stood in the middle of a canoe raking up seaweed. In a swimsuit and tennis shoes, gripping a rake with a twelve-foot handle, she'd float near the public dock where we swam. Then she'd heave up mound after mound of stinking, slimy weeds. She was strong enough to hold it over the side to drip and then plop it at her feet.

"Want to join me?" she asked. "There's another rake."

I tried it. Once.

But the seaweed brought up muck from the bottom, and you'd get splattered from your toes to your thighs, as if you had spent the day pushing a truck out of the mud.

"You don't mind the smell?"

"Oh, it doesn't bother me. I'll take a swim to clean off when I'm done." When the canoe was so weighed down that the sides were only about an inch above the surface, she'd sit down and paddle it around to the side dock. Then with a pitchfork she'd unload the seaweed on the shore. "That's good fertilizer, I think. I'll have to plant tomatoes and try it out.

"Come join me later for a swim if you like."

One of the more terrifying moments of my childhood occurred while eating dinner with my grandparents; I must have been around eleven at the time. We were finishing the meal when my grandfather—my mom's father—spoke up. "No cake for me. I'd rather have more corn. Corn will be my dessert." I watched as he happily spooned more kernels on his plate. He appeared to be serious.

Now I was beginning to wonder if my mother was the same way with work. Just as my grandfather preferred vegetables to cake. Could she possibly believe that slaving all day was just as good as taking time off?

It was hard to know what motivated her. As an adult, I have often wondered if my mother would have chosen a different life for herself if she hadn't fallen into this one, with my father, on this miniature golf course. If she has been as happy as she claims to be working so hard.

Then again, I could be mistaken. When one is talking about one's mother, it is easy to confuse your desires for who you wish she would be, and her own desires for herself. And, I suppose, vice versa.

* * *

I stood on the dock in my swimsuit with a beach towel wrapped around me.

"You want me to go in first?" Mom said, walking past me to the ladder. She always went in first.

"Sure," I said. She gripped the handles and backed down the ladder. One step, then the next step. Once at the bottom she flung her arms behind her and—*whoosh*—she was in the water, her head above the surface. Never taking her eyes off me.

"Not too bad," she said.

"I don't know. I think I saw your lips quiver."

"No, it's quite warm."

"You looked like you were about to say something."

"It's not as warm as yesterday, but it's really not too bad."

It's the game we played; she pretended the water was fine. I read her face for any signs that she was lying and would scream if she were a normal person.

"Didn't the rain cool it down?" I said.

"It did. A bit. But it's fine. Come on in," she said, treading water.

I stepped down the ladder and stood on the last step. "I don't know. It doesn't feel that fine."

"Hurry up," she said. "I want to move away from the shore."

"Okay." I flung my arms out behind me and plunged. "Ack!" I screamed. People heard me across the lake and probably thought I might be dying. I have never been good at keeping my emotions a secret. "It's not warm at all!"

She laughed. "Just think, if the lake was always this cold, we'd think this was normal. We'd still go swimming."

"That doesn't mean it would be fun."

"Just keep moving. You'll warm up," she said, moving out into the lake. "A person can get used to about anything."

Take a break for some fantastic COTTON CANDY!

The Secrets of COTTON CANDY:

Cotton candy is made from heated sugar and air. Now you know. You can put down the book and die easily. That's the big secret. Ta da. You're welcome.

People don't ask us very often how it all works. If they do, they want a brief answer: "We put sugar into the receptacle and then it melts and spins out—" "I knew it!" they say, triumphantly returning to their family with an I-told-you-so and a giant pink wand of fluff. No customer—not one that I remember anyway—has asked to step into the Snack Shack to take a close look at the cotton candy machine. If they did, they would see what looks like a washing machine crossed with an Airstream trailer: squat and silver, curved and aluminum, bulky and ancient. Ours was born sometime around 1959.

However, customers do sometimes ask "What's *in* a cotton candy?" because that's a different question. They don't want a lot of *detail*; they just want to know how much guilt to have with their treat. These are the people who look over the ingredients on a Kit Kat candy bar, finding relief, presumably, from the *act* of reading the fine print, rather than finding any particular toxic chemical included or omitted.

"Cotton candy? It's a scoop of sugar with a little bit of flavoring," we say. And the customer is satisfied and requires no more explanation.

It is not magic—it is only a wonder. But if magic is craved, and you are stuck in Wisconsin, this one will have to do. The people who buy cotton candy at Tom Thumb do *not want to know* how it comes together.

There may occasionally be a sulky man who "comes along" with his family to Tom Thumb. He considers it embarrassing to actually *play* miniature golf, so he prowls the corners of the course. While the rest of his family forms a foursome, he kicks at tee-off pads. He zips and unzips his windbreaker, then knocks his fist a couple of times on the wooden fence to test its construction. And this man, who has not let himself be caught up in the excitement of getting a hole-in-one on The Airplane, or winning a free game on #18, may be wondering how cotton candy is made, but he will never ask me. I am a sixteen-year-old girl. This would never do.

Recipe for cotton candy sugar: (1) one teaspoon cotton candy flavoring powder, (2) one five-pound bag of sugar from the Piggly Wiggly. Stir the two together. Place in a red plastic canister from the 1950s labeled FLOUR. Carry it out to the cotton candy machine and park it on the Snack Shack shelf. Done.

The flavoring powder comes in a one-quart tin that pries open like a can of paint. It gets rusty around the edges before we order a new one—which is about once every five years—from Badger Popcorn Supply. The ingredients on the tin: "Sugar, artificial flavor, red dye number 40."

The best flavor is grape, but we never make grape. "People want pink," Mom says, and it's true. Another mystery.

The flavor for pink is vanilla.

When you are making a cotton candy, you have a choice of two methods for gobbing that floss on the cone: (1) You can stand there while the sugar spins out a thick layer into the machine, then poke in your cone, take one step backwards, and like Zorro brandishing a sword, whip the pink loop into the air. *Fwooop.* "Ooh!" and "Ah!" People will love you. But you must consider how hot the machine is at that point, and also your level of cotton-candy-maker confidence. Spectacle may get you attention, but if you misjudge your twirl you can end up with "flop." You can't sell the flop because it just looks heartbreaking. Or (2) You can lean over the machine and rotate the cone in the palm of your hand—circle the bin clockwise, rotate counterclockwise—as tediously small amounts of floss are emitted, accumulating layer upon layer, like calcification on a stalactite over yeons of time. It's a safer method. This is what my dad does. It's a little bit boring.

The rest of us use a combination of both methods, a little Zorro, followed by a little stalactiting, depending on our mood and, of course, humidity—the Dark Enemy of cotton candy.

The cones for the cotton candy come in a box large enough to conceal a small child with her arms at her side during a lengthy game of hide-'n-go-seek. Since it is so huge, the box stays in the porch. We replenish the Snack Shack with cones every week by marching down the steps holding up a stack of cones like the torch on the Statue of Liberty and singing "From the Halls of Montezuma." We don't know why holding a stack of cotton candy cones makes us want to do that. It is just another secret I'm admitting to you.

More Mysterious Truths about cotton candy:

If you have just washed your hair, customers will appear out of nowhere and order about two dozen. As if out of spite, the fluff will fly directly onto your head. Afterwards, your mother will pull off pink floss with her fingertips, and you will feel like a couple of monkeys. Your hair will have been clean for all of fifteen minutes.

Your dad will offer to take a turn making a cotton candy during dinnertime, because he says he doesn't mind getting up and walking out to the Snack Shack. Your mother will remind him, "Don't make it too big this time," and he will say, "I won't," but he will. He always makes the cotton candy too big.

And that is the ultimate mystery about cotton candy: how it is able to mesmerize you. When you are standing at the machine, twirling the floss onto the cone, layer after layer, it's hard to know when to stop. When is enough? Now? NOW? You finally pull the wand out, and then you see that the cotton candy will be bigger than you thought. It will be *too* big. All our cotton candies are too big.

And you may feel generous as you hand it out the window—"Omigod, that's beautiful!" the customer says—and you feel god-like for a moment having made something so magnificent, because the cotton candy you're presenting truly *is* beautiful. But that moment is fleeting. That giant pile of fluff will be too big to eat, as the customer—and you—will soon discover. Fifteen minutes later you will hear the dull thud of a half-eaten cone falling into a waste bucket. The now-heavy sugar hits the bottom and sticks. You learn that there is a limited time to enjoy magic, about twenty minutes. And then humidity takes over. Life is not ever-lasting. There is a limit to beauty, thrills, and magnificence. The customers are sad they couldn't finish eating their treats, or are sick to their stomachs from trying. You are sad that you'll have to take out the garden hose and blast out the garbage pails before the raccoons get to them. You will realize that *moderation* is not a bad word, not a word solely for grown-ups.

Next time, you will try to make your cotton candies smaller. Your customers will be happier in the long run. You are not God. You are not the president. But there are things you know as a cot-ton candy maker. You have been trained to accept the responsi-bility of making such a magical thing out of sugar and air. It is a duty of sorts, making magic for other people.

They'll wander away, dreaming, pulling pink clouds onto their fingers. They may leave the earth entirely, and you have to call them back to the window, because they have forgotten about the existence of money.

"That'll be seventy-five cents," you say.

And once they're out of earshot, you scrape the butter knife around the walls of the machine to get it ready for the next time.

Squish the scraps into the Tupperware container—it holds a lot when you push the lid down. Months later we'll cut out hardened chunks of the leftover cotton candy sugar and use it to sweeten our Kool-Aid and strawberry Jell-O and rhubarb crisp and jars of homemade raspberry jam, which will all glow pink, as if radioactive.

CHAPTER 12

THE BARRELS

Captain Ahab stood erect, looking straight out beyond the ship's ever-pitching prow. There was an infinity of firmest fortitude, a determinate unsurrenderable wilfulness, in the fixed and fearless, forward dedication of that glance.

—HERMAN MELVILLE, *Moby-Dick*

Delicate leaves of the water willow flutter along the edge of the back nine. A small forest of them grow behind the picket fence; and beyond it is the lake, reflecting clouds in the sky. A chipmunk peeks out between the fence slats, then runs back into his private woods. And in front, enjoying this lovely backdrop, are The Barrels. Four wooden tubs turn gently in the sun, the light glinting off the golden oak.

Have you ever made something so beautiful that the next morning you got out of bed, ran over to it, and just stared at it for a while? When I stopped doing comedy, I taught myself how to paint on canvas to give me something to do with my evenings. From comedy to tragedy, you might say. But one night I made a painting that came out so well that I couldn't take my eyes off it. Some kind of miracle. Hole #12 is this for my father. He built it more than twenty-five years ago, and he hasn't looked away from it since.

My father made this hazard from strips of oak that he beveled himself, one at a time, so you know he has a lot invested. He attached the oak to four metal cans he got for free from the bakery in town. The cans once held thirty pounds of lard or butter or frosting; now they are lined with AstroTurf.

He attached the four barrels to a central spoke, added a motor, of course, and placed it with love at hole #12. Then he asked us girls to run out onto the course and unplug it. Then plug it in again. And when customers left, unplug it.

Once when my dad was driving around our hometown in the station wagon, he was pulled over by a cop. "You are driving too slow. Speed it up a bit." We've always wondered how slowly he must have been going if even a small-town cop considered it dangerous. My dad was only thirty-five at the time, not old. And our town was small, about seven thousand people. Now this hazard, The Barrels, my father's most beloved, turns so slowly that it often appears to be standing still.

One thing we discuss at mealtimes is how to tell if it is on or off. "I look at the cross bar on the side," Mom says. "It's easier to tell if you compare the barrels to the stationary object," she adds, always ready with a helpful tip.

"Dad, could you make them turn faster?"

"Well, I suppose I *could*—"

"Why not then?"

"I like them like this."

"But look—" we'll say, pointing to the course, where a couple of tourists are pushing on the hazard to make it spin faster.

"What are they doing!" Dad will say, dropping his fork, and running out of the house to stop them.

Dad finished the barrels with a coat of varnish, even though varnish isn't waterproof. "But it looks better," he said. So The Barrels have a special blanket we pull over them at night. It's actually a rain tarp, and it also goes on whenever it starts to rain. The tarp is dark green and heavy with grommets on the corners, and may have once been on a soldier's back in Vietnam, we aren't sure. But regardless, each morning, like a flag, we fold it dutifully in our arms. Then we drape it over the white picket fence behind The Barrels, where it lives the rest of the time, though no one ever sees it. Like a Vietnam vet, in camouflage or no, it completely disappears from our everyday life, into the cattails and water willow.

"I'll go cover the barrels!" one of us will yell, which is how we announce to each other that is it starting to rain.

"Has anyone covered the barrels?" one of us will ask, which is how we say, "Rain is on the way."

Because this is what my father wants. The Barrels are my father's firstborn, as far as hazards go. And so we do what he says. It's easier that way.

And that's why hole #12, The Barrels, is about Rules.

When we arrived at Tom Thumb, "Risk" was a board game. We had no idea what trouble to expect. We had never dealt with what you could call "the public." But there were clues scattered around in the objects we discovered. One summer, behind several cans of adhesive and faded cardboard posters in the garage, we found a sign:

NO BEER ALLOWED ON THIS COURSE.

"Well, I guess we should put that up then."
"Greg must have."
"Yah."

There were brackets attached to the front fence which we had left unused, expecting one day to know their purpose. This sign fit them perfectly, so we bolted it there, congratulating ourselves on our powers of deduction.

Several days later, Dad came running into the house. "That group out there is drinking out of wineskins!"

"Well, technically they aren't drinking beer," Mom said.

"But they're still getting drunk!"

"I saw a guy stumble on the two-by-fours of #14 and almost fall into the clown on #13," I said.

"That would have killed the clown," LeAnn said.

"I think so."

We had a new topic for mealtime discussion, namely: what kind of person carries around a wineskin? "They saw the sign. They came prepared," we concluded.

Now, a mini golf course is a dangerous enough place when you're handing chrome weapons to a bunch of people on vacation—one of four of whom will take a full swing claiming to have learned from Jack Nicklaus—without adding the extra entropy of drunk people.

I was working when two middle-aged couples in swimsuits approached. They read the sign, filled plastic cups with beer, and then lined them up on the ticket booth counter. "See, the beer is not ON the course," they said, smiling. Then they went out to play, trusting I wouldn't spill their cups when poking out putters to people. Between holes they returned to the ticket booth for a sip, as if it was a bar, which would make me the bartender. I was probably thirteen years old at the time. I stared dumbstruck, unsure how to enforce a rule that they were technically following.

"Well, I'm impressed at how determined they are," Mom said, when we discussed it at the next meal. Yes, impressive. And surprising the interest in semantics from your average Wisconsin beer drinkers, who seem intent on analyzing the meaning of each word. When it's in their best interest, of course. "Yah."

Mom took down the sign and handed it to our local sign painter. "Can you fix the wording?"

"Sure," he replied.

But she probably should have been more specific. One week later it came back, in lovely black script, with the grace usually reserved for wedding invitations:

NO INTOXICATING SUBSTANCES ALLOWED ON THIS COURSE

The next day when people arrived, they stopped to read the new sign. "Intoxicating substances?"

"Does that mean beer?"

"How about aspirin?"

"I think that just means heroin," they decided, hoisting a six-pack of Old Milwaukee on the fingers of one hand.

"I think it means you, babe," one amorous man said, squeezing his girlfriend. "You're intoxicating *me*."

We took down the sign, and Mom drove it to the sign painter, handing him yet another fifty-dollar check. This time she was more specific:

NO ALCOHOLIC BEVERAGES ALLOWED ON THIS COURSE.

A lot of things can go wrong at a mini golf. There was a lot for us to worry about, and by *us*, I mean *Dad*. He worried about The Swinging Pole, when people pushed the pendulum the wrong way: "Too much strain on the supports." He worried about the ball retrievers left in the water overnight: "They'll rust." (I thought they appeared to be aluminum.)

But let's take a moment to point out the many things that Dad *did not* worry about. He didn't worry about children crawling under the slats of the white picket fence to fall into the swamp and drown. He didn't worry about the guys who ran across the road to piss in the woods, which took them, and their bare legs, through the moat of poison ivy. He didn't worry about lawsuits.

Mostly, he worried about the motors.

Before we came to Tom Thumb, Dad had extra concern about our schoolwork and grades and achievement. Just kidding. He worried about lightbulbs. "Are you using this lamp?" "Are you done in this room?" "Were you going to turn off the light?" Now, at Tom Thumb, he was very concerned with preserving the motors. It started with The Barrels . . . everything started with The Barrels.

One day he brought home modules, plug-in devices, so we could turn The Barrels on and off remotely using a control box— one placed in the porch, another in the ticket booth.

"I don't want you girls running out there all the time to plug and unplug them—"

"That's so nice of you—"

"Too hard on the plug, I think."

He crafted a wooden box to cover the module. Then a special hook-and-eye to hold up this box on sunny days so the module wouldn't overheat. Excited by this success, he added switches inside the ticket booth to control all the hazards, then added signal lights like on a dashboard to tell us whether a motor was on or not. Care and adoration spread in this way, from The Barrels to all the hazards on the golf course.

"Looks like an airplane cockpit in there," some of the neighbors said, looking inside the ticket booth. "Are you going to try to fly this thing? Take the ticket booth on a joyride around town?"

When a new group started, we turned on #2 and #4. After a few minutes we ran back to turn these two off. When people got near #12, we could run to either the ticket booth or to the porch. Then run again to turn that one off and switch on #15.

And back to the ticket booth to turn #17 on. And this was just for one group.

We were a thin family.

"Can't we just leave them on all day, like most mini golfs?" I asked.

"I don't want that!" Dad objected.

"Couldn't it actually wear down the motor more to turn it off and on?" I said as calmly as possible, because I knew it would be the most irritating. "Rather than just leave it running for fifteen minutes at a time?"

"Just turn them off!"

I've generally been the type who follows the rules, usually after making it unpleasant for the person who made them. When you are the one in the middle, there is little purpose in stirring the pot. Who would notice? So instead, you might tip the pot a little to either side on occasion, slosh it around, just to see what happens. But it was not in our best interest to make the pot boil. If Dad became too upset he would go into the house, put headphones on his head, and tune the radio to Mexican music—*oompah, oompah*. We never understood how a tuba could be relaxing, and thought it best to leave him to his own devices when we could.

It was the beginning of a Saturday evening and Bass Lake gleamed with the color of a pea green crayon. The breeze tickled the branches of the locust tree near #5.

"Nice evening," we said, finishing supper.

"Could be a busy night," Dad said.

"I'll warm up the fogger." Mom scampered out of the house.

There were rules for Us. And rules for Them. One of our rules was that Dad got to work on Saturday nights, taking command of the ticket booth once there were three or more cars in the lot. "I like to keep an eye out when things get busy," he said. But I suspected he claimed weekends because they were the most fun.

As the sun crept lower behind the woods, the course was taken over by young people: teenagers and college kids, girls dressed in their shortest shorts. Dad even changed the radio to rock music once the people who might be offended—that is, families with young children—had all gone home. It was seven o'clock, and all around the course teenage boys posed with faces of great pain and sexuality as they strummed the invisible guitar strings on their putters. "Taking Care of Business," by Bachman-Turner Overdrive, blasted—at a moderate volume—over the speakers.

"Can I work?" I asked.

"No," Dad said.

"Please can I work?"

"No."

Dad positioned himself in the corner of the ticket booth with one hand on each of the two counter edges, as if resting his hands on the wheel of a ship.

LeAnn considered herself first mate, and took the seat in the back of the ticket booth. Mom paced the corners of the course, shooting a cannon of mosquito fog into the grass. Carla and I were deckhands, that is, we wished we had better jobs. We sat behind the Snack Shack on metal garden chairs—ready to help— but mostly we watched while everyone else had fun. I was sixteen, in other words, miserable.

Tom, the cook, wandered down from camp and sat next to us. "Terrible week. So many strange requirements. No soup! No hot dogs!"

LeAnn leaned out the Dutch door. "June! Go in the house and turn the light off in the porch."

"I'm not the one who left it on."

"Do it anyway!"

"Why?"

"Mosquitoes!"

Generally, I don't think that the military allows siblings to serve together for the simple fact that it's so unpleasant to take orders from a sister. But I did it anyway, after making a terrible face at her—which was my usual fee.

"We're here again! Two in a row. I hope you're not tired of us," a happy group of customers said to Dad.

"I'm here too," he said with a smile.

"Do you ever take a vacation?" they asked.

"Of course we do," he said, raising his eyebrows to indicate that a punch line was coming. "Sometimes we go to Ogdensburg." This was his second favorite joke.

Dad's face was smooth, his nose was perfect and narrow, and there were no scars or acne to speak of. It was as if each element of his face had thought it just easiest to stay in line. He wore a long-sleeved shirt with skinny red and blue stripes, the cuffs rolled up to his elbow.

A high school boy slowly approached the ticket booth with a shy girl beside him. He pulled out his wallet and in a quiet voice said, "Two please."

"So, different girl tonight, huh?" my dad said, deliberately and without smiling, as he handed back the change.

Then Dad came back to tell us all about it. ". . . and I said to the boy, 'Different girl tonight, huh?'" He slapped his leg, laughing.

"Did you remember him from before, George?" Mom asked, resting the fogger on the grass.

"I had never seen him before! You should have seen his reaction!"

"Dad, can you let me work?" I asked.

"No. I want to be out here!"

"Too much fun for me!" LeAnn said, and drove off to a party of her own.

* * *

Rules are usually determined by the most outspoken person in a group. And secondarily, by what's actually printed on the score-card under "Rules." These guidelines go ignored, for the most part, until something goes wrong—a ball is stuck or flies into the lawn. It is at this point, when the foursome has encountered trag-edy, that one person flips over the scorecard, makes the discov-ery, then rises like a member of the Greek chorus. "Listen! Listen!" He steps up onto the two-by-fours along the green and balances there on his flip-flops. "There are rules!" he will say. "Listen!" Then finding a voice inside which resonates to all the heathens in range: "Ball off carpet, place at point of exit, add one stroke." And then he steps down, and the game resumes.

Rules have complications: "I shouldn't get a penalty. I'm the youngest."

And there is the imperfect reality of the game itself: "What if someone knocks you away from the hole?"

"What if someone else knocks you *into* the hole?"

"Of course that doesn't count."

"Why?!"

"Because I said so."

A mini golf course can be a land of squabbles and confusion.

Each family has its own version of what is allowed and what is forbidden. Sometimes a family will come to play Tom Thumb and choose not to follow any rules at all. These groups will putt as many times as they like. They won't keep score. When a ball rolls off the carpet they will pick it up, put it back any place they like, and then shrug, instead of taking a penalty.

And you know what? These people don't have fun. The game goes fast. They are done in twenty minutes. And they argue. They grumble. Some members run on ahead, so when you look out on the course you can't tell that there is a group out there, or just four separate players, playing a game on their own.

Our rules had exceptions as well. Dad was allowed to squirt

honey on his peanut butter toast from a height of two feet above the table, to see if he could hit the bread. The rest of us were not allowed to do that.

By eight o'clock the course was nearly full. Cars drove in, and peeled out again, just to check out the action. When the seas looked fairly calm, Dad poked his head out of the ticket booth. "I need to run in the house for a minute. Can someone—"

"I'll watch!" I said, jumping up.

He waved me to come into the ticket booth. "That group on #9 is going rather slow, so there's no hurry turning on The Barrels—"

"Okay."

"And we're running low on children's clubs, so you can give them medium ones if you need to—"

"Got it."

"And you know we got these new men's clubs," my dad explained, "for adult men who want a heavy club, probably not women unless they ask, and for people who look trustworthy, like, perhaps seniors."

Most mini golf courses have two sizes of clubs: short and tall. Child and grown-up. At Tom Thumb, we had more than a dozen. Actually, it's difficult to count how many categories we had, as Dad tried each year to match up a customer's need with the perfect putter: there were light ones and heavy ones, skinny heads and fat heads, putters that were just one-half inch taller than the next size beneath.

But, of course, what are rules but just attempts to get the world to look like you wish it would, in your most idyllic dreams? In your swimmingly fishiest visions? Everyone plays well together, respecting each other, and they appreciate the beauty of the new hazard you've put out this year, and tell you they enjoy either its beauty or the surprise of a new challenge, or perhaps both.

Perhaps rules are less about trying to control others, but instead the ill-fated attempt at idealism. Life is easier if you don't have visions, ideals. Or so I gather, because I've never had the pleasure/relief to be without them.

Along the back wall of the ticket booth were the putters Dad had set aside for the customers who appeared a bit rowdy—the boys he considered "a crew." They might have arrived in loud cars, or joked too much between them as they paid for their game, or just acted a bit too . . . lively. Cracked handles and rusted metal, the old clubs were in terrible shape. He kept old balls too, so he wouldn't have to give them any new ones. "Here are older balls you can hand out if 'a crew' shows up."

"They don't have any bumps left on them," I said. "What damage can a guy do to a golf ball anyway?"

"Just do it."

I sat on the kitchen stool and, with great flair, used a putter to flick up the switch on #17. Soon after, an old black Mercury drove in with loud music coming out the windows. It brought a group of boys, three out of four of whom were stunningly gorgeous. "Hello," I said, trying to smile—but not too wide, keep it calm. "That's one dollar each. Here's your change. How about these colors for balls?" I said, too completely overwhelmed to stray from the usual script. Along the back wall, I saw the old putters. I looked back at the boys. *They don't look violent.* Unable to actually speak, I "flirted" by handing them four decent putters. They would never know the honor bestowed onto them. "Here you go. Thank you!"

"I'm back," Dad said, returning. He looked out the window. "That group on number three looks like they have good putters. Did you wait on them?"

"They didn't look that rowdy to me."

"Did you get a good look at them?"

As a matter of fact, I had noticed their fine dimples and wind-tossed hair, so yes, I had gotten a good look at them. "They didn't look like bad kids, really."

Dad scowled at the boys as punishment for a crime they didn't know they had committed. "I'm here now. You can go," he said, dismissing me with a frown. I slunk back to the metal chairs.

He didn't trust teenage boys, but it was a hard one to figure. My father had been a high school teacher all his life and was well liked by his students, despite a reputation for being strict. One year he had a "necktie contest" because of the large number he owned. He started the school year telling his students he was going to wear a different tie each day. Whoever noticed when he repeated a tie would win a prize. And the students apparently loved it. Many of them took notes.

Besides, the putters weren't that fragile and broke only about once a month. The balls were so cheaply made, there wasn't a reason to protect them. They got nicked easily by just about any-one, and the person to blame was the mini golf equipment man-ufacturer.

Dad wasn't really trying to protect the putters and balls, I don't think. When I look back on it now, I wonder if he wanted the rowdy kids to get old putters as a form of punishment. The rowdy kids made him worry. About what they *could* do out there. About the risk to the hazards.

Because all the while, on the edge of our existence, turned The Barrels, out on the horizon, by the shore, next to the watery part of the world. Whatever happened, we must protect The Barrels.

(Which is to say, Dad.)

Oh, the parents. Oh, the burden they become. Oh, the heavy weight around one's neck. Oh, heartache, thou art nothing to an angry dad.

* * *

I probably should have rebelled. Perhaps I should have given my parents a harder time. Run off drinking. Carousing. I should have found a bad boyfriend. Given them something to worry about. But to be honest, there was so much screwy behavior from the tourists that acting up seemed crass. Like something that *they* would do, not us. Perhaps even tacky.

But now, ladies and gentlemen, my big act of rebellion. A few minutes later, still pouting, I went to the laundry room, stepping over the large frog sitting on the concrete slab outside the door. I looked at the set of main switches on the wall. There was a breaker labeled MAIN. *It's only eight o'clock. But it really is looking like dusk. I know Dad won't like it, but really now, it's for the best.*

I flipped up the switch, and all the lights went on above the mini golf course: flood lamps, the light above the parking lot, and my favorite, the string of colored lightbulbs that ring the course along the road.

"To-to-too soon!" Dad said, when I got back to the ticket booth. "Who turned the lights on? It's too early!"

"It's not too soon!"

"It's just barely eight o'clock!"

"But the colored lights will attract business!"

"I don't want them on yet," he said.

"Actually," Mom added calmly, "they also attract mosquitoes."

"Well, gosh," I said. "I just wanted people to be able to see. Should I turn them back off?"

"No, no." He turned away from me and back to the front window.

"The lights!" Tom said, from where he sat by #18. "This place is my refuge! Tom Thumb! The lights!"

*　*　*

There has only been one day that Dad was willing to be away from
Tom Thumb. The day of his father's funeral. When it was time for
LeAnn to go away to college, my parents asked my cousin Judi to
drive her there. It was two states away, and they weren't sure they
could leave Tom Thumb in anyone else's hands. "Sure," Judi said.
And LeAnn didn't mind.

"Now they're playing a hole backwards," Dad said.

"Who?" Mom asked.

"Oh, that group that was messing with the barrels."

"Oh, George."

He sighed.

"Do you want *me* to talk to them?" she offered.

"No, Jean. I'll just—" He sighed again. Sat on the stool. He was
the only one of us who, when sitting, kept one foot on the floor,
so he leaned to one side, like a man ready to spring into action.
Or like a man with one wooden leg. Ahab. Always on watch. He
awaits the great whale.

CHAPTER 13

THE AIRPLANE
(formerly THE CLOWN)

Rejoice with your family in the beautiful land of life!

—ALBERT EINSTEIN

The first drops of rain pat the ground with gentle fingertips. They touch your forearm to let you know they are on the way.

There are no birds, no wind. Everything is still. The air seems yellow. The bright crayon colors of the golf course—purple, red, and blue—look faded in sepia now. For two days we have sweltered under pressure from the heavy air—Dad getting impatient from the heat, Mom trying to sooth him—my eyeglasses sliding down my nose. Now the lake has turned black as oil, just like the smoke billowing from the pontoon boat as it speeds away towards shelter.

Then from beyond the hill, it sounds like a bowling ball has been dropped; then a rumbling as the ball rolls towards us.

"Is that thunder?"

"I think that's thunder."

"It's definitely going to hit us!"

There are three groups playing on the course.

"I'll go cover the barrels," one of us says.

The rain begins to find the leaves, a few drops on each, pattering, pattering. Bigger drops thump the roofs of the cars. Customers start playing more quickly now, without taking aim. They swat the ball and step quickly over two-by-fours. "You go!" "What?" "Hurry!" After they pick up their ball from the hole, they stay hunched over, protecting their faces from the raindrops.

You hear the wind before you feel it. The metal clip on the flagpole is lifted up, then falls back again clanging, and clanging again.

The group from #4 flees to their car, still carrying their putters. They are going to wait to see if the storm blows over. The ground itself is shimmering from the rain on the pavement.

Several holes away, a group calmly gives the swinging pole a push. "You're next, Sarah," one of them says. They are not rushing; they are not looking up at the sky. They are like actors from a scene in a completely different movie: one where it isn't raining.

"But it has started, hasn't it?" we ask each other, looking out onto the lake. You can always tell if it's raining by the surface. The lake is not a body of water but perhaps a second sky that lies closer to the earth. You learn you can predict the weather by looking across it, what the wind is doing, how many raindrops. Yes, there are white dancing puddles and Frisbee-size crests. The lake never lies, never denies the truth; the customers, on the other hand, are prone to wishful thinking.

Then, *krarkk!* The sky finds a rip and is splitting itself in half.

Mom runs out onto the course. "You'll have to quit now!"

"We want to keep going!"

"But there's lightning! You're holding lightning rods!"

They run to the ticket booth, laughing, waving their arms over their heads. They fling wet balls and putters onto the counter. "I made it!" they hoot. "Come on!" they yell at the teenager who is still putting on #6. One more crack of thunder, and he dashes under the eave, holding out the wet scorecard. It flops over like a skinny pancake. "I was losing anyway!" one of the girls says. "You were!" "It's all your fault!" The rain is falling harder now, and they huddle under the roof of the ticket booth like one large umbrella. We laugh with them from the inside; we are sharing the same roof-umbrella. They show off the water dripping from their arms: "Look at me!" We hand them free-game cards. "So you can come back another time."

The wind picks up; it's stripping weak branches and leaves from the trees.

"Here it comes!" Dad says.

"I'll get the windows upstairs!"

"I've got to put some things inside the garage."

"Someone get the lawn chairs?"

"I got The Ferris Wheel," LeAnn says. And we take off our sandals and chase across the course, leaping barefoot through puddles and the familiar two-by-fours. We are laughing at the rain that is falling on us, as if it is ribbons from opened packages. "Whoo, baby!"

And then the large droplets fall. It's a roar above us. The storm is taking over.

"Hallelujah!" Mom says. "Maybe it will cool things down."

"One! Two! Three!" the customers say, and then they scream and splash together to their cars. They squish inside together— "I wasn't sure you were going to make it!"—giggling and punching each other like they have just stepped off a roller coaster at Disneyland.

We have money boxes under our arms, and Mom pulls the ticket booth door closed. "Now we need to just get inside."

"I think we might get wet."

"Ya think so?"

"Ahhhhhh!" we scream as we run down the path, then step through the screen door with raised eyebrows of disbelief. "Look at it out there."

"I think we have a new lake by hole #3."

"Where's Dad?"

"Oh, no! He's not still out there?" Mom says.

The rain is coming down now as if it has forgotten to rain in months. It is a waterfall pouring over the eaves of the porch. Just beyond it we can just make out the blur of a silver-colored pith helmet. Dad is coming up the path, slowly, deliberately. He walks over to the windows, stands there, grinning. We are inside looking out; he is outside looking in, the water pouring off his big black poncho and the rim of the helmet. He brings his hand up to his face. Gives us a goofy wave. "Hello," he mouths.

"Dad!"

"Oh, my gosh. He's out there in the rain."

"George, get in here!" Mom yells.

"What are you doing out there?" we call out, laughing.

He holds his hand out and looks up at the sky, as if to say, "Has it started to rain?"

"What is he doing?" LeAnn asks.

He shakes his head, squints as if to say, "Why are you all indoors?"

Dad finally steps through the door, grinning like a teenage boy who just performed a great stunt involving a bicycle. He takes off his helmet and reveals the boyish cowlick on the back of his head, which now is wet and sticking straight up. "I was coming in, and then I remembered I left a car window open."

"Did you get it in time?" Mom asks.

"Well, almost!" And then he laughs, and his whole face is given over, and his eyes crinkle like that, you can't help but smile too, because when the happiness overwhelms him it is a canoe swamped by rapids and you are in the canoe and you are drenched too and it is wonderful to be drenched together.

The roof begins to roar. Water pours off three sides of the porch. "Whoa!"

The winds pick up, and arcs of water ten feet high are blown across the golf course. On Bass Lake we look at the turmoil in the soup. The rain beating the water. Pounding it, pounding it. The wind bends the branches of the birch tree into contortions. Green leaves and small branches are falling onto the lawn. A river of brown flows down the vinyl pathway along the garage. It is chaos as all the world gets pummeled into new shapes. "I think we might be closed all day." This makes us smile even more than before.

As the rain slows to a steady rhythm, the AM radio on the table pipes up: "There is a severe weather warning for the city of Waupaca." And we almost kick ourselves with laughter. "Gosh, do you think it *might* storm sometime soon?" Then there is a flash, and the yard is green-yellow light.

"Has anyone seen the cat?"

"Not since this morning."

We are inside watching. We forget to breathe because the power of the storm is crazy. *KRARKK!* We jump. Together. Our feet briefly leap off the striped carpet. We are safe and we are wet and we are laughing together, and the sheets of rain create a wall between us and the golf course. We know it is out there, but it has vanished behind the rain. And I don't know if I will ever be this happy again.

A lot of people say that hole #13 is their favorite. Here you can get an easy hole-in-one. The hazard has the face of a clown painted to resemble Bozo, the star of a children's television show back in the 1950s when this golf course was built. He has a big open mouth; there is a narrow steep ramp going up into it. If your aim is straight, and you get your ball up this incline, it will travel through the clown and then plop into the hole from above. Hole-in-one. We already have a clown on #18, so Dad built a beautiful blue airplane to replace Bozo, but the obstacle is the same: aim up the narrow ramp to the cockpit, then your ball will get funneled inside the plane. I love the sound of rain, but a close second is the satisfying sound of your ball bouncing around inside the funnel-shape just before it drops into the hole. Hole #13, The Airplane (formerly The Clown), is about Joy.

By the way, after the sky cleared up, we discovered the cat. She was sitting inside the mouth of this clown on hole #13. Her paws were draped over the lip where the clown's tongue should be. She yawned at us. She was unmoved. Unconcerned. Un-damp. Instead of running away, she had chosen to sit out the storm inside the clown. Happily.

CHAPTER 14

THE PURPLE ONE

Forward.

—Wisconsin state motto

Hole #14 is flat. There is no little building. There is no motor or turning what-cha-ma-gig. And yet it is probably the second hardest on the course. (After #3, The Mole Hole, and possibly #10, The Outhouse.) This one has a bunch of different names, but for now, let's just call it The Purple One.

The obstacle here is the fairway itself. This one zigs. And then it zags. Across this zigzaggy path are boards blocking your way. There are several "mouse holes" of different sizes cut into these purple boards. You'll notice there is more than one way to get through. You can choose your path, and because you will fail, you'll probably get several chances to try. Fun, huh?

Sometimes when people ask me a question, instead of one reply, I answer with too many words. I can't say, "My time in college? It was definitely interesting, and I made great friends." Instead my mind wanders back, and I might mention my regret at not changing my major to art, and I will talk about the campus and walking barefoot a lot, and I will be thinking about the time Greg, who shared an apartment with me, left a note on the kitchen table asking if we should perhaps lose our virginity together, as long as we were roommates. (I said no.) But the question was simply: did you like Washington University?

This hazard is like that. There is no straight line. Okay, there appears to be a straight line from the tee-off to the hole because, you know, my mom paints it there. She puts down two strips of masking tape and then runs a paintbrush between them each time she replaces the carpet. The paint is yellow, and one year she thought it would be fun to paint it in dashes.

14

CAN YOU FOLLOW

—the yellow brick road?   ● Par 3 ●

Sounds good, but honestly you can't putt down that line. You might try, and that's how we know you are new around here. It's nearly impossible to get through the first mouse hole if you follow directions. It's best to take a chance and invent your own way through. (I usually put my ball on the left and take a bank shot between the first and second barricades, knowing I'll need a second putt to make it to the green.)

Hole #14, The Zigzag (or The Purple One), is about Finding Your Path.

If you become a stand-up comedian, which I eventually did at age twenty-five, people ask you about your childhood. If you are a guy, they expect you were the class clown, a charming and witty boy who delighted everyone around you, including parents and teachers. (Which is not usually the case, by the way.)

If you are a woman doing comedy, they figure that at some point you were kidnapped by pirates and lived life in an abandoned shack. Or something. Terrible. Actually, I never knew what people wanted to hear. But they asked all the time.

People want *reasons*, that is my theory. They want to know how you got from point A to point B. Or in my case from point A to point W. Are they trying to pigeonhole you? No, I think people just really want it all to make sense. Even though their own path has been more jiggety than a jiggedly-jag-jag, for some reasons they expect *other* people's paths to be logical. Why is that? Does anyone's life really ever happen exactly as expected? Isn't it enough just to get somewhere? Is it supposed to make sense?

After a show it's nice when audience members come up to shake your hand. You want them to say, "Good job! You are terrific!" This is much more desirable than "So, why are you doing this?"

"No really! Normal childhood!" I said, which always left them disappointed. "Not from an orphanage! Happy!" But of course, I was lying.

It's an average Friday afternoon during the month of September.

My father is making a blindfold from two white socks and one brown sock, knotting the toes and heels together, and passing it over his head until the lumps rests on his eyes. "I hope no one pulls us over and thinks I've been kidnapped," he says, chuckling, pushing his pillow into the passenger-side door. Then he pulls up a sock and squints at us. "I'll tell them I'm being held for a really large ransom." He chuckles again. Like many families trapped together in a car, we are taking turns to see who can be the most annoying. My mother responds by sliding her lower jaw forward into a grimace as she slides the car onto the highway.

The summer is over, we have closed up Tom Thumb, but after a week of school we are heading back north again—two hundred miles. LeAnn claims the front seat each time, which is her strategy for irritating. "You know how I get carsick."

"That was eight years ago!" Carla says.

"LeAnn, feel my shirt right here," I say.

"Why?" she says, reaching back to put her fingers on it.

"Dog drool."

"Yuck! Why did you make me touch it?"

Carla and I are stuck in the backseat. Bo, our collie, is in the far-back of the station wagon, in a dog-shaped space between suitcases and boxes. He expresses his discontent by drooling on our shoulders. "Gross."

We stop halfway for gasoline and ice cream cones. Carla and I eat quickly because our shoulders are aching from Bo pressing his skull into them. He is drooling even more. Then it's time for Round 2.

"Who wants a sandwich?" Mom says. "Oh. It looks like LeAnn was sitting on them."

"Again?"

Raising the stakes somewhat, Carla and I begin speaking in the Arb language. "Harbow arbare yarbou?"

"Arb-I'm farbine. Harbow arbare yarbou?"

It is like pig latin. You add the sound *arb* to every syllable, after the first consonant sound. So my name, June, becomes—

"Jarbune. Darbo yarbou warbant sarbome carbandarby?" (Do you want some candy?)

"Sharbure." (Sure.)

"What's wrong with you?" LeAnn says.

"Wharbuts wrarbong warbith LarbeArban?" (What's wrong with LeAnn?)

"Arb-I darbon't knarbow." (I don't know.)

Mom has watched *The Sound of Music* too many times and tries to get us, as a family, to sing together. "Come on! It will be fun!" She sings a sad song about the moon. We sing with her. *I see the moon and the moon sees me. The moon sees somebody I wanna see. God bless the moon and God bless me. God bless somebody I wanna see.* And then it gets quiet in the car. There is nothing like a sad song about the moon to remind you of your lonely life.

"We should watch for deer," Dad says.

"Girls. Watch for deer. Everyone watch for deer."

"Well, I see a lot of dead ones on the side—"

"Live ones! Watch for live ones!"

Even though the summer season had ended and the tourists had all gone home, our work was not all done. There was closing up to do, nailing boards over the Snack Shack windows, storing hazards in the garage, and raking, lots of raking. It would have been different if we lived in Wisconsin year-round. But we lived in Iowa during the school year. On Friday evenings in the spring and fall we would sit together in the dark, facing north, driving up to the cottage. On Sunday night, we would sit together again, this time facing south, driving back home again.

We arrived at 10 pm, sometimes 11 pm, then unpacked the car quickly—there was school the next day. Not every weekend, but many weekends, since I was ten. Now the route to Tom Thumb was more familiar to me than the hallways of the high school.

In Wisconsin, one of the first signs that winter is coming to an end is the widening of open water where the lakes connect to each other. Ice fishermen finally give up and drag their shacks to shore, leaving dark holes in the ice. A sign that the lakes are finally melting is the formation of thin long crystals of ice—they call them candles—that pile up along the edges.

The other sign is our station wagon pulling in late one Friday night, my mother waving her arms in the headlights to direct the car between the trees. "A little to the right. No. Stop," she calls out, as my father tries to park near the cottage for the first time since the snow melted.

It is March or it is April, and we open the car doors slowly, step out from our warm seats and snug pillows into the cold, barren land.

The sound of gunshot from the darkness. Then another.

"Is it a thunderstorm?" Mom asks.

"No, I don't think so," Dad says, looking up at the dark fingernails of tree against the night sky. There are only a handful of stars, looking scared themselves between tree trunks, but enough to prove that the sky is clear. It couldn't be a storm. "It seems to be coming from the lake," Dad says. "Could be the ice melting."

Then an explosion, like a band of elastic is stretched from the opposite shore to ours, one brave person pulling it back and letting it fly—a zap near us, then an echo on the opposite shore, tectonic plates of ice, one shift causing another, ice cataclysms ricocheting across the universe.

"Time to carry in, girls."

We drop pillows and suitcases on the worn velvet couch, while Dad lies down on the gray linoleum floor. The cottage has no furnace, just a space heater in the living room that he is attempting to light with a match. "Fudge," he says. Forty-five minutes later, he is going to give up. "Girls, you're just going to have to sleep in your clothes tonight." LeAnn carries her two sleeping bags up the stairs and says good night.

Mom pulls cold quilts and blankets from the hall closet and layers them on each of us, one on Carla, another on me, one on Carla, one on me, like dealing out a deck of cards. We lie underneath like mummified mummies, unable to turn over because of the weight. Dampess makes things cold too, and it is difficult to tell if the chill is from the winter-laden blankets, or from the dampness of being in the wrong place at the wrong time. We listen to the squirrels running through the walls.

The next day we rake. In October we raked the maples, the

willow leaves, and the crab apple. Now we've come to rake the oak leaves, which took all year to finally give up and fall. They are wet by this time. Heavy and burdened.

There is no sun or even clouds. Instead the sky is a light steely color like a movie screen that glows gray in a semi-darkened room when you have stayed too long after the picture is over. We have metal rakes and bamboo rakes and the thing to do is just keep going. The temperature never rises over forty-eight degrees. I am wearing three layers, but it is not enough. Mom says, "If you're cold, go put on more clothes."

"I didn't bring any more."

"Well then, you'll just have to keep busy."

I hear a bird screaming in the trees just north of us; I swear it's calling out, "Help, help."

Like loads of hay, we haul leaves to the neighbors' in the back of a wagon. Twelve loads, thirteen loads, we begin to lose count. Dad pitchforks them into a pile that is thirty feet long.

Sunday morning we go to church, and then we pull rakes the rest of the day. It is Easter.

The pioneers of this country followed the wagon ruts across the prairie. For them the destination was the West. A new home. A new life. They shot animals for food and nestled together in the wagon for warmth.

We sleep in our own gray corners inside the cold gray house. We don't have a destination. I want a chocolate bunny.

I look out past our yard of naked trees to the cottages and houses in the distance, imagining that inside each one is a dining table under a bright cheerful light, with cups of colored dye and a bowl of boiled eggs and happy kids with blue and red fingertips.

I watch my parents as they lift a black plastic tarp of leathery leaves up above their heads— "One, two, three"—then they dump it into the trailer. "Let's do one more."

*　*　*

We keep an eye on #14, The Zigzag.

People get frustrated when things don't work out the way they planned. You think you know where you're going. You've picked out a path and—whomp—you're on your way. But then, powie, you start hitting things. Hole #14 is where people blow it.

Even those who've been playing a nice, respectable game will suddenly go nuts. They stop aiming. They swing at the purple cross-boards. They leave little triangular divots of despair by slamming their clubs into the carpet. "People don't realize. Those holes don't go away," Mom says. "Not until next time I put down new carpet."

It was strange being away from our hometown so much of the year. While I was away, it seemed like the rest of my classmates had gone through some kind of Jaycee Halloween Fun House, and come out the other side with manly voices, and boobs, and beer parties in the corn fields. When I walked through the high school, the other students sounded like this:

"How jeeb the wombats last night?"

"Oh, about seventeen!"

Uproarious laughter.

"Next weekend far flung the pernicle barrier."

"Glabulous!"

"She sure is!"

Ha, ha. Heh, heh.

Okay, not exactly like that, but to be honest, I couldn't understand what everyone was talking about. Another problem was that I didn't know who to relate to. After spending the summer taking care of needy tourists:

"We've locked ourselves out of our car."

"Do you have anything for a bee sting?"

In the classroom, I felt more connection to the teachers than the students:

"I brought the wrong book."

"Do we have to take this quiz?"

"How late are you open?"

"Can we get out early?"

"Can I get extra sno-cone syrup?"

"How about extra credit?"

Before we bought Tom Thumb I had some good friends back in Iowa, but like houseplants you forget to water for a few years, they withered.

Grown-ups do a lot of stupid things during their life. If they are lucky they will beget children, who after some nourishment will grow up to become teenagers, who will tell them one day, like a prophet with a vision, just how stupid the parents have been. I don't remember one specific time I questioned my parents, because I'm not sure there was a time when I didn't.

Why are we doing this?

Because there is raking to do.

No, but why are we doing this?

Well, we've got to do it sometime.

No, but why? Why. Are. We. Doing. This?

No one else is going to do the raking for us!

"Tom Thumb just fell into our laps," they had always said, which might be true, but at this point we hadn't taken a vacation for seven years. Our spring and fall weekends were taken up with chores. The raking never seemed to get done. Since I was ten years old we had spent every Easter vacation in an unheated cottage. No one was thanking us. Our customers only came in summer and never saw the work we did. We were not making money. I wasn't sure if my parents enjoyed suffering, or if they simply didn't know any better. Either way, they were dumb.

I was smart.

When she is in Wonderland, Alice encounters a party where everyone is celebrating their Unbirthday, which is every day of the year but one. You have 364 Unbirthdays every year, they explain to Alice, who is understandably thrilled. When I was seventeen I realized that I was, indeed, finally and at last, inherently different from my parents. This came as wonderful news. I had no idea who I was, or who I would become. All I knew was that I was NonJean and NonGeorge. But that left it very open to me as to who I actually *was*. Being *not* like your parents made the possibilities limitless. And limitlessness is what dreams are fueled upon.

(Also, okay, and some discontent.)

And now I will tell you about what makes a stand-up comedian, the one part of our childhood that we do seem to share: at some point in our lives, we realize we might be "outsiders."

In school I got good grades because it gave me something to do. While other kids passed notes to each other, I entertained myself by learning to write backwards. I did a lot of kissing, if you count drama rehearsals, with a guy who I always suspected was gay.

When I think of myself as a teenager, I picture myself doing crafts in my bedroom. It's a weird thing to want to be alone at a time when you are also simultaneously lonely. It's like being tired of milk, so to solve the problem you are pouring yourself another glass of milk. Who would do that?

"You had it too easy with me!" I have said to my mom.

"Yes, it's true. We had it easy with all you girls," she admitted later.

In college I majored in electrical engineering. I don't often admit this, because then people say, "Electrical engineering? Really?" which sounds a lot like, "Why are you doing this?"

My parents couldn't attend my college graduation—it was

Memorial Day Weekend, one of the busiest weekends of the season—so I didn't attend it either. But when I got back to Tom Thumb, Dad cleared a space in the garage where I set up a "studio," a place for me to write songs on my keyboard, while people putted just outside on hole #17. I had decided I was going to become a professional musician.

If I wanted to become famous, I needed a couple of things, not the least of which: self-confidence. I should be able to look people in the eye. So, before I pursued my dreams, I prescribed for myself a giant trip abroad. I would return a new person. I'd be ready to go. Then become a famous rock-and-roll musician. As a backup singer person. Maybe on the keyboard . . . or something. I was still working out the details.

I traveled for a year in New Zealand and Australia. I went backpacking. I tried hitchhiking. It was marvelous.

When I returned to Tom Thumb the next summer, Mom told me that my cousins and aunts and uncles had sorted through belongings from my grandparents while I was away. There were only a few things left behind: some Pyrex bowls, a rubber spatula, and my grandfather's accordion. I took them all. "Nobody wanted this accordion?!"

"Well, you can't take it and just sell it," she said. "You'd have to play it."

So I put an ad in the classified section of the paper, and once a week drove out to a farm nearby, where an eighty-year-old woman in a wheelchair gave me accordion lessons. She kept me late telling me about her polka band in Milwaukee. "We had satin uniforms! No one else had satin uniforms!" For six weeks the customers who played mini golf tried to concentrate to the sound of "Lady of Spain," played at a slow and halting pace, coming from the house. Shrug. The customers should know us by now.

I sent out résumés and cover letters to firms in California. I'd use my engineering degree to land a sweet-paying day job. But no one replied. When the summer was over I was still living with my parents, and I moved back with them to Iowa. It was my father's last year teaching.

Finally in January my parents drove me to the Minneapolis airport. Against all odds, LeAnn had found someone she considered her equal and had married him. They had a little boy named Ryan who rode on Perry's shoulders as we walked to the gate. I was leaving for San Francisco. Dad wandered away somewhere, while we waited for my flight.

"Are you excited?" they asked in turn.

"Sure."

I had thirteen hundred dollars and the address of the youth hostel where I planned to stay while I got started. "I'll look for a job and then probably an apartment."

"Well, we'll miss you," Mom said.

"Do you have quarters for a pay phone in case you need it?" LeAnn asked.

Dad finally returned, blinking back tears, which is how he said good-bye, this time and all the other times to come.

I moved to San Francisco to become a rich and famous rock musician. This is what I say, and it is true. "I arrived with a suitcase in one hand and my grandfather's accordion in the other." That's the other thing I say. It is also true. I know it sounds funny, which is one reason I say it; and it helps after the fact to admit your naïveté quickly, before others discover it ahead of you.

Why did I pursue my dreams? Let's be honest, I had no idea what I was doing.

And I believed I'd be a success because I was different from my parents. They were not a success.

Parents = Not the Type to Win

Me ≠ Parents

Therefore:

Me = The Type to Win

And so, I reasoned, success was inevitable. I hadn't learned much in engineering school. But I had learned logic. This. Was. Logical.

After I checked into the International Network Hostel in the Mission District of San Francisco, I crawled into my bunk and stayed there for a month. I was known as The Girl Who Doesn't Leave the Bed. The girls who cleaned the room each morning vacuumed up around me. "Sorry," they said.

"No, don't worry about it," I replied, from the bed, too terrified to move, too scared to even eat. I needed to find a job. And everything.

It was here at hole #14 several years later—and I'm not making this up—that I had a conversation with my former high school guidance counselor. I was home for a week visiting from California. He was one of Dad's fellow teachers from the high school back in Iowa, and he and his wife were driving through Wisconsin on motorcycles. They just decided to drop in, unannounced, after hearing about Tom Thumb for many years in the teachers' lounge. I went out to say hello. "Nice course," he probably said, because everybody does.

He was also the parent of one of my former classmates. His son, Jeff, was in most of my classes and was co-valedictorian with me at graduation. He told me that Jeff was now married and lived outside of Chicago. He was happy working as an engineer, or computer guy, or something.

"That's nice," I said.

"How about you?" he asked.

I don't remember if I hesitated or if I just blurted it out. Because I never felt ashamed about my choice. I told him I was living in California and pursuing a career in comedy.

"Stand-up comedy?" he said. "Really? I thought you used to be smart."

Take a break to eat some delicious hot POPCORN!

It's day-old.

Not fresh.

Sorry. But isn't it wonderful? Warm and crunchy. Hard to believe it was made yesterday.

We think.

At night, we scoop up what is left over and carry it into the house. The next morning we dump it back in the machine—something we do before customers arrive. They probably don't want to see popcorn poured in from a white kitchen trash bag. But an hour or two under that lamp, and you probably can't tell the difference. Fresh—almost fresh. And it's Monday. People's expectations are always lower on a Monday. (Or at least they should be.)

We won't sell popcorn more than two days old. But the days kind of run together. Sometimes Mom will ask us to taste a sample, which is like carbon dating.

"I think it's fresh," one of us will say, meaning it was made yesterday.

"It could be from the day before," someone else will suggest. We'll have a scientific discussion.

We won't sell popcorn that we wouldn't eat ourselves. But the thing is, we aren't picky. We love popcorn.

When the popcorn is two days old, we dispose of it by eating it. When the popcorn is three days old, we'll probably still eat it, but we shrug first. Four-day-old popcorn we feed to the ducks. Or we feed it to the turtles. Unless we are mad at the turtles because they've been feeding on the ducks. Or we hand the leftovers to our cousins, who are always happy to receive it and get all excited about a white trash bag full of old popcorn. This is another reason to like your cousins: they make your parents' choices appear sane and normal.

There are days when Mom will go into a morning panic. "Did you put that popcorn back into the machine?"

"Do you mean the bag that was sitting by the toaster?"

"I think that's from Tuesday!" she'll say, it being Saturday. She'll dart out the door to outrun a group of canoers who are strolling towards the Snack Shack. Canoers love popcorn. Like a fifty-yard dash run from two different directions, she'll try to scoop it into the trash before they reach the window. Or if time is short, she'll turn off the light so the popcorn machine is dark— maybe they won't notice. Then she'll stand in front of the machine, blocking their view. "What can I get you folks?" she says, giving them a gentle smile. It would not be easy to explain why the machine is full of popcorn but you aren't allowed to buy it.

We eat popcorn every day. We eat it in the ticket booth. We eat it around the firepit. We eat it on rainy days because it's the best way to get rid of it. We devour popcorn as if it's part of our duties, like goats led out in the gorse to eat back the weeds. Eating popcorn, you see, is actually part of our job.

Sometimes Mom will ask us to eat popped popcorn "in a conspicuous way if you can" because she popped too many batches and no one is buying. So we will take turns marching around the golf course, eating the stuff, smiling. Then people will come to the Snack Shack to buy some. Popcorn is contagious.

It's impossible to putt while also eating popcorn, but people try it every day. They hold the club with one hand, the popcorn bag in the other, and then they run out of hands. So they grip the white bag between their teeth and shove their faces inside, like a horse in its feedbag. *Very* sexy. A lot gets spilled. A bag hits the ground about twice a day. The popcorn scatters across the fairway or flies across the green. "Oh, no!" they say, looking over to the ticket booth, as if we are their mom or dad and will know what to do.

Popcorn isn't easy to sweep up, so we use a special vacuum cleaner. His name is Bo Jangles. "Bo! Popcorn!" This is how we start up the vacuum. Our vacuum is a collie. When he hears the word *popcorn*, he comes running.

"Bo! Popcorn!"

"Maybe we should change his name to Popcorn," we say.

"Maybe he'd obey better."

Bo's main talent is running away. But he can also vacuum up one-half bag of popcorn at a time, which tends to be the quantity that most people drop.

The dog prances out onto the course, his white tail swooping the air. He straddles the spill and unrolls his tongue—he knows the white fluffs will stick to the wet surface. Then he rolls them back in his mouth the way an elephant feeds with his trunk. You can listen to him crunch.

"This dog likes popcorn!" the tourists will say. And then they will pour more on the ground, having decided it's more fun to watch the dog than eat the popcorn themselves.

The popcorn machine isn't cleaned all that often—maybe once a summer—but we get away with it anyway. Because my mom has nice-looking legs.

"No, no. You girls! Don't say that!"

But it's true. Once a year the state of Wisconsin sends out a guy to inspect the Snack Shack, to see if it's clean enough, to see if they should renew our license to sell food. You don't get a warning. He just shows up: surprise. But he never seems to "inspect" that much. He never notices that we "wash" our hands by dipping them into a bucket of stagnant water from under the sno-cone machine that's used to catch drips. Or the soft ring of scum that forms inside that bucket because we don't dump it out very often. He doesn't see that we have ant poison on scraps of aluminum foil on the windowsills.

Because he thinks Mom is sexy. He thinks Mom is cute.

"That isn't true!"

"We've seen him staring at your legs, Mom."

"Girls! Don't say that!"

It's weird how this guy flirts. She doesn't ask for it, and never wears makeup, except for lipstick she applies on Sunday on the way to church. Also, Dad is just around the corner by the garage.

Mom doesn't know she's attractive. She has convinced herself that he renews our "confectioners license" because everything *is* okay, that the Snack Shack is in good shape. "I DO clean out the popcorn machine. Not all the time. But sometimes." And then she remembers. "Actually, he did tell me last time that I needed to dump out the old maids more often."

"What do you mean?" we ask.

"Those holes in the metal tray? At the bottom of the machine? The unpopped ones fall through there. Apparently there's another tray you're supposed to empty out every so often. It was kind of embarrassing. I probably had two years' worth."

⅓ cup kernels
¼ cup oil
½ teaspoon Flavacol

These are the ingredients. We know because Mom inked this recipe on a yellow card and taped it to the machine. She doesn't need measurements; this is for us. She wants us to be able to make popcorn, but we won't do it. We wait for her. On desperate evenings when she is away, Dad will make the popcorn.

"What's wrong with this stuff?" we'll say, having a taste.

"Dad made it."

"Oh," we say, dumping it in the fire. One thing you should know, popcorn burns quite well.

Mom's popcorn is by far the best. We do not know why this is. It's just another Mom-mystery, like how to bake a turkey.

People think our popcorn is good because we have a special popcorn machine, the kind they've seen in movie theaters, as if the equipment itself were magic. "But it could be the oil," Mom says. We use 100 percent coconut oil. You don't want to use 100 percent coconut oil at home, or ever. Sure, it tastes good, but it is 100 percent likely to clog your arteries.

"I think it's the Flavacol," she says. Flavacol is what we use instead of regular salt. It's bright orange and powdery and comes from our secret supplier. It's toxic, we are pretty sure. It's full of chemicals, we know. For one, they won't sell it in the supermarket. You need a business license to buy it. We have studied the paragraph down the side of the waxed milk carton it comes in, and the list doesn't end until it's halfway to the bottom. Preservatives, MSG, BHT . . . one of the wonders of chemistry is that there are chemicals so rare and toxic, only businesses get to have them. We take a carton of Flavacol home to use all winter, so that's how it is for us. Chemicals year-round.

Popcorn. A miracle, the kind that lasts for days on end. The sky hath opened up, and God hath sent down little puffs of heaven for us to crunch between our teeth. Crunch. Gnash. Scoop it! Use your cup-shaped fists. You can chaw all night long before your stomach will get full. Plus oil and salt. Everything becomes heavenly with oil and salt.

CHAPTER 15

THE FERRIS WHEEL

*You can discover more about a person in an hour of play than in
a year of conversation.*

—PLATO

A spider is walking across the archway between my living and
dining rooms. He gets to the middle, and then he lets go. Head-
first he plummets to the floor, trusting the tether is attached, putting all his faith in the line that has just come out behind him,
even though he can't even see it. Once at the floor, he turns
around and climbs back up the way he came. Then skiddles to
the right and leaps again; as fast as gravity, he falls towards the
earth. This is the job he is designed to do, to spin his web. This is
his destiny, to trust the invisible cord he has made behind him,
and then to jump. Towards death, in order to sustain his life, that
is, find food.

I am like that spider in that I have always assumed I would
be caught. Saved. By whatever invisible thread there was behind me.

When you look out on #15, sometimes the first thing you'll see is
a kid running up to it. "Ooh, this is my favorite," the little girl
says, setting her pink ball down on the tee even though it's not

her turn to go first, and the rest of her family is still playing the previous hole. But who can blame her? This is The Ferris Wheel. There are eight chairs swaying gently as they sweep down from the top: red, yellow, green, blue, purple, orange, white, and light blue. Candy, it could be made of candy. Like a dream it is turning, and you can picture yourself four inches tall and sitting on one of the benches; they are wooden and look so solid, you'd be safe as you were carried up and around on this magic wheel, flying four feet into the air.

The Ferris Wheel. The Fairies Wheel.

Miniature golf is about putting, and it is about imitating the game of real golf, but additionally, it is about creating the illusion that you are in a magical wonderland. A fantasy world. You can forget about the fact you have a dead-end job or that your roof needs to be replaced. Everything seems so different. This is magic (or at the very least, kooky).

Well, the sign for The Ferris Wheel isn't actually true, but my parents couldn't come up with anything better (and when they phoned Greg, he couldn't recall the wording on the original sign). If your timing is off, your ball won't get swept into the ride. When the chairs come around, the most they can do is give your ball a smack. If you want your ball to get a ride, you'll have to plop it into one of the seats. And, of course, many people do. Because they want it to be true.

People put their balls into The Ferris Wheel seats all the time, not just kids—parents, grandparents, men wearing beer hats—everyone wants their balls to experience the thrill of a carnival ride. Then they watch, the way a parent looks on as her child rides the mechanical rocket outside the grocery, smiling, wondering how it must feel to grip the steering wheel, imagining you are jetting off through space.

Because what is the ball, if not an extension of ourselves? "I'm blue," people say. And "I'm the orange one," people claim. "You're in!" people say. They don't mean *you*, they mean *your ball*. We are the ball we have chosen—or that has been chosen for us by being the last one on the counter after everyone else picked first. (Yellow is the least favorite color, by the way. Yellow is always the color of the person who picked last.)

Hole #15, The Ferris Wheel, is about having a place to Play.

My Adventures in Terrifying Myself led to a much skinnier me—I bought "day job" clothes in a size or two smaller than my usual. I sent out résumés to every company in Silicon Valley, with a cover letter prepared on a cheap typewriter I bought in the Mission. "Seeking an entry level job . . ." I never heard back.

When my savings were sufficiently dwindled, I signed up with a temp agency. I worked as a secretary. When I rode the public buses, I was afraid to pull that string, because I didn't want people to notice me. Instead I waited in the back of the bus, hoping someone else would signal the driver in time for my stop.

It never occurred to me that moving to a strange city might be a bit scary. Never realized it might be, you know, stressful.

I was lonely. So I signed up for a course in comedy with one goal in mind: meet men. The first day of class I learned that the course was not about sketch comedy. "Stand-up? This is a course about telling jokes?" I would have walked out, because I considered stand-up comedy beneath me, except that I had already paid for the class, and also, I had nowhere else to go.

Three weeks later I was in love. Not with a man, but with doing comedy myself.

Life is weird like that. You go into life expecting one thing; you get something else entirely. It's not like muffins. I like muffins. You can throw anything you want into that pan, and no matter what you do, it comes out muffins. It never comes out meat loaf. (That was one of my jokes from my act.)

One day at the end of class, the crotchety comedy teacher wrote down a formula. "I can predict who will be a success," he said. You take the number of times that comic gets onstage in one year, "open mics, anywhere. It doesn't matter." Then you divide that by the number of days in the year. "It's a simple calculation," he said. "If you have less than fifty percent, forget it. Seventy-five percent, maybe. But the people who hit it big are out there every night. Their numbers would be like eighty to one hundred percent."

I worked as a secretary during the day, I went to comedy clubs at night. "I get two days out of one!" I remember bragging. I waited all evening for my five minutes onstage at a small comedy club in the Richmond District. The Holy City Zoo. About the size of a living room, it was where all the famous Bay Area comedians started out.

I told jokes about being from the Midwest. "No one takes me seriously. I have a face that screams 'I Like Corn,'" and then I would mug at the audience. It might surprise you to know this was one of my more reliable jokes.

I was living the "simple calculation." I was racking up my percentage, which was my way of pursuing my dreams. I was still shy, but it was different onstage. It was easy because you knew your purpose: *I am here to make them laugh. I can do anything I want, as long as there is a laugh every five seconds.*

After a couple of years in San Francisco, I was sucked into the downdraft that pulls all entertainers to Los Angeles—some kind of California gravity.

Hollywood was a strange place. I would dress up to go to parties, and eventually a nice-looking guy would sidle up to me. "It's a buddy picture, but with a twist, because one guy is actually a donkey . . ." He'd look over my shoulder then, to see if there was someone else in the room to whom he should be talking instead of me. I went to parties hoping for a date, but it seemed men went to parties to pitch their movies.

But I loved doing comedy. Getting ready for a show. The excitement. Putting on the "performing clothes." Gathering the set list, the props, the water bottle. Running out the door. Arriving to see the crowd gathering. Then afterwards standing around with the other comics, the outsiders, the observers. The truly sarcastic ones.

I used to think I did stand-up because I was a middle child and had a few things to get off my chest. But now I wonder if I had just been too serious as a child. Perhaps, I just wanted to play. Like a roller-coaster ride that ends too soon, your time onstage is much too short, but so thrilling you get back in line to do it again the next day. And the next day. And the next. That's what stand-up comedy is all about, a roller-coaster habit. And eventually, one day, you have accumulated enough material to actually get paid. But this is secondary. It's about play.

When you live on the West Coast, you learn to shrug a lot. There are people who believe in fortune-tellers, auras, the power of vegetables, the wisdom of smells, and I don't know if I could invent things here that would go much beyond the actual beliefs. California also holds a lot of people who just drifted west, always searching for a place where they might fit in. With enough misfits, they form groups, doncha know. And after I had been performing stand-up comedy for a number of years, I was invited to perform at the Elysium, the local nudist colony. I said no.

"They pay seventy-five dollars. You should do it," friends of mine said.

I said no. The next month I said no, and the following month I said no.

"It's not a bad gig," friends told me. They were folksingers as well as comics, and had performed there themselves. "It's hidden in the canyon, and you don't have to be naked yourself."

"I know that," I said.

"It's 'clothing optional.' So it's optional!"

I said no.

Several months later, one folksinger said, "That nudist colony? I did that gig last winter. No one was naked. They all wear clothes when the temp drops below sixty-five."

Winter . . . Maybe I need to be more open-minded, I thought. When in Wisconsin, you go to the corn roast. When in California, perhaps you go to the nudist colony. Just once.

The next time I got a phone call from the activity director at the Elysium, I gave in. When the night of my gig arrived, I was terrified.

My friend Andrew came with me; he's a reassuring force, a gentleman, and everyone's favorite singer/songwriter/optometrist.

You do see strange things at a nudist colony, first of all, a "gift shop." Incense, dream catchers, and the usual hippie stuff. I picked up the free newspaper, which seemed intended for nudists around the United States. In the back were advertisements for couples who wanted to "swap wives."

"Hmm," I said to Andrew, "so maybe this isn't only about nudism."

But I had to do the gig. We went to the small "community room," which was about the size of a family den and had wood paneling just like one. There was a fireplace on one end, and twenty bean bag chairs on the floor. Out the window you could see the gray hulking shape of the backyard sweat lodge. Each bean bag chair was draped with one senior citizen, who in turn was draped, more or less, in a bathrobe. *This is what it looks like in a nudist colony?* For months I had pictured a much more—uh—awake group of people who might heckle me with "Take it off" or something of that ilk. But these people had smoked a lot of pot, either earlier that day or cumulatively over the previous forty years.

There was only one naked person, and unfortunately, he was the host. A jocular man in his early sixties, he had gray hair and a rather biggish belly, and walked to the front of the room absolutely, bouncingly naked. "Our performer tonight originally comes from the Midwest . . ." I stood in the back amazed; it was my first time being introduced by a naked person.

It is traditional for the performer to shake hands with the host as the microphone is passed. And so, as expected, he extended his hand. In front of a semi-live audience, I shook his hand, keeping my eyes firmly on his eyes, pretending his private parts weren't just inches from our friendly grasp.

The set went fine, as far as jokes go when delivered to a group of people whose faces, due to the nature of bean bags, were mostly aimed at the ceiling. I did my schtick clothed in a skirt and a cute, perky top that exposed a couple of inches of tummy—my consolation to the naked community, my attempt at "reaching out."

When the show was over, Andrew and I were invited to enjoy their outdoor swimming pool, which we did, clad in swimsuits. We lingered along the edge as stars glittered through the oak tree above us, when the host walked by. "I just wanted to thank you again for coming out to perform tonight," he said, putting his hand out and leaning over the side so I could shake. It was a simple gesture, except that leaning towards the pool thrust his personal parts just inches from my face.

"You're welcome," I said, pretending everything was normal, which is another thing you learn to do in California.

"Okay, let's get out of here!" I said to Andrew. "I think he did that on purpose."

"Um . . ."

"Did he do that on purpose? I think he did that on purpose!"

"You may be right," he said, reluctantly. "That could have been on purpose."

When I moved to California I came with a suitcase with colored notes my mother stuffed into the corners: "Go, June!" and "Watch out, you California boys!" I also had a full bank account of Trust in Humanity. Now there was less.

My parents retired from teaching four months after I moved to San Francisco. They sold our house in Iowa, packed up everything, and moved up to Wisconsin, about the same time I found my first apartment in the Haight. My parents demolished the old cottage and laid the foundation for their new year-round house, about the time I first tried stand-up comedy.

"It crumbled like dust," Mom said.

"When I saw the first wall come down, and all that dust, I knew we had made the right decision," Dad said. "Starting over. With a new house."

We had been spending our summers in a cottage made of cardboard, something Carla and I already knew, having pushed sewing pins into the bedroom walls to hold up pictures we cut from *National Geographic* magazine.

The new house had a furnace and insulated walls, so they could live there all winter. It also had windows on the side, so while eating breakfast my parents could watch a family of ducks walk across the lawn. Sandhill cranes. A great blue heron feeding in the channel. A misty fog on the water until the air above it began to warm. They mailed me glamour shots they had taken of the yard and the lake, showing the change of seasons, the leaves turning, the snow all around. They took so many photos, like parents who bring home a new baby. Clearly they had fallen in love with Tom Thumb, again.

One year I was performing at a major comedy club, and the show must have gone well because I got phone calls from all the major networks, ABC, CBS, NBC, and a couple of big-time production companies, about casting me in a sitcom. Maybe even my *own* sitcom. *I'll be the next Mary Tyler Moore.* I went to dozens of meetings. Ate at fru-fru restaurants. I was so sure I would be successful that I turned down an audition for *Saturday Night Live.* "Thanks, but I don't really do that sort of thing, put on wigs and play weird characters." My career was being managed by the best managers in town, whose roster was made up entirely of celebrities—and me.

I didn't get my own sitcom that year, but I had gotten so close that there was good reason to continue. *Maybe next year.*

But I always felt as if it was continuing somewhere—summer, at Tom Thumb—like a parallel universe, and another version of me—much younger—was waking up on a July morning to discover that Mom had already cleaned out the pools and Dad had already fixed #14, and LeAnn was painting chairs, and I was wondering what to eat for breakfast. That it was going on. Still. That time had not stopped but was going around and around, one continuous summer.

If I could afford only one trip home, I came in the summer. Like the motors themselves, time moved slowly at Tom Thumb, one year like the next, the faces on the other side of the window still familiar, only taller, older, the teenagers now grown-ups, the grown-ups now grandparents. The tourists still parked too close to the fence under the sign PLEASE PARK CLOSE TO FENCE. The cotton candy still got too large to fit out the front window. So reassuring to see Tom the cook, the Camp Onaway boys, or The Cotton Candy Family. And the WROE-fans. "Hello, there!" I'd say. "How's life in Milwaukee?"

"Good! How's CALIFORNIA TREATING YOU?" Faith said a bit too loudly. "Are you famous yet?"

"Almost!"

Just as Tom Thumb continued to run season to season, I had rhythms of my own seventeen hundred miles away: acting classes on Wednesdays, voice lessons on Saturdays, new publicity photos taken every two and a half years.

Meanwhile, my sisters married men they met at college. At a reasonable age, they started making babies. They bought homes. They settled in the Midwest. They baptized five boys. Three for LeAnn, two for Carla. Her last one, Ben, was blessed right here in Beasley Creek as I, the godmother, held him, standing in my bare feet, the hem of my summer dress splashing in the water. Responsibility and irresponsibility. Figure of authority and casual indulgence.

Every Friday night I performed at the Comedy Store. I opened with a joke about my small breasts. "I prefer to call them 'travel-sized.'"

They visited their in-laws on holidays.

I made soup using ramen noodles, adding beet stems, which made it pink (and which I could get for free if I asked nicely at the farmers' market).

They send out cards at Christmas with pictures of their families standing together.

I started using a violin in my act which I referred to as Dr. Violin.

They breast-fed their babies.

I wrote a song about how cats cough up their food.

They bought school supplies in the fall as each of their boys began kindergarten.

I acted the part of a green space alien in a movie.

They didn't ask me questions about my life in Hollywood, probably for the same reason I didn't ask about how they got their kids to bed at night. Because I had no idea that it might be difficult.

"My favorite hazard is the boat," one of the nephews said one Christmas. "Whatever you do, don't replace the boat." The boys looked out the window at the snow covering the yard. "It's too bad we can't play mini golf right now."

"All the hazards are put away, you know," my mom said.

"Yeah," the boys sighed.

"What about snow mini golf?" I said.

"What's snow mini golf?" one of my nephews asked.

"I'm not sure, but I think we should play it."

"What in the world?"

I wasn't a mom. I didn't have to be normal. It was my job to be the artsy aunt.

"You need putters?" Mom asked.

"Of course!"

"I'll find the ticket booth key."

"Be careful you don't lose the balls in the snow," Dad said.

Bundled in coats with hats and scarves over our faces, we tried to find evidence of the mini golf course under the snow. "How about . . . here." I plunged my mittened hand to make a hole somewhere in the vicinity of hole #4. "Why not? We'll never find the real holes!"

And we whomped at the balls, which traveled only a couple of feet each time. It wasn't really doable, playing mini golf in the snow, and that was half the fun. So ridiculous. These boys always responded to the absurd—smart kids, all of them.

"Hole #3 is actually easier to play now," one nephew said. "The snow has leveled out the molehill!"

Sixty feet away there were ice fishermen lying on the ice on Bass Lake. They lifted themselves up off the ice to look at us. Then they looked back into the hole they had drilled into the lake. "Who spends Christmas on their bellies staring into a hole?" we asked each other.

"But who plays mini golf in the snow!"

On Christmas Eve Dad would read aloud from his devotional. "The title is 'Live a holy life.' You should be a light for other people. Live so that they will see the good things that you do . . ."

On New Year's Eve I'd make my own resolution: to look in the mirror more often. I wasn't really good at paying attention to my appearance and too often would discover hair sticking up on top of my head as I left an audition, or something brown between my teeth, or a bristle from my makeup brush sitting happily on my nose. I vowed to wash my hair more often, and not just brush it in a way that I'm hoping no one will notice.

The problem with Hollywood wasn't that I failed; the problem was that I kept getting *close*, over and over again. Like a gambler at the slots, I found it hard to know when to walk away; harder still, because everyone I knew was also gambling.

Los Angeles: You can have an argument with a friend, and then you never see that person again, you never cross paths. This is a city. But there is no buzz, just hustle. We are all vying for the best parking. The least blemished fruit. No one has dinner parties. No one has the time. We are all hungry to be remembered and loved after this. Today is not what we live for. The present is never enough in Los Angeles. The air is brown, and the drive is horrendous. We are living, like fundamentalists of all kinds, for the coming afterlife . . . In the case of this town, for fame, for future fortune. For the days when our talent will be recognized and money will pour in, and we'll get the house of our dreams high up on the hill, or so high on the hills it's in the Pacific Northwest, just outside of Seattle. Los Angeles is not a destination. This city is just a path. Days are not to be enjoyed for the day-ness of them. Days are small clumps of clay into which we must fashion a tile of our own to pave the path to our future glory.

All over town there were actors and writers putting sticky notes on their bathroom mirrors. "You deserve it!" one note says. "You are beautiful!" says another, on the dashboard of their car. "God wants you to be rich." Back home the farmers prayed for rain or sun, or a good soybean yield, so perhaps I shouldn't be so judgmental. Still, praying to God to make you a celebrity always seemed a little crass. You know, for God to deal with, in the big picture of things. In light of droughts, hurricanes, and bedsores.

Some people added a rationalization. "Once I'm famous I can help people. After I get my own sitcom!" But I would think that God might see through that kind of bargaining. One would hope. For him to be the Almighty and all that.

Not that I was above praying for help with the rent.

Once, as a birthday gift, a friend gave me a crystal on a string. "This will bring you good luck and success," he said, putting it over my head.

"Well, thanks. What is it?"

"A crystal. Powerful stuff. Crystals can bring you all kinds of good vibes."

Does that include salt? You know there are a lot of crystals in table salt.

"Thanks," I said, but I never wore it. I'm from the Midwest; if I ever start believing in something weird, I'll have the good sense to keep it a secret.

After thirteen years in Hollywood I have an address book filled with friends I can't call anymore. Some of them have died, suicides, drug overdoses. Others are names of people who have become too famous. Like the dead, the famous friends are also removed from your life. They no longer live in the cracking apartment building just around the corner. They are in another world now, arisen, to a place much better than ours.

Each year I drove up to Sequoia National Park. I'd set up a tent and spend a week or two, camping alone. I'd walk through the trees, write in my notebook at night. After all those years of going to the state park with Carla, this seemed the right way to celebrate a birthday.

For months I've been having the same dream, over and over. I am driving an old car up a steep road. But the hill is so steep that the car is almost falling off. As I drive, it is almost tumbling over, falling below, me with it. There are a group of houses high up on the slope, and that is what I am aiming for. But the roof of the car is being pulled backwards by gravity, lifting off of its tires. How did the people in those houses get up there in the first place? And once they are there, is it nice to live in such a place? Do they dare ever leave? I keep driving, but I'm having second thoughts: Is this a good idea? Is this not a good idea?

It's about Hollywood. I mean, I think that's what the dream is about.

A few years ago I stopped performing comedy. It felt as right for me to stop as it had for me to start in the first place. These days I write mostly poetry. I still perform but on different stages now: coffeehouses and literary festivals, poetry slams here and in Europe. The goal is still the same—be entertaining—but there is no chance of getting rich. It's a modest life. But I love the other poets. Who would be so dumb as to write poetry in Southern California when you could be writing a screenplay? Why write for free, people tell us, when you could be writing the next blockbuster? Who would give up the chance, however slim, to make a zillion dollars?

We would. I love the poets, who are as crazy-idealistic as I am.

Once in a while I get a phone call and drive across town for an audition. HGTV needs a host for its new show. "Someone who knows how to use a microphone and is also familiar with arts and crafts." *That's me!* I think, getting my hopes up. But nothing ever comes of it.

Somehow I turned forty.

Life is absurd. Life is unpredictable.

My parents would say that it is all ruled by God. And that may be. It seems to be that God embodies just about everything that I don't understand. And that is, truly, a vast amount.

I don't claim to have any answers. But I like admitting that. That was what I liked about comedy; your job was to be the fool, to go first, so everyone in the audience could follow and be a fool right along with you.

But now, I have lost the reason to be here in Los Angeles. Like an expatriate who spends fifteen years working in China, teaching English perhaps, and then one day wakes up and realizes, "I am not Chinese." Then where does he go? Back home? Who would he be able to talk with about dim sum and red lanterns? Who would understand him now? Would he be even more a foreigner in his own land than he was living in China for those years?

Almost every day I drive past the Capital Records building in Hollywood, which is shaped to resemble a stack of records. There is even a needle on the top, so it looks like an old record player with 45s. *That would be an interesting hazard, a stack of records. Dad could attach a motor so it would turn.* Even in Los Angeles, when I am living half a continent—and what feels like half a century—away, I am thinking of hazards for Tom Thumb. This too will be coming to an end.

CHAPTER 16

THE WEIRD BLUE PIPE THING

Hello. Tom Thumb.

—My mom, answering the phone, 1974–present

I have a strong propensity in me to begin this chapter very nonsensically, and I will not balk my fancy.—Accordingly I set off thus:

—Laurence Sterne, *The Life and Opinions of Tristram Shandy, Gentleman*

We used to have a goldfish when I was a kid. Then one morning when I came down to breakfast it was dead. And I said, "Well, that's dumb."

So too is August.

August always comes as a shock. Summer is almost over, and there is nothing you can do about it. After flourishing for months, everything is going to turn brown at the same time. And then die. You are supposed to be okay and not freak out about that.

But what's really breaking your heart isn't the loss of green things and warm weather, it is realizing that you are running out of time. Summer is going to end. You haven't accomplished all you had hoped. Not gone boating as many times. Not swum in the lake often enough. Not visited your parents, your grandparents, your college friends. The deck may not get stained. The walls washed. The nephews taken for an overnight camping trip. There are still a couple of weeks left, but not enough for all you planned.

Los Angeles. It's August 6. There are twenty-seven days left this summer before we close Tom Thumb for the last time. I want to talk to you about grumpiness. I am grumpy. The best thing about being grumpy is the opportunity to use the word *grumpy*, which remains one of my favorite-sounding words. Also, the observed fact that when you tell people you are grumpy, they seem to be happy to leave you alone.

Sold. I don't want it to be true.

The night I got the news, I went to a retro club to go dancing with my friends Aimee and Annie, but I couldn't dance. "We've had the mini golf for thirty years," I tried to yell over the 1970s music, "and now it's going to be GONE." People like 1970s music these days the same way they like to put on a shirt that they wore when they were fourteen. So odd but innocent. Memories are also so.

Mom and Dad are surprised that you seem the one most sentimental of all of us about losing the mini golf.

Yeah, me too.

Is that because you've moved so far away? LeAnn and I have been living much closer. Do you think that's the reason?

I have no idea.

Even though it's been for sale for over a year now, the reality of letting go of Tom Thumb Mini Golf is oh, so slowly trying to creep into my reality. Can you use the word *reality* twice in one sentence? And if you do, pray tell, what does that indicate?

Inevitable. Tragic. Hopeless. How can I eat? Wanting to run to the rescue. Wanting to play the message back, "We've decided to keep Tom Thumb forever." A miracle! The other message must have been my imagination or a strange quirk of the Samsung playback.

Bob disappeared from my life sometime in June and, two-months-of-silence-later, called yesterday. Left a message: "You'll never guess where I am! On the way to Las Vegas! A friend of mine's having a party . . . blah blah blah . . ." I'm not calling back. I don't want to sound crass, but it's too late. I don't care anymore. I would rather be swimming in the lukewarm lake.

"It's really warm now, June," Mom said on the phone this afternoon. "I mean, it's still cold, but it's warmer than it's been all summer."

"I'll be there," I said.

Tomorrow, early in the morning, I fly home. One last time.

Welcome to #16. (Go ahead and scream.) It doesn't look inviting. There isn't very much level ground before the ramp rises in front of you. It almost looks vertical. In any case, your job is to make it to the top. It usually takes a few tries. (I highly recommend using some "follow-through.") When you get to the top, you really don't have any control over what happens next. What happens next is that you'll be "sorted."

On top there are two concentric circles, smoothly rounded into the concrete and painted light blue like a swimming pool. There are two pipe openings: one in the center, and one in the back. Your ball, if you're lucky, will fall into the middle one. Then it will rattle marvelously through a pipe and emerge gently, delicately, onto the green, like a well-behaved violin student who stands up on cue for her recital and plays perfectly for the adults who clap their hands with equally apt timing and precision. Ta-da. Your ball rolls out towards the hole. Not a guaranteed hole-in-one but lovely nonetheless.

There is also a second pipe. No one likes the second pipe. If your ball bounces too hard up the incline and rolls right over the center opening—it's going too fast!—you'll watch it get funneled through a short pipe into a second green behind it. This is not the green you want. There is no cup here. Let's call it what it is: purgatory. You will have to take another stroke just to get your ball to the "actual" green. That's where you'll find the hole.

You really, *really*, need to avoid falling into purgatory. The strange truth is that most people who land here never find their way out. It doesn't look that hard to exit—one putt should do it—because the opening to the real green is wider than a foot and a half. But there is something about the purgatory green that is so *disheartening*. If you miss the exit on the first try, it's likely you'll never leave at all. You'll putt again and again, swinging at the ball to watch it rebound off all the walls of purgatory, because once hope has left you, so does your aim.

The main obstacle of #16 isn't the steep fairway or even the two pipe openings on top. The hazard here, nearish the end, seems to be inside your own head. (I don't make the rules. I'm just reporting what I have seen.)

Hole #16, The Weird Blue Pipe Thing, is about Bewilderment.

In the parking lot there are brown maple leaves, a stem from a pair of sunglasses, a smattering of cigarette butts, a metal washer, and bubble gum wrappers. Along the shore the cattails look like half-eaten corn dogs with white fuzz foaming from the bitten-off top. August. It has always looked like this. Except this year there is a Century 21 Real Estate sign out by the road. SOLD.

"Closed Labor Day, huh?" says a semi-naked man. He pulls his arms behind his back to take a big ape-stretch; his bare belly says "hello" in front of him. There is a six-day beard under his mirrored glasses, and it is clear this man has not forgotten about the purpose of a vacation: to relax a bit, let go of any tendencies to be uptight about one's appearance. He reads again the hand-lettered sign on the ticket booth:

CLOSED AFTER LABOR DAY

—

THANKS FOR A GREAT SUMMER!

(AND ALL 30 YEARS!)

"Yeah," Dad says, leaning a bit on the front ledge to answer him.

"Boy, I hope they're open next year, so we can buy this kind of stuff." He looks over at the Snack Shack, nodding. He means he wants to be able to buy treats.

"Well, as far as we know they'll be open next year," Dad tells him.

"Well, good. We'll be here to find out."

It is August 7. There are twenty-six days before my parents close up the mini golf for the end of the season. The new owners will get the keys four weeks later, after my parents have moved out.

I am walking around the yard, by the creek, and along the shore. Just yesterday I was at the Hollywood Sav-On Pharmacy, standing in the "households" aisle, wondering whether I could afford to buy a package of mothballs. Now here I am, in the most beautiful place on earth, and I am thinking of it as mine. This is wrong in the first place; it belongs to Mom and Dad. And I have come home on a flight they paid for, which is wrong in the second place.

August has always been the month when you look at things

differently. Leaves. How they may not always be green. Your blue
jeans. They have been folded at the bottom of your dresser. "Oh,
hello," you say to the jeans. "I remember you," as you take them
out for the first time since May.

My parents have sold Tom Thumb. For just over half a million
dollars. The land has gotten so valuable that it took four people
pooling together to buy it.

Right now, I have about two hundred dollars in my savings.
I am forty years old, but I am even more impoverished than
my parents were back in 1973, the year they bought this land.
They already owned a small house they could mortgage to get a
down payment to buy a second place. They had a brother who
urged them, and they also had naïveté and boredom. Of all
these things, the only one I have is naïveté. Or a wished-for
naïveté.

The sun overhead heats the back of my neck as I stand at the
front counter of the ticket booth. I lean my chest on the felt top,
then I kick my legs behind me, the same way I did when I was
fifteen. Just to remember. This is what I used to do.

"That same old cash box," I say to Mom, who is coming down
the path. "I can't believe it's hung in there all these years."

"Just barely," Mom says. "Don't lean so hard on the counter."

"It was here when we bought the place, right?"

"Oh, I'm sure. Greg left it for us." She grabs the checkbook
from the ticket booth and turns to leave. "Oh, by the way, we're
keeping the money box open this year. Don't close it after you
wait on someone. Dad put some screws in, but the hinges are
almost giving out. He's worried that it might not make it all summer, the strain of opening and closing it."

"Aren't you worried about people reaching in and taking
money if you leave it open?"

"We're just not worrying about it."

"But sometimes Dad doesn't close the front flap of the ticket booth—"

"Oh, he's always forgetting to close that thing."

"But someone could . . ." I reach my fingers under the flap to try to unlatch it from the outside like we did when we were bored teenagers. Fingertips from the side, turn the latch counterclockwise, push up just a touch—click.

"We're just not—just let it go, June. We only have about three weeks left."

"If someone only takes a twenty, well, you know that could probably buy two new fishing tackle boxes."

She ignores me and starts walking towards the house. I hold out some twenties. "Well, at least can I hand you some of these extra bills?"

"What do you want me to do with them?"

"Put them away someplace." I say that I'm from the Big City now and I don't like a lot of money sitting around.

She comes back to the ticket booth, steps inside, and looks into the money box. "We need these. We get fifties every once in a while, and even a hundred—"

"Seriously? People are paying with hundred-dollar bills these days? For mini golf?"

"Some of these folks carry around just incredible cash. The guy who bought our little fishing boat. He had a billfold full of hundreds, and he peeled out three just like that."

"Really?" I gasp. "That old rowboat? I remember when I rowed it over to Long Lake—"

"Maybe we shouldn't have gotten rid of it." She pushes the Dutch door open and steps out of the ticket booth. "I'm going inside the house."

"I'll watch." I sit down on the kitchen stool, look out onto the course, then check the cheat sheet to remind myself what to charge when people come: Four dollars for adults. Three dollars for children. It's been thirty years since we came here, and the prices are still way too low.

A woman and a young boy approach the counter. "I see you guys have a SOLD sign up," she says. "The new owners, they're going to keep the mini-putt and everything?"

"Yeah!" I say. I am trying to sound cheerful.

"I'm thrilled. When we saw it was for sale we were kinda sad," she says. She bends below the ticket booth counter to talk to her son, then she looks up at me. "He said, 'Mommy, I wanna buy it.' 'How much money do you have in your piggy bank?' Not even enough for a golf game, let alone enough for the whole thing." And then she adds, in what has to be the supersweetest mom-voice, "But we can still come back next year because somebody else bought it. That's right, huh?" she says to me. "But it'll never be as nice, probably."

"Well-errr." I'm not sure what to say. "We hope it will be."

"I've been coming here since I was his age," she says, glancing down at him. And then she gazes out at the course. "Yeah."

"Yeah," I say.

When you talk to customers, there is a lot of time spent looking out in the same direction at the same time, not speaking, like a couple of cowboys in the saddle, pausing to view the rock outcropping up ahead. "Yup," she says.

She must be just waiting for someone else to arrive. But she is not leaving, and I cannot get away.

"This place actually even got nicer over the years," she says. "I remember coming here when I was a kid and it wasn't—" She stops. "I think it's awesome now. It's wonderful."

"My parents have really put their hearts into the place." I let my voice drop at the end of the sentence like I have learned from years of acting classes. It says, "I am done speaking. So leave me alone now. That is my final word."

"Did you grow up here?" she asks.

"Yes."

"It must have been like growing up at Disneyland."

I laugh. I am starting to feel irritable. This customer seems to be taking the sale personally. She wants to get all sentimental and talk about it. But I'm not in the mood. What am I supposed to do, admit that I'm falling apart?

There are twenty-one days to go. It is August 12. My shoulders ache and my eyes are red, and I look as if I stayed up all night watching zombie movies. There is a breeze in the trees and a red-faced turkey vulture overhead. He looks like me, or me like him. I set my alarm for 8 am, trying to get up early to help this morning, but the California in me was awake all night long. Now I am on my hands and knees at #17 dabbing white paint onto the spots that I patched yesterday with wood-fill. Mom is scraping the back window on the Snack Shack, getting ready to paint it. Dad is replacing a blade on #17.

It feels like business as usual. We are making repairs as if we plan to stay forever. "Isn't the place sold already?" asks Jim, the retiree who lives around the corner and comes in every day on his motorcycle. "You're gonna get the place so nice you're not going to want to leave!" There is an actual "to-do list" of required repairs that the buyers requested after the house inspection, but we aren't doing those. These are extra.

Things keep breaking now that the end is near. Dad had just attached the blade to The Paddle Wheel Boat when a young boy fell onto The Airplane on #13. The whole wing assembly broke off and was lying on the grass, and before we had even looked up from our own jobs, my dad was over there with his wrench and kneeling on the grass to fix the thing. He takes it all in stride now. He looks at the object; he assesses both the cause and the cure. He takes it back to his workbench, spends the next six hours tightening the bolts, and complains about it the rest of the evening. It's like that. "Someone must have sat on it. The brackets were bent!"

Dad is stressing out, spending more time these days resting and listening to Mexican oompah music on the headphones. Perhaps this is the right time for them to sell after all.

I had planned to become a whopping success in entertainment, and then I'd sweep in and buy this place from Mom and Dad so they could retire. I never expected to, you know, fail. And I never expected the property value to, you know, skyrocket. Sometime in the 1990s the secret got out about this area—the crystal clear lakes, available shoreline for summer homes. The word spread, somehow, and people from farther away started to come here. "They are coming up from Chicago and buying up the old cottages. They tear them down and build these huge monsters," Dad has said. "Did you see that mansion on your way in?" Mom will ask. It was built by some hockey star or football star. It's an ugly house. Whatever. But with the demand for land, property values have kept rising and rising. "Our property taxes are quite high now," Mom has told me. "We could never afford to live here if we didn't have the business; not on a teacher's pension." This was how my parents look at it. They have never taken a salary from Tom Thumb; there isn't much left over after expenses. "But we get to live here! In this beautiful place!"

My parents are moving to a house five miles away, on the edge of town. It is not on a lake. They will have "lake access," which means you don't get to see it out your window, but you can walk down the street a ways to get to a dock you can call your own. The taxes are cheaper that way.

Last night I got to meet two of the four new owners when Matt and his wife came with their kids to play mini golf. Matt looked like a sportscaster, all his hairs combed too neatly to one side, but I can't hold that against him. His wife smiled a lot. She said she played at Tom Thumb when she was a teenager and worked as a babysitter for some children up the road. She said she thought she remembered me waiting on her. I told her I didn't remember her, but I said, "It's quite possible," because I thought I should pretend not to hate them.

As the new owners finished their game, Mom and Dad hovered around like a couple of hyperactive Girl Scouts— embarrassingly helpful. "We are just so grateful," they said, and "Let us know what we can do." And they sounded so cheerful, and Matt's family was cheerful, and it was all so painfully cheerful.

Then new owners introduced their two daughters. One is six and, as it turns out, the other one is ten years old. The same age I was when *my* father purchased this mini golf course. She was dangling her putter over her feet and wiggling her bare toes in her flip-flops. Like a kid. She smiled and twisted to the right and left, a little-girl belly poking out from under a white tank top. I used to have a tank top that like. I used to have that same girlish belly. "I'll write down some things for you," Dad was saying to them, "about the motors and such."

I ducked into the ticket booth. She is me! The back window of the ticket booth is always covered in dust and spiderwebs, and that's what I looked through to stare at her. Ten looks so young. This is the age when I started waiting on people. I looked that young when I started here?

While the grown-ups were talking (my parents to her parents), she walked up to the ticket booth to turn in her club. Here was my chance to talk to myself! Or rather, her. "So what do you think?" I said, or something equally dumb. Gah! It is always impossible to find the right words when the right words are actually right in front of you, but you can't say them to a complete stranger, like "Do you have any idea what you're in for?" or

"What do you think about your family moving to a mini golf course?" or "You probably don't realize the workload that's ahead or the holes on your bedroom ceiling where the squirrels will drop bits of leaves. Or what it will be like to spend Easter with a rake in your hand, wearing damp "work clothes," and piling load after load of leaves onto the bed of a truck borrowed from a neighbor, and you forget until Sunday night that you have American Studies homework and a test the next day on the Louis and Clark Expedition, something you remember while you go to the creek to fill a bucket with water . . ."

Instead, "Tomorrow is the first day of school for you?"

"Yes!" she exclaimed, obviously very excited about school, just as I used to be.

"What grade will you be in?"

"Fifth!" The same grade I was in when my parents bought Tom Thumb.

"That's cool," I said.

She doesn't know what terrible things might come. I don't know if I wanted to warn her, tell her that she was going to be okay, or if I just wanted to crawl inside her brain and find out who I used to be, before this all happened. "Are you excited about living here?" I asked.

"Oh, we aren't going to live here," she said. "We have a house already."

Of course. We don't know who, among the new owners, is going to live here, but it doesn't matter anyway; it's not going to be the same as it was for us. This new house doesn't have holes from squirrels. They won't need to dedicate whole weekends to raking—most of those trees are gone. And then I hear her parents joke that they bought the place hoping it will improve the little girl's score when she plays real golf . . . Maxi golf? Not work? But so you can play golf better? *So you aren't like me at all, and this isn't at all like it was for us . . .*

* * *

There aren't many days left here. I know that selling Tom Thumb and this land is a terrible idea, but I haven't figured out a way to stop it. We'd have to hire someone else to run Tom Thumb so my dad could retire. We'd have to get some place in town for him to live. And Mom too. But I don't have that kind of money. Okay, I don't have *any* money. And I have spent the last umpteen years developing excellent skills for which there is no job.

It is August 14. There are nineteen days to go. Mom and I are swimming in Beasley Lake, just the two of us, as usual. It's a slow leisurely breaststroke, a gentle swim as always. Our heads above the surface. Our hair stays dry because we never go underwater.

"How far do you wanna go?" I ask.

"Oh, let's just see how it goes, maybe across the lake," she says.

There is the sound of warblers and the buzz of an occasional red-winged blackbird. The water is lighter in color near the edge, not because it's more shallow, but as it reflects the grass along the shoreline.

"Have you ever swum underwater?" I ask.

"I swam underwater when I was a counselor at Girl Scout camp. Back in high school. To get your junior lifesaver license, you had to dive."

There are a couple of boats sharing this small lake, but they are on the far end. So we swim straight out from shore to the buoy in the middle. It is white and cigarette-shaped with a faded orange circle on one side. It is supposed to warn people they aren't allowed to speed through here, but the words have all faded in the sun. Instead of SLOW NO WAKE, all you can see is the letter S.

"But after the second surgery on my ear—it must have been in my twenties—the doctors told me not to go underwater anymore. It wouldn't be good for it. Anyway, I'll be all healed in heaven."

Today the lake is dark blue and rippled. As I look out across it, I feel weightless.

"In heaven I'll be able to swim underwater," she continues. "I'll be able to *breathe* underwater. The lake feels colder today than yesterday, don't you think?"

As I move my arms in little strokes, the water falls in small droplets, like the sound of wavelets on the shore of a lake after a small boat passes. I am the small boat.

This is not a big lake, but we have plenty of room to ourselves. Fifty feet below us. The shorelines far to either side. It's like infinity. The lake makes no sound. It is stillness. It is like the coming of evening. Like the cool end of the day. And we kick underwater without splashing.

In Los Angeles I go to the Hollywood YMCA. I still haven't adjusted to pool swimming. It's hard to think of it even as swimming. It is so different from this lake. First, there are definite limits; you have to pay attention. You lose track of yourself and you'll crash into concrete. Also, people are watching. You can't just stop and look at your toes, all green-looking five feet beneath you. And the loudness. It's best to just accept it. Try to think of it as excitement rather than what it really is: noise hitting tiles, to rebound against another set of tiles, and then more tiles. Just like you in that pool, hitting one wall and turning around to fly towards another.

Here in Beasley, what we love the most is not paying attention. We float. We coast. We look up at the sky. "It's hard to believe that heaven will be more beautiful than this, but it will be. It will be."

There is something about being in this lake, the luxury of this water, that makes my mom think of heaven. She likes to talk about heaven when we swim.

I listen.

I mean, for the most part. I don't know for sure if there is a heaven or not, but she is so happy when she talks about it. The last thing in the world I want to do is say anything to spoil her dreams about it.

"Heaven will feel more like home than our home does. Let's wait for that pontoon boat to pass us," she says.

We stop to tread water, and I stare at my hands coming up out of the lake, the nails so white. Dirt finally and magically all soaked away. And the sea creatures they appear to be, monsters, or the appendages of monsters rising from the depths, all pink, wrinkled, faded versions of the fingers I used to have.

There is no reason to try to tell her that heaven might not have all the specific things we don't get to have here on earth. Or that I have a lot of doubts about preachers who try to "sell" their religion by telling people that heaven will give them everything they desire. I want her to be happy, but a lot of what she says about heaven sounds like wishful thinking.

"In heaven you will work—it will be fun, but you will work. You spend your life working, why wouldn't you have a job in heaven? Once we find out we're good at something, we get to do it in heaven too."

What am I good at? Being sarcastic. That sure will be a fun job in heaven. Perhaps uncommon and therefore very much needed.

My mother is a better person than me. It is true. She is kinder; she is more thoughtful. She worries about total strangers on a regular basis. She prays for people she sees in the news. If she is having trouble falling asleep at night, instead of becoming anxious (like me), she thinks through everyone in her family and says a prayer for each. If she gets through the list, she starts praying for friends and people in her church, then people she has seen in town.

When I have a hard time falling asleep, I pour myself a glass of red wine and sip it faster than I would like. I read a book under the covers.

"It's hard to imagine eternity," I say. "Our own lifetimes seem so long."

"But boy, when you get older you realize how short it is. It goes faster and faster as you get older, you know. It goes by so fast. I don't feel like it's such a long life at all. Let's just splash a bit as we go to make sure those boats see us," she says, and I let her go ahead of me.

I look down at my legs and feet. The water makes them appear smaller than they are, as if they are farther away from me, disappearing in the distance.

"And yet sometimes when you look back," Mom says, "you can see where you were at different points, that there were different chapters or almost different—almost like a different life there and there and there."

And we continue out farther from the shore, heads above the silken surface like turtles, or crocodiles, or icebergs, or the dry ends of sticks that are mostly submerged.

"You know, June, of all you girls, I've always thought that you remind me the most of me."

"But—" I mumble something.

"You probably don't want to hear that. But of all you girls," my mom says, "I always thought that you were the most like me."

"I don't—I'm not—" But I don't bother finishing the sentence. I am treading water, my legs circling out away from me, two gears that don't quite meet, spinning against each other, but threatening to fly off in either direction.

CHAPTER 17

THE PADDLE WHEEL BOAT

The best way to cheer yourself is to try to cheer someone else up.

—MARK TWAIN

Hole #17 is The Paddle Wheel Boat. If people take out their camera only once at Tom Thumb, it's to take a picture of this hazard. It is, in a word, spectacular.

The boat looks like something you would see floating down the Mississippi River one hundred years ago. Dreamily, lazily, with a Dixieland band playing on the main deck; perhaps Mark Twain himself looking over the rail. The Paddle Wheel Boat is a big hazard: seven feet long, white, and tiered like a wedding cake. There are three decks in all, and rails strung along the edges made from tiny chains attached to little white posts. The lower decks have windows with bright red trim, and panes of yellow plexiglass that glow at night when we turn on the light inside. In front, facing the green, is an elegant staircase so the tiny passengers can wander between the decks. On top is a red pilothouse, and two great big smokestacks.

The obstacle, of course, is the turning wheel in the back. Your ball will need to pass beneath it and travel through the boat to the green. The paddle blades are dark green and purr as they turn. One of the blades is solid, the others are not, and that is what you aim for, the space in between.

Greg made this boat by hand in his workshop almost fifty years ago. My father has spent the last thirty years keeping it up. He replaces the parts that break, the pieces that rot, and installs new motors when the old ones give out. This week he told me something that I hadn't heard before: The Paddle Wheel Boat—a shining piece of "Americana"—is powered by a motor that happens to be very American. "It's a spit motor," Dad said.

A what?

"For turning that thing, whatever you call it, a rotisserie? On a grill."

"Are you kidding?" I said, watching it turn. "This is a motor for a barbecue grill?"

"Cost me a buck a piece. At a garage sale. I think I bought three."

"When was this?"

"Oh, ten, fifteen years ago."

And thankfully by this time I have matured enough that I don't scream in a way that would alarm the customers. I don't shout, "Are you telling me that we've been turning this motor on and off for years, to make it last a long time, and it actually cost you only a dollar?"

Okay, actually, I said those exact words. But nicely. And then he chuckled.

Hole #17, The Paddle Wheel Boat, is about Nostalgia.

It is August 15. There are eighteen days left before we close for the last time. At dinner, Mom asks me for my opinion about a new personalized license plate.

"Do you have to change it?" I say. "Can't you keep the one you have?!"

"We can't drive around with TOM THUMB on our car. We have to leave that for the new owners, if they want it."

I suppose.

"What about this: BLESSED," she says, writing it on the back of an envelope.

"That kind of sounds like you're bragging," I say.

"I don't want to sound like we're bragging."

"It *kind of* does," I say, but I realize I'm probably being picky.

"Hmm," she says, taking the pen and trying out a few others which sound even more Bible-centric.

Does she really remind me of her? We really don't seem that much alike, my mom and me. I mean, not in the obvious way. I'm kinda private about God-stuff. I wouldn't put my beliefs on my car and drive it around town. When we were swimming, I should have asked my mom what she meant, that she is like me, I am like her. Well, what I *should* have said was *Thank you*. What's wrong with me? I don't know if I want her to explain. Does she mean she would have liked a life like mine? Traveled more? Pursued her dreams? Does that mean that she has dreams that she *didn't* pursue? If this is true, I don't want to know. Letting go of Tom Thumb is enough for me to handle. I don't want to know if she would have rather been doing *something else*.

But maybe that's not what she means at all. How are you

supposed to compare yourself to your parents? By your desires? By what you've achieved? People only rarely see a physical resemblance between us, and when they do, I always reply, "Really?" She will always be taller than me. Her arms stronger. Her faith, unsinkable.

August 16. Only seventeen days left of summer.

Why is this place so hard to let go of? Why am I sentimental about the blue and red dots that stain your fingers from sno-cone syrup?

Carla arrived this morning along with her husband, John, and their two boys. She is playing a game with Luke and Ben, ages seven and six. The sun is directly overhead, and shreds of white cloud move over it, thin, like cotton candy. Ben puts his blue ball into the tee-off of #8, sets his teeth into his lower lip, and swings.

"Oh, Ben! That was so close!" Carla says. "The course looks really good this year. Mom and Dad have really been working hard."

"Yup. I would have to agree on that." I tell her about the repairs we've been doing, getting it into even better shape. "I should have come here earlier. I wish I had spent the whole summer here, all three months. Just to go through a whole season again."

"Really? You would? Good one, Ben! I guess it's my turn." She takes aim and putts exactly the way I remember her doing, swaying her lower body towards the hole while leaning her upper body away. "Oh!" she says.

"So close!" I say.

A biker rolls past down the road, and I can't help myself from blurting out, "Remember how we went to the state park? And snuck into the campground for my birthday?" Then I do sort of a burp-laugh, the kind of sound you make when you are admitting something that is a little embarrassing.

"I've told my boys about it," she says, laughing. "But they don't believe me." The boys give her a quick glance, and she puts on a serious face. Then speaking deliberately, as if reciting a fact from history class, she says, "On June's birthday, we celebrated by sneaking into the state park to take showers." There is a look children reserve for times when a parent is acting crazy and should be ignored—Luke and Ben give her this look. "They think I'm making it up!" She laughs so hard, she reaches to balance herself on the writing stand of hole #6.

"I know, I know!" I say, laughing a bit too loudly, then looking over my shoulder to see if anyone on the course is staring. "But we loved it. That's what's so funny!"

"I know! I looked forward to it every year!" She is bent over at the waist in hysterics, her putter banging against the stand.

"Oh, my God. We were such protected children," I say, catching my breath.

"Easily amused children," she adds.

LeAnn drove in this afternoon from Minneapolis, where she and her family live. Her husband and their three sons will come later, for the very last weekend. She is still talented at giving out orders, but now she has Max, a golden retriever, who cushions us from the brunt of her commands. "Max! Sit! What are you saying, June? Sit!" You just have to filter out which commands are directed at you.

Carla, LeAnn, and I have fallen into our usual habit of sitting in chairs that face the mini golf. "We'll watch," we say to Mom and Dad, offering to keep an eye on the ticket booth. Branches of maple arc above us like a leafy green chandelier, and black squirrels race along the limbs.

"That workshop is a sight," Carla says.

"It's bad. It's really bad. He says he's not ready to start packing," I say.

LeAnn says, "I just wished he'd let me help."

Then we talk about Mom. About how she doesn't seem excited about moving, that she would probably stay a few more seasons, that the move is mostly to benefit Dad. "I'm just so glad Tom Thumb didn't sell right away. I needed a year to get used to the idea." We all agree on that too. So glad it took a year to find a buyer.

LeAnn says, "And we can come back next year and play."

"Do you really want to do that?" I ask her. "Come back here? Next year?"

She mumbles. "Well, I don't know. Maybe." She cranes her neck to look out on the course. "Are the barrels on? They are. Okay. Well, you know, if this place is still open next year."

I know what LeAnn is thinking, but I don't want to hear it.

"Well, look at this place," she says. "One of the new owners is a realtor. That guy, Matt? He knows exactly what this place is worth." She says that they might be planning to move the course somewhere else, to less valuable land.

Move the mini golf? "Is that even do-able? I mean, it's concrete," I say.

"There are two lots, right? They might want to build a big house here, or two houses. Or they could run it one year, then change their mind," she adds, "once they find out how much work it is."

We sigh. This is true. No one knows how much work it is.

I tell them about repairing the boat, and the other painting and touch-ups we have been doing since I arrived. "Mom and Dad want it in as good a shape as possible."

That must be the reason, we agree. They want the new owners to make it. Not quit. Not be overwhelmed by the workload. Not tear out the mini golf after all these years.

"I'll turn on the boat," LeAnn says, heading to the ticket booth.

One year ago, when my parents first talked to a realtor, he recommended that they take down the mini golf. "Then sell the land!" He told them the sad truth: that the property is worth more than the business. Lakeshore has become so valuable that the land would actually demand a higher price *without* Tom Thumb. It could be developed, condos, a mini mansion, and then would actually gain in value. "You could become millionaires!" he said.

Of course, my parents said no.

But what about these four new owners? How many people could resist that? At least one of the buyers is from Chicago—the Big City, I know that world. They said they plan to run Tom Thumb, but they could be lying. After they get the keys, they can do whatever they want. My innocent parents don't suspect a thing. I wish I could do the same.

Dad comes out of the garage carrying a large tin box my sisters and I have never seen before. It's rusted on the corners, faded yellow, with painted green script. *Bread.*

"What have you got there, Dad?" LeAnn says, as Mom comes down the steps to join us.

He sets the box on the ground and jimmies up the lid. Inside is a toy train set. "I just found this in the garage," he says. He lifts up a graying cardboard box and pokes out the car inside. "My first paycheck in the service. I bought this." He picks up a couple of tracks and sets them gently in the grass. He kneels beside them. "I had always wanted a toy train. I had seen them in the store in Blair. When I got my first paycheck from the army, I got this one."

It is beautiful and untouched. "Really good shape still," he says, pulling the engine out of the box.

"Probably worth some money," LeAnn says.

"Dad always takes care of his things," Mom says. We agree, nodding.

"That might be an understatement," I say.

* * *

August 19. Fourteen days left this summer.

This morning while I was working, a guy came up to the ticket booth and asked if he could walk around taking pictures of each hole, professional-quality photos, "sometime in the afternoon, when the light and shadows would be better." I asked him if it was for personal use. "It's for my dad," he answered. "He is into Americana." (The guy was not bad-looking but, alas, was wearing a wedding band.)

I don't think my parents are aware of the term *Americana*, but they seem to have understood the importance of tradition, and how comforting it is to see the same toys and games that you played with as a child. They may have even understood, better than I realized, exactly what they were doing.

Now it's time for the first of our many good-byes. "I don't want you to go," I say to Carla as I grab a couple of bags to help carry out to their car. John is already packing the trunk. He is eager to get home to Iowa City.

"I know," Carla says.

"But you might come back, right? If you find a sub to work for you?" I say.

"Not likely. On a holiday weekend," she answers.

"How many people call a crisis center on a holiday anyway?"

"You'd be surprised."

Mom says, "You girls might want to take a couple of things with you when you go. Maybe you'd like to have a putter or two. Or a couple of balls."

"Good idea." Carla takes a sno-cone cup, a scorecard, a free-game card with GEORGE MELBY AND FAMILY printed on it, a couple of clubs and balls. She will tell me later that she put the blue ball on her dresser, where she can see it in the morning, like a piece of fine porcelain or a mirror. "Blue. My favorite color ball."

* * *

August 23. Ten more days, and then my parents will lower the flaps. The front one goes down first. It is the same old musty, smelly plywood flap that was hanging there when they bought the place thirty years ago. I was ten, Richard Nixon was about to be discussed on national television in so-called hearings, much to the dismay of myself and my seven-year-old-sister who also enjoyed watching game shows.

The Last Ten Days of Mini Golf.

It feels like a bomb exploding and I am watching every dreadful moment. When the ticking stops and we lower the flaps on the ticket booth, everyone in my family will be fighting back tears, and we will be saying dumb things like "Where should I put the brooms?" "Do you want to take a broom?" "Should we leave a broom for Matt [one of the new owners]?" As if no one were fighting back tears. *Matt* is like a metaphor. *Matt*, who is the future, who is unknown. Will he run it? Is he lying? Is he even capable of doing what my parents have done?

Running a business without the intention of making a profit went out . . . well . . . I'm not sure if that was ever in style, but it was certainly more common in small towns, say, a Swiss hamlet in nineteenth-century Europe. The jolly baker sells his bread too cheap, everyone in town eats, and when the baker looks all mopey because his wife is deathly ill, the people in town finally stop being so selfish and help him out, usually with gifts of live chickens and leftover zucchini from their gardens.

You're supposed to make a profit, aren't you? You're supposed to, you know, respect the rules of business. Otherwise you'll be taken advantage of, right?

August 29. Only four days left of summer. (I am freaking out.) It feels like a NASA countdown at this point, very important, and affecting the entire free world if they know what's good for them. I still don't know why I care so much. Is it the detail? The interesting-ness of the place? But I walked into the ticket booth this morning, and it smelled damp from the rain of the night before. And that sugary smell. The cotton-candy-in-the-vicinity smell. This is the smell of my childhood.

It's our last weekend. LeAnn went home more than a week ago; now she's returned with her husband and their three boys, fifteen, eleven, and nine. They are rushing around, grabbing balls and clubs. "Stay away from holes where there are already people playing," Mom says, in her grandmother voice. Our last days here will not be quiet, and that will be just fine. My nephews are all redheads and a bit hyper, which is to say, perfectly distracting. LeAnn is documenting the weekend with a video camera. Mom is taking snapshots. We are all taking photos, only I don't own a camera, so I sit along the edge drawing on a pad with colored pencils. One of my nephews sits next to me; he is drawing too. I feel like I am nine years old.

The paddle wheel of this hazard was changed some time ago. Dad rebuilt the back section so balls wouldn't get caught underneath, but it also made the hazard slightly easier to play.

My parents have done this, made the hazards easier over the years, as they became grandparents for my sisters' children, and everyone else who comes to play. My parents are becoming softies. And I've tried to get them to stop. Each year they talk about the latest change. "We were trying to make the hill on #3 less steep—"

"No!"

"—but then we found out we would need to bring in a backhoe—"

"Good! Keep it the way it is!" I don't like changes to the hazards. I don't like any change. I don't know why that is, because my life has been all about trying new things and taking on new jobs. I've backpacked alone, hitchhiked alone, and done stand-up comedy because apparently I enjoy scaring myself to death on a regular basis. But I guess I don't want *anyone else* to change. Is that okay with you all? Just stay the same? And never change?

August 30. Three days to go. It's our last Saturday here. Ever.

The course is crammed with cheerful people. They hoot and scream and laugh from every corner. "Ho!" and "Ha!" ring out as people celebrate their missed shots. Time is running out, but everything looks annoyingly normal. It is like having the most perfect summer day to shine down upon your own funeral.

In the cartoon drawing of me today, I am a roundy dwarf, wearing a green conical cap, graying beard, and shoes I am using to kick chair legs, stones, and overturned mugs of dwarf-ohol. All of them are empty. My head hurts. There is a balloon above my head, but it looks like a spill or an ink blot test. *Stomp stomp stomp.* Dwarves who tiptoe get no respect from the other dwarves. We argue over the spelling of the plural, *dwarfs* or *dwarves*.

"I thought we might have the course to ourselves!" says a woman in a flowered scarf.

"Not today," my dad says.

"Lots of folks coming to say good-bye, I see."

"So far, no one is saying good riddance!" He laughs.

I could poke myself in the eye with the blunted pencil from the last hole.

LeAnn is assisting Dad in the ticket booth, as always, taking in clubs from customers who are leaving, while he waits on the customers who arrive. My nephews have played mini golf plenty of times over the years, now they're actually fighting over who gets to work. This is their last chance to learn how to make cotton candy. "Okay, but one at a time," my mom says, promising to teach them. "Hey, you're going to have to take turns, boys. One at a time in there!"

I sit on a metal chair trying to draw a picture of The Gumball Machine, the hazard that is now at #1. Mostly I'm trying to pretend that I find this whole situation normal.

"How are you doing?" Mom asks me when she gets a break.

"Nothing," I say, because I am feeling contrary. A dark green dragonfly alights on the arm of my chair, stares at me through the motorcycle goggles of his eyes.

Customers keep coming. It's been steady all day. Late afternoon, and the sun makes a steep slant across the course. It lights up the white picket fence along the lake which glows like a row of tightly clenched teeth.

Is it true that you get ahead in this world by being selfless? Is it true that if you put your heart and soul into something, without any thought of reward, you'll actually come out ahead? That seems too far-fetched. That seems impossible. But this is what has happened.

Dad is rubbing his hands together as he looks out on the course. "Hi, there."

"Hi. Two adults, two kids."

"Eight plus six is fourteen," Dad says, as they hand in bills.

"Excited about moving?"

"Yes, I am." Then he pauses and lowers his voice as he does when he is making a confession. "I'm getting too old for this," he says. His head is at an angle, and he is nodding with each important word. *Old. This.* It is his intimate, teacher's voice, the voice he used when he would take a pause from his lesson plan, stop during the lecture, sit down on a chemistry lab stool, relax into something like a contra-posto pose, and tell them secrets that us kids had never heard. We would hear in study hall the next day. "Your dad was talking about what he regrets in life." "He was?" "He was talking about what it was like to be a father." "In class?" And usually I didn't ask for details because I knew it would be embarrassing. I wasn't sure what the other kids had learned that I didn't know.

"I just don't have the energy that I used to," he continues. He is apologizing. The father, in his thirties and fit, listens intently from behind his dark sunglasses, white baseball cap, and white t-shirt with an America flag on the front. My dad is good at commanding respect.

"Let's see," Dad says, looking up again at the family through the window. "Someone hiding behind you?" A child appears behind his father's legs. "Here you go," he says sweetly, handing out a putter. And then another. "How is this for you?"

The customers look at each other trying to remember when they first came to Tom Thumb. "Was it 1969?"

"Nineteen sixty-eight," the woman says. "We'll miss you," she says to my dad.

"Thank you," he replies, handing out their balls. "And it's time to move on."

When my dad takes a break, I wait on a few customers. A guy tells me his story, about how his dad built a cottage on Beasley in the 1950s. "I started walking down here when I was nine or ten; sometimes we'd cut through the woods, be adventurous. Greg was so generous. I think he let us play for free half the time. This is my daughter—she asks to play every time we come up here." He nods, looking out on the course. "They keep it in such good shape. Looks just like it did in 1965."

Mom takes a look at my sketch of The Gumball Machine. "You know," Mom says to me, "that gumball of yours was very visible most of the summer in there."

"Really?" I say, setting down the tablet and skipping over to the first hole.

Dad made this hazard years ago, when we agreed we wanted "something less scary" than an unexploded bomb (aka: The Rocket) at #1. It's larger than a real gumball machine and has clear plexiglass sides so you can see the "gumballs," which are actually colored golf balls. I remember sitting around the dining table painting golf balls, the way we used to dye Easter eggs, to get enough to fill the "machine" in the colors we liked. I painted my name across the side of one, and it has lived inside the gumball machine ever since.

I lift off the square wood top and dig around inside. I haven't seen that ball in years, and I need to know if I should be embarrassed.

Then I find it. For the first time in twenty years or so I hold it in my hand. In pale green paint, *june.* Uncapitalized. Uneven. What year was it? I wonder. I must have been young—at the age, anyway, when you would paint your name on something like a ball. Letting the world know you exist.

"You should take it with you," Mom says.

I toss the ball back in with the other balls. "I think it should live in there," I say, reaching up on tiptoe to pile other golf balls over it, burying it deep.

September 1. Monday. Our last day at Tom Thumb.

Most families gather around the kitchen. We hover around the ticket booth. Instead of a stove, there is a money box. Instead of food, twelve cans of bug spray. We take care of the constant stream of customers, each of whom says incredibly nice things to my parents.

"Take care," they say. "Good luck on your new home!" they call. "Thank you so much!"

When there is a break, we gather between the buildings. "I just remember trying to rake leaves, and there would still be ice inside the leaf piles," LeAnn says.

"Oh, man!" I say. Mom shakes her head in disapproval. "Those were hard days—want something?" she says to a young boy who is digging through his pockets at the front window.

"Is everything on?" we say, looking over each other's shoulder. On the floor of the ticket booth are two bags of golf balls that my dad bought. One bag of red-and-white; one bag of blue-and-white, unopened. We have no idea what he's saving them for.

Standing by the pop machine there is a young man looking at his father. They are about the same height now. The father has the same hair, only thinning. The same nose, only longer. The same chin, only exaggerated. The two resemble each other like a young man and a caricature drawing made for him by an artist on the street in an amusement park—the features exaggerated somewhat but the resemblance unmistakable. This too is something I'm so accustomed to. Not just these hazards but this view, of the people.

This is how it has always looked. These colors. The same ones in the box of six crayons you were given in kindergarten to start off your coloring life with gusto and with strength. Red! Orange like the sun! Blue like sky! Yellow like bananas! Green like all the world after the first spring rain! Subtle hues and uncertainty will come to you later in life, but for now, enjoy the shouting of these paints—they are as familiar to me as my own two feet.

LeAnn says, "Remember that garage? Oh! That was a hoot!"

There is the sound of balls banging into the clown. "C'mon, c'mon. We gotta get it in the nose!"

"He's the winner."

"I'm the weiner!"

"They know us more than we know them," Mom says to me. "They tell us how their summer wouldn't be the same without a visit to Tom Thumb. It's part of their annual tradition."

"Thank you for a fun thirty years," says a man in a Green Bay Packers t-shirt.

"Great. I'm glad you enjoyed them," Dad says.

"It was very, very enjoyable. Thank you."

"You're very welcome."

"Good-bye," adds his wife.

Dad turns to us after they leave. "I sit back here by the pop machine sometimes, and I just listen to people. And they are so amazed when they see the doors of the castle open for the first time. 'Oh, it's opening!' they say. It's unusual in this day and age, you see. Most miniature golf courses don't have the mechanicals."

LeAnn says that she misses the radio, the music we used to play.

Dad explains that he turned it off two years ago.

"Why?"

"I enjoy hearing people out here." He gestures with his thumb. "I sit here with the newspaper, and you just hear people laughing their heads off. But with the radio on, you never hear that."

A man with a thick Wisconsin accent leans against the front counter. "So you're moving on after this year?" The word *on* almost sounds like *ahn*.

"That's correct," Dad says.

"This is it, huh?"

"Yep." He's answered this questioned twice an hour for the past one and a half months. "We just bought a place about five miles away."

"Oh! Good!"

"This has just gotten too much work for us."

"Sure. When you're open ten to ten. That's long days. Someone bought it, though?"

"They told us that they're going to keep it going."

Another man calls out to the one leaning on the counter. "They're going to have the golf course next year?"

"They're going to have it next year," the man at the counter replies.

"All right!"

"As far as we know," Dad says.

"Good!"

"As far as we know. I'm so tickled to tell people, that yes, it will be here, so"—he laughs—"so I hope it is!" The guy laughs with Dad.

"I don't know who that was," Dad says, as people leave. "But they remember me. So I just smiled!"

I step under the canopy of the red maple tree near the tee of #5. Its roots form a platform on which to stand as I sharpen a broken pencil. A group of eight or nine people herd together to hand in their clubs to my dad after their game; they joke about their scores and who might have cheated. They look like campers: no makeup, just rosy cheeks, ponytails, and pullover sweatshirts. "We just wanted to thank you for keeping this place going all these years!" He says thank you, but they keep talking. "It is such a wonderful place!" they say. Then they begin to bow. They bow to Dad first; he is inside the ticket booth. Then they bow to Mom, who is standing outside by the Snack Shack. "Thank you, thank you," they say. They see me with the pencil sharpener, and they bow to me too. "Thank you so much." Their heads bob low in their hoodies. "Summer would never be the same without Tom Thumb—"

"Now, okay, I want you to do me a favor," my dad interrupts them. "When you come back next year and there is a new person sitting in here, I want you to say the same thing to them. We're tickled they are going to run the place. I want you to thank them for keeping it going . . ." He deflects the kind words from the campers. This is more gratitude than he needs; he'd rather share it with the new owners. He knows they'll need the encouragement to get them through the first year, and the year after that . . . and the year after that . . . "Don't thank us. Okay? We are glad they are going to keep the place open."

"We should have had a guestbook out there," I mumble after they leave.

"What's that?" Dad asks.

"We should have gotten a guestbook. For people to sign."

"That would have been a good idea."

I am very good at coming up with good ideas that come too late.

Then a man in a baseball hat leans into the front window. "Excuse me, could I take your picture?"

"Sure," Dad says, stepping out the ticket booth door.

"Your wife, too, if she's handy."

Dad nods and pokes his head into the Snack Shack. "Jean? Someone wants a picture of us." He leans one elbow on the front counter, under the ADMISSION sign; Mom comes up to stand beside him. They smile at the camera together. Dad so comfortable, so at ease—this is his front counter after all, each of the tacks that hold up the screen were tapped in by his hand. "Hold on, one more," the man says. This is how they've always looked. Dad's eyes crinkle as he smiles, leans leisurely, his weight on one foot. Mom standing to his side, a calmer smile, her legs so straight, almost as if they were in braces or connected somehow into the ground all the way to the center of the earth.

After they leave, Mom says, "I think people took it for granted that we would always be here. Until they saw the SOLD sign. Then they started to worry."

A boy about twelve tees off at #5, then leaps into the air. "It's going in!"

Two young girls in pink crowd together in front of the Snack Shack.

"Can I get you something?" I ask.

"One cotton candy!" they call out.

"Coming right up!" I say, going into the Snack Shack and switching on the machine.

Is it true that it's okay to be humble? To not try to grab more for yourself? They've made so many people happy. After thirty years of *not* trying to advance their own lives, my parents are getting a check for half a million dollars.

And they don't give a hoot about the money. They are buying a humble house, instead of making wild plans. They are opening a bank account called "Benevolence" and plan to give a lot of it away. What kind of American dream is this? If you live your life in a generous way, ignoring the pressure to be selfish, will you actually come out ahead?

I don't know if it is true, but I want it to be true.

I want Los Angeles to be wrong. I don't want it to be true that you get ahead by lying, being super-aggressive, and discarding the friendships you have along the way.

I want my parents to be right. More than anything in the world right now, I want them to be right.

"Here you go," I say, carefully tipping the cotton candy at an angle so it fits out through the front window. The first girl reaches for the paper cone, the top finger of her hand brushing against the lower finger of mine.

It's half an hour too early to turn on the lights, but no one's going to yell at me tonight. I walk down the path to the laundry room. There has always been a frog on the concrete outside the door, every evening. All these thirty years. I'm eager to see if there is one sitting there tonight. "Hello, you," I say, stepping over him as I always have.

It's only 8 pm, but we will be closing in two hours. It is the last two hours of Tom Thumb Mini Golf.

Switch.

There it is—Christmas.

CHAPTER 18

THE CLOWN FACE

The wine glasses are empty except for that one undrinkable red
spot at the bottom.

—AIMEE BENDER

It is modern and trendy not to pine for the past. But I do anyway. And pretending that I don't would be lying. But perhaps being sentimental isn't being mushy or emotional. Perhaps I am sentimental because I wasn't paying attention the first time things happened. I didn't appreciate floating on inner tubes. I complained about the condition of our bikes rather than enjoying the freedom of picking wild blackberries along Rural Road. But I am not the only one. This is what it is to be an adult, to realize the best program in the world was being broadcast, just for you, on your own private movie screen. And you were looking away—in my case, complaining about the sun/wind/fairness of life.

Does sentiment live next door to nostalgia? Are they cousins? Are they the same? Being sentimental, perhaps, is expressing emotions now that you didn't bother to experience the first time around, when you should have taken care of it. Like doing the laundry thirty years too late. I'm finally getting around to enjoying my childhood. And this is why, perhaps, I am wondering if my being sentimental is just another form of greed: I want it all back. It is us, and we are it.

Take The Barrels. When it starts to rain, someone in my family will always run out to cover them. So comforting that old army tarp, with grommets on all four corners, except for the one that's been torn. Dad made these barrels in the basement one winter, and they have turned around and around every summer since. And they are us.

And The Wishing Well. When we first arrived, we talked about removing the old plywood deck on the thing, so it looked more like a well. Or trying to smooth out the ridge across the green that made balls appear to magically stop right alongside the hole. But it remained the way it was. The Wishing Well is our unrealistic hopes in 1973 of the things we thought we could change but learned were unchangeable. That is us.

We are the ground. After it rains, Mom vacuums the puddles in the grass wearing rubber galoshes while the electrical cord drapes across the water. "I don't want you out here without shoes on" was her only warning, and she would resume vacuuming water from the grass.

And it is us.

And The Covered Bridge. How balls sometimes catch inside it.

The Paddle Wheel Boat. How people will say, "My ball is lost," and we reply, "Have you checked the hole?" And then we hear them scream with surprise; they discover they have got a hole-in-one. That is us too.

The bats that live behind the sign at #10 (GO IN THE RIGHT HAND HOLE—OR YOU'LL BE SORRY) and the time when I was taking it down and realized there were bats just inches from my face. I dropped the sign on the grass and injured one bat, who then crawled away slowly, and I felt bad for it—but mostly bad that it couldn't disappear faster because of its new limp.

There used to be another sign here, on hole #18. What did it say? Dad must have taken it down so he could see out the ticket booth window. I can't believe I have forgotten what was on that sign. It is so important right now to remember.

Because that sign is me. All the signs are me. That was my job. Putting up the signs, taking down the signs, keeping track of all eighteen little signs, hand-painted in beautiful script and attached to the hazards each year. At the end of each summer I carried them into the house and tucked them under the bench in the porch. In the spring I carried them in my arms back out into the sunshine, then searched in the garage for the cottage cheese container where I had tossed the screws, nuts, washers nine months earlier.

And the sound of cars hitting the parking lot gravel. When three cars pulled in, we knew we had more time before we needed to run out of the house to get them, because the more cars that come together, the longer it takes the people to gather at the ticket booth. You could pour yourself some milk, stand up and drink it, and still get to the ticket booth at the moment they did.

And that is us too. The timing.

We know too much about time. The revolutions of each mechanical hazard. What looks normal, what looks wrong. "I think The Ferris Wheel is slipping," we could say from fifty yards away, and Dad would go out and tighten the pulley.

And how long it takes people to play the back nine, if we'll have time to finish dinner first. And how long it takes storm clouds to produce actual lightning so we'd need to chase people off the course. How long after the rain clears before people reappear in the parking lot.

The ticket booth, how it leaks sometimes. How squirrels make a nest in the eye of The Clown each year. That is us.

And that old cottage. The place on the third step that creaked so loudly, we took a long stride to the next step up when we knew

Dad was resting in their bedroom. Now there is the new house, and that is us too.

Everyone feels attached to the house where they grew up. We are no different. It's just that our house is different. And colorful. And there are lots of little gadgets and motors involved. And people, hundreds of people. Or is it thousands?

Hole #18 is called The Clown Face. Or sometimes simply "The Last Hole," or as some kids say, "Darn, It's the Last Hole!" Which is a bit ironic, I suppose, because there is no actual "hole." There is no green, no metal cup, and instead there's a box. Like every other miniature golf course built since the beginning of time, or at least since 1930, the last hole is designed to take your ball away. You're going to lose it on this one.

What you aim for is a clown face. It could be anything, but a clown is convenient, it's happy. It reminds you of a circus. And it's difficult to think of an alternative that would work. You don't want to slam your ball at a baby bunny, would you? Or an elf? Or a princess? But a clown . . . We have mixed feelings about clowns, and so it is a target that most people don't mind whomping their ball at.

There are four openings: two large eyes, the nose, and a mouth. There is a one-inch wooden "lip" along the bottom that can funnel your ball into the mouth. At many mini golf courses, the lip catches *all* the balls. You only get one shot. Automatic hole-in-one. But not at Tom Thumb. This is a more challenging course. Your ball can bounce over and roll back down to you. But then, people like a second chance. They are happy to try again. Because even if your game has been lousy, and your aim has been "off" since about hole #6, after all your misses and your miscues, your sixes and your water splashes, and the fact that you have already said, "Don't bother adding up my score," there is still this possibility: you could win a free game. Just hit your ball in the nose.

Imagine the beauty of the bell as it rings out across the course, telling everyone of your success. See people smile at you from all across the course. "It was me." You smile back; you might even wave. Your family cheers and slaps your back. All your bad luck on the previous seventeen holes is forgotten. You are the winner now. This is a truth that every mini golfer understands: getting your ball into the clown's nose and winning a free game trumps everything.

There is hope. One last chance to save you. That is why The Clown Face, hole #18, is about One Last Chance for Redemption.

It's the last evening of our last summer here at Tom Thumb. Only two hours left. Just one group on the back nine. No new cars for a while now. There is nothing to do but wait. The sky over the golf course is lighter than the sky over the lake, which it always is during sunset. And it focuses our attention in that direction, which it always has.

We pace between the ticket booth and the firepit. "I'm surprised there isn't more business," I say.

"It might be easier this way," Mom suggests.

"Yeah, I think so," LeAnn adds. And we all agree.

The phone rings, and I rush to answer. Carla. "It looks just like every other night here," I tell her. "It's really really weird! I wish you were here!" She says that she is actually glad she had to work, because if she were at Tom Thumb on the last night, she's not sure she could take it. *It's easier to answer suicide phone calls?*

"Don't pull the cork all the way off, just wiggle it to the top," LeAnn explains to Dad as we gather around the firepit. "He wants to try opening the champagne," she says, then pulls the bottle away from him. "Don't point it at Mom!"

"Like this?" he asks, pulling the cork all the way off in his hands. The cork does not fly; there is only a mild pop. Mom and Dad are so unfamiliar with champagne; we have to show them how to celebrate.

"What's this thing?" Mom asks, picking up the metal cage that was around the cork.

"Thats what they use to hold the cork in." So much to teach them. We pour champagne in plastic cups.

Dad pulls up his favorite webbed chair to the fire. "I was okay until I saw June crying," he says, rubbing the corners of his eyes.

"I'm afraid what will happen if I get started." Mom stares blankly at the fire.

The hazards have been covered, the money boxes brought inside, and the modules unplugged, but the lights still blaze and The Windmill still turns. We poke sticks into the flame, as we always have. And this is when I decide to give my little speech. I'm going to try to sound all Martin Luther King–like, you know,

as if I'm giving a speech that doesn't sound all dorky like I usually am, but which will be impactful and remembered.

But I'm not Martin Luther King. I'm just a starving artist with
freakishly long hair. "Mom and Dad, I'm just so impressed by
you," I begin.

"I am just so impressed with all you've accomplished. You're
the most successful parents a kid could ask for." I really say this.
Because I'm a total dork. Then I hug one and then the other.
I repeat myself, because I've been drinking, and to be truthful,
because I've been holding it in. "You set out to create a place for
families to play together, and you did just that. I'm so impressed."

"You did!" LeAnn chimes in.

"In the past couple of weeks, well, I just realized how much
you know and what you've been able to do . . ."

And then we all sob. "I'm just so happy for you," says LeAnn,
dabbing the back of her wrist at the edges of her eyes. "For the
new life you're going to have. Group hug!" she calls out, so we join
arm over shoulder. It's the first time we have ever done this, hug
in a circle. We say how much we wish Carla were here. We kiss
each other's cheeks like they are wineglasses that needing clink-
ing one by one, in turn.

"Remember the day we opened?" Dad says, as we step back to
find our chairs. He clicks his tongue. "We had no idea what we
were doing!"

"But we didn't know!" Mom says.

Whenever we talk about Tom Thumb, Dad mentions the First
Day. He is getting repetitive, which is probably what you'd expect
at seventy-six. But then again, maybe he keeps bringing it up
because we haven't yet figured out how we actually survived.
And now that we are at the end, this being the Last Day, we are
still talking about the First Day, because the end reminds you of
the beginning, and the beginning is also an end.

The conversation turns to reminiscing about the vacations we took before we had Tom Thumb, about camping in the pop-up, the trip we took to Texas, reminding ourselves of the life we had before this place.

When Dad goes to get more wood, Mom turns to us. "Looking back," she says, picking up a twig by her feet and dropping it into the fire, "do you girls regret having spent summers here instead of back in Decorah? I mean, a lot? Or do you think maybe it was a trade-off . . . ?" Her voice trails off at the end, like she's not sure she wants to ask the question, or hear the answer.

"Well, it was an adjustment," LeAnn says. "But probably a trade-off. We had so much fun here with the cousins. And being away, we missed out on a lot of that teenage angst."

I look at a log burning almost blue in the flames. Then I say, "LeAnn, when people talk about their teenage years, do you find there's a lot of stuff you can't relate to? Because we missed out on that stuff?"

"Yes. I do think so."

Then Mom turns to me. "June, how about you? Do you regret summers here?"

There is the purr of a prop plane overhead, far away, barely discernable. And the soothing sound of cicadas, our built-in lullaby at night.

"I have a hard time answering that. It's sort of like saying, 'What was it like growing up as a girl?' Well, I never was a boy, so I don't know the difference. I don't . . . I don't know."

The lights go dark over the golf course, and Dad reappears coming out of the laundry room. We hug again in the moonlight.

September 2. It's the next morning. It still feels like summer, but it looks different somehow. The light through the trees is slanting yellow. The ticket booth windows are closed, which always looks so strange. Mom is carrying buckets to the Snack Shack to clean out the cotton candy machine. "I want to get it done right away."

LeAnn drives off in her minivan as Mom, Dad, and I wave good-bye from the parking lot. I have one more day here, because my flight back to Los Angeles leaves tomorrow. Mom and I will play Scrabble, and I'll try to persuade her to let me help pack, and we will put on our swimsuits. "Are you sure you want to?" Mom asks. The water could be quite cold.

"We can always back out!"

"You won't back out!"

"No," I admit. "I won't back out."

We walk together down the path towards the dock. It is the last time we will be able to swim together in this lake, and I'm trying hard not to say that out loud. But one problem I have after years of doing comedy is that I have a hard time biting my tongue. I tend to blurt out the most obvious thing that's going on: Last time. Here. This lake.

"Whew, it sure isn't warm!" she says, grimacing as she plunges in. It must be really cold because she isn't bothering to pretend otherwise. "We can keep it short." She spreads her arms out behind her.

But we swim. We want to. And while we push off towards the center of the lake, I am thinking about Los Angeles for the first time in weeks, because I go back tomorrow, and so I start to tell her about it, the difficult year I've had. Very few auditions because my agent dropped me more than a year ago, during the actor's strike. Still get a few calls from casting directors who remember me. Roles I don't have much chance at because the other women are ten to fifteen years younger than me. Spending three hours of an afternoon driving across town, to find out it's a role I'm not suited for. "But I don't know what else to do. I don't want to be a legal secretary full-time . . ."

I keep talking while we breaststroke. We are getting near the buoy now. I tell her how I don't know how I'm even going to pay rent the next few months, and as of a few weeks ago, I'm single again. I'd like to leave Los Angeles, but I don't know where I'd go—

"We are all hoping you move back to the Midwest, June."

"Really? But what could I do here? I can't see myself working at the Piggly Wiggly."

"Teaching?"

"I don't have a degree for that."

She nods; she may not know Hollywood, but she does know the world of teaching.

Where could I live now? What use is there for a voice-over actor? Or a poet in a small town like this? Meanwhile, most of my friends are writers these days, I tell her, and they were smart enough to go to graduate school during their twenties, so they have steady teaching jobs, and I'm older than they are but I'm behind the curve with them too. How can I think about graduate school when I don't even have enough money to fix the transmission in my 1988 Honda, let alone pay for tuition—

And then in the middle of Beasley Lake I begin to wheeze.

"Breathe," Mom says. "Take a deep breath in." Her legs spin out treading water next to me while I gasp. "Huuuuuuhh. Huuuhh." I'm not getting any air. "I don't know what's going on," I say. "I can't breathe."

"Just keep breathing."

Is this a panic attack? We are one hundred feet from shore, and I can't breathe and I have no life preserver. What is happening to me? As I wheeze I remember that this happened once before, when I was in New Zealand and signed up to go swimming with dolphins, only it wasn't like I had seen on TV, in a peaceful lagoon, instead they boated us out into the deep waters of the ocean and then told us to jump in—*And when the dolphins swim*

past, do some tricks to attract their attention—then a flock of dolphins darted past, but just as quickly were gone—*Chase after
them, they said*, as I started to panic. I don't do tricks. The rocky
coastline was miles away, and I'm not a trained swimmer. I do
the breaststroke, but we were in the ocean, and I stopped to tread
water and gasped for air—

"You can make it. Keep breathing," Mom says, leading me back
across Beasley. I can't stop wheezing, but I can't stop talking
either, how I had been in denial about dating someone younger
than me, but now I'm going to be alone again at age forty—

Mom gets twenty feet from the dock and says, "Why don't
you get out first this time." I swim past her, misjudging the path
between the seaweeds which are grabbing at my ankles. I grip the
bars of the blue-enameled swim ladder and swing my body up
the steps. "I made it!" I say, and I actually feel as if I accomplished
something.

Mom sits in the car, engine running, waiting to drive me to the
Appleton airport. "Oh, Dad, it's so hard to say good-bye," I say,
hugging him in the driveway. "Take care now," he says, tears falling on his cheeks. I pull out the Kleenex in my purse to dab at
my eyes. "Oh, that's why I didn't bother putting eye makeup on
this morning." As Mom turns right, out of the parking lot, I look
out the window at Tom Thumb, as if taking one last picture with
my eyes.

"Just be as good to yourself as you are to other people," I say
to Mom at the airport, sounding, yet again, as if I'm preaching
the Gospel of Selfishness.

Several hours later, I am in a car with my friend Steve, heading up Sepulveda Boulevard. Palm trees. Billboards. Stop lights.
"It feels like it shouldn't be so bright," I say, as he drives me home
from the Los Angeles airport. I blubber and blubber about my last

days at Tom Thumb while he patiently listens. "It's only three pm?" I say. "It feels like it should be night."

He waits as I unlock my door and drop my bags inside. "Thanks for picking me up," I say, handing him a package of cheese curds. "You eat them warm. Then they'll squeak." And then I collapse on the bed.

There were another three agonizing weeks before the real estate deal "closed." My parents never knew that I spent those weeks trying to figure out a way to keep it from happening. "I'm having second thoughts!" I phoned my sisters. Each night we talked; we brainstormed. I don't give up easily. Without a job or family keeping me in Los Angeles, it seemed my destiny to save the day! I would sweep in and end our terrible state of mourning about the impending loss of Tom Thumb! Maybe I could take a class in motor repair from the community college, so Dad could finally relax! I would find a job in the winter so I could afford to live in Wisconsin! Then again, I have no idea what that job could be . . . But once I buy a house in town for Mom and Dad to live in, I could run the mini golf! Of course, that would be difficult on my budget . . . Or maybe I could ask our cousin Phil if he'd be interested in running Tom Thumb? "But I think they just built a new house in Seattle." "Oh, then there's no point in asking them . . ."

Then it's September 30, 9 am, and Mom and Dad have just arrived at Tom Thumb to walk around one last time before they drive to the realtor's office to hand over the keys. They are crying in the backyard. This is what I picture. I am staring at my alarm clock watching the red minutes click by. As if by looking at them closely, like animals running through the woods, they will freeze in their tracks.

But you can't actually stop time. Even if you have a lot of money. You can't will it to be so. I can't stop the sale. I'm going to have to accept that it's over. I can't buy Tom Thumb to give my mom this lake that she loves, this heaven to enjoy now. I can't take over the family business so that my dad doesn't have to let it go, just like the farm where he grew up, and which fell to the ground in disrepair. We're going to have to trust Tom Thumb, that is, our home, to the new owners, and to the future. I set out with great gusto to become a success, you know, at something or another. Funny how it didn't happen.

So, I'm setting out now to be nicer—like my parents—and do good things for people. A woman I just met who needs emergency surgery and doesn't have insurance just heard me volunteer to accompany her to the scary county hospital. And after a friend told me on the phone that she and her husband are really broke—"I can't buy more groceries until Dave gets paid on Friday"—I put a twenty-dollar bill and a happy card in an envelope and sent it off to her. I guess I had to wait until there was proof: it's okay to be nice. Which is the better road to happiness: Pursuing your dreams, that is, going after happiness selfishly, like it's your own personal goal? Or generosity, that is, finding your own happiness by helping *others* find theirs? It's time for some experimenting.

And I remember the very last time I played, the day *after* we had closed for the summer. We had just finished eating supper, and Mom said she had sorting to do, and Dad said he wanted to try again to repair the dishwasher, which he had already spent the whole day trying to repair—just another thing he wanted to do for the new owners.

"Well, I'm going to play a round of golf before it gets too dark," I said, heading outside to get myself a putter.

"I think Dad and I both are going to join you," Mom said, coming down the path. She went into the Snack Shack and lugged out the large bag of popcorn kernels.

"Can I help you carry things?"

"No, I'm just leaving it out here," she said, obviously *not* leaving everything out there. But I can't fight my mom. She is stronger than me, as always.

The motors were still turned on, inexplicably. We got our putters; then we waited and we waited . . . "Dad went to feed the birds again. Do you know he gives them jam three times a day? Sometimes four or five!" We decided it was best that we start without him. I missed my second shot. "We could just start again!" I suggested. "If you miss too, we could both just start again when Dad comes." Ah, the beauty of cheating. Another thing we'll have to give up when we no longer have the word *proprietor* after our name . . .

"I just wish we had played more often," Mom said, setting her ball on the tee. "I don't know why we didn't play more. Until you girls came home, I don't think we had played more than two or three times all summer . . ."

Dad joined us, and we were on hole #3 when a car drove in: a man and woman with a kid. They got out of their car and walked to the fence. "We have the CLOSED sign up, don't we?" Mom said.

"Yes, but they probably saw the windmill turning," Dad said.

They looked at each other, "Should we let them play?"

"Well, we're out here. The motors are already turned on."

So, of course, they let them play. "But we don't have money boxes out here, so do you have exact change?" Dad said to the couple.

"How much?"

"Eleven dollars."

"Thank you so much!" the woman said, as my parents gave them balls and a scorecard. "We tried to get here last night, but we had a car wreck and I promised"—she, gestured to her ten-year-old boy—"that I'd take him to play mini golf."

* * *

Dad shot a 38, his best score ever on the course. I wrote the date on the scorecard. He kept it. I put a handful of colored golf balls into my jacket pocket to take home with me. We waited until the couple and their son had finished.

"Same flaps," I said, as we closed up the ticket booth.

"They've hung in there a long time," Dad said. "Since we opened. June, do you remember that first day?"

"Of course."

Like a child repeating his favorite joke, Dad was talking about the first day again.

"We didn't know a doggone thing! Remember that carpet sweeper?"

"Oh, my goodness!" Mom said.

"It was murderizing the carpets!" Dad shook his head and raised his eyebrows, then he looked over at her. "We had no idea what we were doing!"

And they laughed together, my mother and father. It was like a duet. A melody and a harmony, entwining, wrapping around each other, finding new notes and adding them to the song. Musical laughs, the kind you can only have when you are laughing at yourselves, at a moment of humility seen from a safe distance, after decades of time, and one that is shared together.

THE TICKET BOOTH: EPILOGUE

The ticket booth is the place where you start and the place where you always return. Like home. This is where you add up your score. Proclaim yourself the winner or make a face if you don't like the result. And here is where you will hand back your putter—you can't take it with you. You may be the kind of person who forgets or who gets accustomed to holding on to things. You may walk across the parking lot to your car, discussing the scores, until one of your friends or family yells out, "Hey! Forgetting something?"

You'll smile in embarrassment. "What? I don't get to keep it?" you'll say, waving the putter, trying to cover your embarrassment. Or you might jog back to the counter apologizing, "Oops, sorry," hoping we won't think you're a thief. But we realize that ultimately, just as with all possessions, in the end what you've called "mine" has been borrowed all along.

Next time you come, you might get the same ball. Who knows? You might even get the same club. We'll keep them here for you. They'll be waiting next year, like summer itself. Until you return again.

When I was in engineering school, they talked about infinity almost every day. About how far things go. And what happens when you take something normal and then put it at infinity and look at it again. Infinity, I learned, is something you can think about when you are the type to take things to extremes. When you like to think of things as being endless. Also, infinity is symbolized by what looks like a two-headed fish. He is swimming away. But he may also be swimming towards you. Towards the end. And towards the beginning. Perhaps the end is the end of time; perhaps it is just another end.

I remember one day when I was in elementary school—I must have been in second or third grade. When school got out, I walked across the street to the high school and down the shiny tiled hall to my father's classroom. He was going to drive me home, it must have been a cold day, but he said he had a few more things to do before he could leave. Asked me to entertain myself for fifteen minutes. On a blackboard on the back wall, just past the row of chemistry lab benches, I took a piece of chalk, and instead of drawing a cat or a house or a sun and hearts, I mapped out my perception of the time. (I was never a normal child.)

I drew a line to indicate morning—the time before lunch. The line was four inches long. Then lunch was half an inch—too short. The afternoon was a line a full eight inches of blackboard before I marked the line for the end of the day. And then I wrote *end!* and perhaps a smiley face.

Having completed this, I mapped out my perception of the year. How the school year was ten inches long, followed by the summer, which had no end. Infinity. The school year so far away.

Remember the time when the world was larger? The streets were larger? The distance across town was vast? The world and the number of countries across the earth seemed infinite. And so you spent time with miniature things, dolls, a toy truck. Or this miniature course. Teenagers seemed like grown-ups. I once was asked what I'd like to be when I grew up; I said a teenager. I had no idea there was life beyond childhood.

As we were about to head for home, my father asked me what

I was drawing on the blackboard. When I told him, he chuckled, and I knew I had done something embarrassing. He left it on the board for his students to see, which I discovered one month later, the next time I got a ride home. The high school students had seen what I had perceived, but I was ashamed.

I was not charting out time, but my perception of time. I knew that the school-day mornings were not actually shorter than the afternoons, but I also realized that the actual number of minutes was meaningless.

Now that we have sold Tom Thumb, we are jarred. When we get together we try to remember which summer each thing happened. "Remember that time when Carla had the bike accident? What summer was that?" "Remember that Jewish camp?" "They seemed so sad, those boys."

We are trying to remember the details of the life we spent together, and we are also trying, for the first time, to admit that it didn't all happen in one endless year. No, that's not quite it. It's just that it seems like it is still happening, as if we are still there, running the place, sweeping the greens, carrying out the money boxes. We talk about Tom Thumb because we have never left it. We are still there, and always will be, and summers continue, and we need to uncover The Barrels because the sun is coming out, and if I were to draw this on the blackboard, the chalk would go off the edge and along the painted wall . . .

As You Drive Away . . .

This is where we are now:

LeAnn still lives in Minneapolis with her husband, Perry. Their three sons, Ryan, David, and Mark, have all finished college, and now LeAnn is training a service dog.

Carla lives in Iowa City with her husband, John, and two sons, Luke and Ben, who are finishing high school and making plans for college. She is a wellness counselor.

Mom and Dad have been living in the house they moved into after they sold Tom Thumb. My mom still has more energy than anyone else I have ever met—she has sewn 994 school bags and backpacks for children in Haiti and elsewhere (but doesn't want anyone to know this, and will be unhappy that I'm telling you). We still swim together when the water isn't too cold.

And me? Two years after my parents sold Tom Thumb, I did finally leave Los Angeles and come to the Midwest to attend graduate school. The year I was about to graduate (and unsure of where I'd go next), I visited my old hometown in Iowa for its Norwegian festival. I met the man of my dreams while watching the parade. We married and now live in the woods just outside the very same town where I grew up. (Another loop.)

My beloved father died on May 24, 2013. Just five months before this book was completed. He is greatly missed.

The new owners have been running Tom Thumb Miniature Golf for the last ten years. They have chosen not to live on the premises, but instead rent out the house to vacationers on a weekly basis. And now, Tom Thumb is up for sale again (as of the date this is being published). Its future is again uncertain.

ACKNOWLEDGMENTS

First, I'd like to give a nod to the regular customers of Tom Thumb Mini Golf. Although we didn't learn all of your names, we knew your faces well. You were part of our summers for so many years, and we miss hearing you play—in groups no larger than four, please—with your families in our backyard. Thank you for the pleasure.

Maxi-thanks to my editor, Caroline Zancan, for her enthusiasm, dedication, and watchful eye. And to my agent, Betsy Lerner, who has smart ideas and a wicked sense of humor, both of which keep me on my toes, and my toes couldn't be happier.

To my mentor-friends: the inimitable knight-poet David Hamilton who deserves an entire page of acknowledgments. This book would not have happened without him. And Kevin Brockmeier, for his friendship, valuable criticism, and reading suggestions. Both are artists with great generosity of spirit. Thank you.

Huge-sized thanks to writer friends Anjali Sachdeva, Hali Felt, and Kate Rattenborg for your friendship and encouragement and everything. To other friends and readers: Maris Venia, Tod McCoy, Robin Hemley, Nancy Barry, Amelia Bird, Maggie McKnight, and Claire Bidwell Smith. Thanks and "two scoops of vanilla ice cream" to my fellow students in Susan Lohafer's class at the University of Iowa.

For their support, thanks to the Virginia Center for the Creative Arts and the Marcus Bach Foundation.

For help with research, thanks to author Tim Hollister (who writes lovely books about fun, kitsch things); to The Waupaca Historical Society, and naturalist Sue Eiler, of Hartman's Creek State Park. To the family of Greg Charlesworth (the man who built Tom Thumb), especially Elizabeth Arsnow, Roy and Ruth Ann Hackbart, and Mary Rodgers. Thanks also to the Charlesworths for the photo on the jacket of this book. (That's Greg and Lucille Charlesworth—who built Tom Thumb—playing on the first hole, circa 1960!)

Large thanks to the Leean clan—my extended family. I am lucky/blessed to be a part.

To former-customers-and-now-good-friends, The Ernsts: John, Faith, Kathy, and Linda Ernst. To Tom Haebig (the former cook!) who is now one of our family; and Dave Sebora.

And a tip of the hat to Gerald Durrell who wrote a wonderful book, *My Family and Other Animals*, which inspired my own, in title and in other ways.

Excerpt from devotional comes from "Grace for the moment, Volume I" by Max Lucado. Thank you.

This book is dedicated to my family. Thank you for putting up with my crazy questions and my tape recorder, for trusting me with this story, which is, of course, *our* story: LeAnn, Carla, and my parents, George and Jean Melby. My greatest reward has been hearing you laugh when you read these chapters. I love you all.

Finally, my husband, Tim. I find myself at a loss for words on how to thank you. For everything.

About the Author

JUNE MELBY received her MFA in nonfiction from the University of Iowa. Her writing has appeared in *McSweeney's Internet Tendency*, *LA Weekly*, *National Lampoon* magazine, and *Versal*, among others. As a poet and spoken-word artist she has toured throughout the United States and Europe. She was awarded a fellowship by the Virginia Center for the Creative Arts, and received the International Artist Award and residency from the City of Hamburg Kulturebehörde (Cultural Affairs Department). In 2002 she was the winner of the Children's Poetry Award at the Edinburgh International Poetry Festival. She lives in Decorah, Iowa.